U0534887

2016年度甘肃省社科规划项目"'一带一路'语境下天水地域文化的双语构建研究"(YB128)终结性成果

天水与"一带一路"沿线国家地域文化双语转换

马英莲　龚金霞 ◎ 著

English and Chinese Bilingual Transformation
on Regional Cultures between Tianshui and Countries
along The Belt and Road Initiative

中国社会科学出版社

图书在版编目(CIP)数据

天水与"一带一路"沿线国家地域文化双语转换 / 马英莲，龚金霞著 . —北京：中国社会科学出版社，2017.3（2019.6重印）

ISBN 978-7-5203-0217-3

Ⅰ.①天… Ⅱ.①马…②龚… Ⅲ.①旅游文化-英语-翻译-研究 Ⅳ.①F590-05

中国版本图书馆 CIP 数据核字（2017）第 073051 号

出 版 人	赵剑英
责任编辑	任　明　刁佳慧
责任校对	沈丁晨
责任印制	李寡寡

出　　版	中国社会科学出版社
社　　址	北京鼓楼西大街甲 158 号
邮　　编	100720
网　　址	http://www.csspw.cn
发 行 部	010-84083685
门 市 部	010-84029450
经　　销	新华书店及其他书店

印刷装订	北京君升印刷有限公司
版　　次	2017 年 3 月第 1 版
印　　次	2019 年 6 月第 2 次印刷

开　　本	710×1000　1/16
印　　张	19.5
插　　页	2
字　　数	291 千字
定　　价	85.00 元

凡购买中国社会科学出版社图书，如有质量问题请与本社营销中心联系调换
电话：010-84083683
版权所有　侵权必究

序

马英莲和龚金霞合作撰著的《天水与"一带一路"沿线国家地域文化双语转换》行将出版。大作出版，照例要有个序。马老师好几次邀请由我来捉刀，理由比较充足：我们是多年的老熟人，再者我多年从事天水地域文化研究，而本书就是和天水地域文化直接相关。我惶恐，理由也比较充足：于旅游文化很少涉猎，再者对"英汉双语转换"介绍旅游景观的旅游文化更是很少涉猎。但及至我浏览阅读本书稿本，真心实意地感到——好书也，我有感想可以发也，序可不自量力斗胆为之也。

有什么感想呢？简而言之，一是如何对外推介旅游，二是推介些什么。

首先来谈如何对外推介旅游。有名胜景观旅游而观览之，可以开阔视野，可以放松身心，可以增长见识，是现代人最热衷的活动之一。顺应这种需求推介自己的"好东西"给别人，让别人来旅游，来消费，以推动经济发展，是宣传领域的大事，有必要做实并做好。天水是丝绸之路重镇，国家级历史文化名城，历史文化积淀丰厚，名胜景观众多，旅游资源丰富。改革开放以来，当地政府在旅游推介方面花了不少气力，想了不少办法。但一直是对内宣传过头，对外宣传不足，尤其是对国外宣传不足。常常是市内、省内自己对着自己宣传。自己名胜景观、历史文化之"好东西"对国外而言，依然是"养在深闺无人知"。不是不足为外人道也，而是足为外人道而没有道及。其最主要的问题是语言障碍。迄今为止，堂堂天水还没有一本研究如何全面推介自己旅游文化的双语著作。现在好了，马老师这本关于古丝绸之路重镇天水与"一带一路"沿线国家旅游文化横向对接的英汉双语对照专著来了，是不是适逢其会呢！请注意，此书书名的关键词之一"一带一路"，其出发点是天水，而视角是"一带一路"沿线国家全域，这是不是又响应了"一带一路"沿线国家发展了呢！

其次来谈推介些什么。如前所言，天水"历史文化积淀丰厚，名胜景观众多"。那么，如何推介历史文化的丰厚、名胜景观的众多就成了问题。当然不能面面俱到而面面不清，而本书的取材很是巧妙，抓住了天水历史文化的五大文化——伏羲文化、大地湾文化、秦文化、三国文化、石窟文化，并兼及天水市主要名胜景观伏羲庙、麦积山等。这很符合我们学习唯物辩证法时学过的"抓主要矛盾"。更难能可贵的是，在推介天水五大历史文化和主要名胜景观的同时，书稿还兼及与天水每个地域文化语境相似的"一带一路"沿线国家主要旅游文化和景点描写，如三国文化对举特洛伊考古遗址、石窟文化对举印度阿旃陀石窟，穿插得相当巧妙。这又很符合我们学习唯物辩证法时学过的事物的"普遍联系"。请注意，本书的描述或推介都是汉英双语对照，而且对文化和景观的介绍推介是按英语国家通行的语篇信息——背景信息（地理位置、社会功能和历史）→主题信息（热门看点）→附加信息（设施和服务、游览指南/建议）层层推进，立足导游，注重实用信息传递。这是不是具有世界视野呢！

总之，读完本稿，我的感受——这是一本向国内外推介天水特色地域文化和主要景观的书，也是一本为天水和"一带一路"沿线国家建立文化交流桥梁的书。立足当地，兼及海外；双语转换，内外普惠；是可满足当下文化传播者及天水出入境旅游爱好者的基本需要，也是当地政府对外宣传的上好资料。虽然本书在"一带一路"沿线国家景观的选择上还有可商榷之处，但不失为一本如何推介旅游文化的好书。

以上碎语，信马由缰，不太像是序言。但基于本书"好书也"的感觉和感想是真心实意的。

马老师为人低调，教学科研认真踏实，不声不响地在双语推介天水名胜景观和地域文化方面做了好多卓有成效的工作。祝马英莲和龚金霞的新著顺利出版，早日和读者见面，发挥其应有作用。

刘雁翔

2017年"五一"长假之际于两可斋

前　言

一　写作背景

随着"一带一路"倡议的实施，尤其是2016年5月习近平总书记在哲学社会科学工作座谈会上讲话精神的落实，位于古丝绸之路第一重镇的历史文化名城天水成为"丝绸之路经济带"甘肃省黄金段的重要枢纽，也使熟练掌握英语的高级旅游专业人才的需求不断增加；传统的一般用途英语（EGP）教学已不能满足当前市场对旅游人才的要求以及学生自身的要求；即将出版的《大学英语课程教学指南》在原来通用英语的基础上增加了专门用途英语（ESP）和跨文化交际的内容，这是大学英语教学所面临的机遇和挑战。为培养能够胜任天水地域文化的英语旅游从业人员，外国语学院和文化传播学院实行跨学科课外合作教学。然而，要实现罗宾逊"利用语言实现一个确定目标"[①]的ESP真正目的，不仅要提高学生的英语应用能力，还需掌握专业领域的英语知识。

另外，以介绍中国旅游文化的汉英旅游翻译只能为入境游客提供帮助且已渐渐不能满足中国游客出境旅游的需求。2016年1月29日，原国家旅游局局长李金早在全国旅游工作会议上提出：中国旅游要从"景点旅游"向"全域旅游"转变。目光不再停留在旅游人次的增长，而更加注重旅游质量的提升。这些潜在游客迫切需要了解旅游目

[①] Pauline Robinson, *ESP（English for Specific Purposes）*, Oxford: Pergamon Press, 1980, p.6.

的地的国情与文化。为接纳中国游客，日本国家旅游局、英国旅游局等有较大影响的外国旅游局开通了中文网站。对于我国来说，在介绍本国国情与文化的背景下，与"一带一路"沿线国家旅游文化的横向对接更加迫切。

二 主要内容

这是一本关于古丝绸之路重镇天水与"一带一路"沿线国家旅游文化横向对接的英汉双语对照专著。主要内容共六章：第一章详细介绍了借鉴的理论基础和翻译策略；第二章至第六章分别包括天水伏羲文化、天水大地湾文化、天水秦文化、天水三国文化、天水石窟文化简述和主要旅游景点情况以及与每个地域文化语境相似的"一带一路"沿线国家主要旅游文化和景点描写；最后运用基于翻译语境说和语篇特质的"相关理论"译文评估解释性模式，客观具体地评判了翻译文本的质量。所有文化均模仿目的语读者熟悉的语篇呈现为一个汉语重构语篇和一个对应的英语书面语介绍语篇及英语口语导游词，满足了文化传播者及潜在的出入境旅游游客迫切需要了解旅游目的地文化和旅游资源的需求。

三 主要观点

(一) 语篇结构分析有助于熟悉不同语篇的构建机制

依据"语篇语法"理论，读者是将语篇作为一个连贯的整体结构来认知和解释的，该结构即关于语篇宏观命题的整体结构。宏观命题是在"删减""归纳""建构"等宏观规则的基础上，对一系列有序的局部微观命题进行推理和归纳而获得的。命题是由主词和谓词构成的逻辑语句，主词通常由名词、名词短语或者另一个命题构成，谓词则主要是动词、副词、形容词、介词短语和语义衔接手段。在逐级演进、生成宏观命题的认知过程中，局部命题本身是其相应上级命题的主词。需要指出，语义衔接手段在段际、句际层面体现为增补、对比、反意、原因、理由、方法、后果、目的、条件、让步关系；在句内体现为小句间的扩展、投射、并列或从属关系；词际层面的语义衔接手段包括替代、照应和省略。可见，体现这些逻辑语义关系的衔接手段是谓词分析的主要对象。与语篇微观命题、宏观结构相对应的是微观结构和上层结构。前者指关于句群、句子、词组、词、词素、语音形式特点的表层结构；后者则指语篇的整体图式化表层结构，比如小说叙事结构、议论文论辩图式等。此外，由于话语主题的相关性被不同程度地分配到语篇微观命题和表层结构，因此，主题相关性是语篇结构分析的参照系数。源语和译语语篇结构对比发现：国内旅游介绍语篇结构程式化、成分单一、语篇中出现的位置也相对固定；而国外旅游介绍语篇结构多样化，游客意识突出，多提供游览指南和服务设施。

（二）重构语境是模仿目的语读者可接受语篇的有效途径

语境的主要功能是对语言的制约作用。一切语言的应用和言语的交际总是限定在一定的语境范围之内，它对语言的语义、词族、结构形式以及语言风格等方面都会产生影响和制约作用。语境意识是译者能否正确翻译的一个重要参数，直接影响翻译的效果。针对天水地域文化与目的语国家旅游文化语域不匹配现象，本著没有简单地把源语语境移植到目的语中而是根据目的语的变化重构语境。为在目的语中寻找在相似的语境中尽可能起相似作用的语篇，笔者借鉴英国旅游网站（www.tourist-information-uk.com）的书面语篇介绍和美国国家公园网站（https：//www.nps.gov/yell）的口语导游词中的语域特征及书面语和口语体特点。在实际的翻译中在语篇层面对原文进行改编，通过调整句子和段落、删减和更改部分内容等，重构语篇贴近目的语读者的思维方式和阅读习惯，更加符合英语的信息结构。

（三）翻译语境是影响、制约翻译决策过程因素的总和

翻译活动是由活动—行为—行动构成的分阶层系统，其中高层元素需通过下层来实现，下层元素则又受制于本层和上层元素。翻译活动的递归性实现过程表明：翻译语境是由社会—文化层面、翻译行为和行动层面诸因素构成的分层功能系统。社会—文化层面的语境因素

包括翻译规范在内的规约性社会规则，翻译行为层面指行为目的在内的情景因素，行动层面主要有语篇功能、规约性翻译问题、译者翻译能力及其语言习惯。实践中，这三个层面的语境因素可具体操作化为：翻译规范、情境性语篇功能、规约性语篇功能、译者的翻译能力和习惯。一方面，行为层面的情景性语篇功能"导向"了翻译规范的制约作用，它使译者决策有了目的性。而规约性语篇功能为规约性翻译问题的解决提供具体策略依据：针对信息性语篇可采用意义为主形式为辅的归结性策略；表达性语篇采用两者兼之的成就性策略；对于感染性语篇，则采用旨在谋求双语语篇语境效果最大近似的替换策略。同时，译者的翻译能力和习惯直接促成了一定文体风格的译文。另一方面，翻译策略选择既要依据行动层的语境因素，同时更要受制于情景行为层以及社会—文化活动层面的语境因素。当各层次语境因素不一致时，则要根据上层语境因素来调整翻译策略。与翻译语境对应的译文语篇特质为"主题相关性"和"关联性"："主题相关性"是语篇结构对于宏观命题及其整体语境效果的相关度；"关联性"是语篇的处理努力和语境效果的比值。只有语篇结构具有相应的"主题相关性"和"关联性"，译文在特定翻译语境中的功能即语境效果才能得到充分实现。

四　新方法

当前天水市旅游文化翻译多是附于文化景点简介和旅游宣传图册的情景性英文片段，本著首次采用语言学方法系统翻译天水"五大文化"与"一带一路"沿线国家旅游文化及相关规约性翻译问题；针对翻译学纯研究和应用研究缺少连接的研究现状，试图基于功能性翻译语境理论和语篇语言学理论，建立基于翻译语境和语篇理论的解释性译文质量评估模式。以应用为导向的描写—解释性研究、英汉双语对照是本著的鲜明特点。通过天水与"一带一路"沿线国家英汉旅游文化对照，读者不仅能充分领悟原文的内涵及其文化背景，而且可以在两种思维和句法的对比碰撞下，激发起英语学习和翻译的兴趣。

五　学术贡献

造成天水旅游翻译数量少、质量低下的原因来自三方面。其一，旅游管理相关部门对旅游景点的翻译活动不够重视。虽然天水旅游业发展迅猛，但旅游部门依然把主要精力集中在境内游客上，轻视甚至忽视了日益增加的外国游客。其二，对译者的水平没有严格的把关。译者没有掌握足够的翻译理论和技巧，翻译水平有所欠缺。翻译是一门艺术，需要译者掌握多种技能，并不是英语学者都可以参与翻译工作，旅游翻译作为一种应用翻译更具有特殊要求。作为翻译主体的译者，不仅要明白中西旅游文本、文化以及语言的差异还需掌握一定的翻译理论和技巧。其三，缺乏相应的审核程序。从各旅游景点介绍语的翻译中存在的问题可以看出，相当一部分的翻译材料未经权威部门或专业人士尤其翻译方面的专门人士的严格审核。

本著将改变天水旅游文化缺少依据连贯方法论施行的系统翻译的现状。打破单一的以介绍地域文化为主的汉英旅游翻译，而进行天水"五大文化"与"一带一路"沿线国家旅游文化横向对接的英汉双语翻译以实现"一带一路"倡议实施前的文化先行。扩大天水旅游文化向"一带一路"沿线国家的展示传播，使其产生与其实际拥有的重要地位相匹配的社会价值。

六　理论创新

天水旅游文化的展示传播还很不够，其产生的社会价值与实际拥有的重要地位还远远不相匹配。天水旅游文化翻译不仅数量少、翻译质量低下，而且没有针对天水旅游文化与"一带一路"沿线国家文化接轨的双语研究。缺少依据连贯方法论施行的系统翻译活动，更缺少一个译文质量的客观评估体系。需要指出，在针对译文评估、翻译方法论构建等问题的应用翻译研究领域，尽管有豪斯的功能主义语言学模式、威廉姆斯的论辩性译文评估模式、斯坦纳的语域分析模式和阿库法伊什的说明性译文评估模式，但这些模式关注的仅是译文的语言特征,并未论及影响、制约翻译策略选择的翻译语境问题,同时其操作性也不强。鉴于此,有必要对天水市旅游文化和"一带一路"沿线国家的文化宣传接轨材料进行系统的汉—英译介研究。整合梵·迪克的语篇结构分析方法和韩礼德功能主义的文本语境分析模式,既强调意义是文本和语境交互的结果,又提倡话语的形式主义分析方法。对天水"五大文化"和"一带一路"沿线国家的文化接轨进行系统的汉—英译介研究既是构建我国传统旅游文化理论的途径,更是探究规约性翻译问题(即由于语言、文化差异而产生的翻译任务)、进行系统旅游文化译介的前提。不但具有应用翻译学的理论价值,而且能为我国西部旅游文化的翻译实践直接提供方法论指导。

七 实践意义

本著将促进天水"五大文化"与"一带一路"沿线国家旅游文化的横向对接,提升境外市场对天水旅游资源的了解和境内游客对目的语国家旅游文化的熟知,重在打造丝路之旅的文化品牌,体现旅游与文化的结合,促进文化的传播。既是高校外语学院和文传学院培养学生跨文化交际能力和翻译能力的跨学科英汉双语学习书目、旅游从业者的指导手册,也是天水旅游文化元素进入国际文化的有效途径。同时为研究者提供大量英汉双语转换语料,为世界旅游组织开展大规模丝路之旅的宣传推介做前期准备,为东西方学者的交流搭建了新的平台,也是对国家"一带一路"倡议的文化阐释。

目　录

第一章　总论 …………………………………………………… (1)
　第一节　天水"五大文化"与"一带一路"沿线
　　　　　国家旅游文化概述 ………………………………… (1)
　第二节　韩礼德语境理论 ……………………………………… (2)
　第三节　源语语篇与译语语篇语域对比分析 ………………… (4)
　　一　语场对比分析 …………………………………………… (5)
　　二　语旨对比分析 …………………………………………… (7)
　　三　语式对比分析 …………………………………………… (7)
　第四节　源语语篇的语域重构及翻译 ………………………… (8)
　第五节　基于翻译语境和语篇理论的解释性译文
　　　　　质量评估 ……………………………………………… (11)

第二章　天水伏羲文化描写与解释 …………………………… (14)
　第一节　天水伏羲文化简述 …………………………………… (14)
　第二节　天水伏羲文化语篇语域重构及翻译 ………………… (16)
　　一　天水伏羲庙 ……………………………………………… (16)
　　二　天水伏羲庙周边旅游景点 ……………………………… (21)
　　三　天水卦台山 ……………………………………………… (37)
　　四　秦安女娲庙 ……………………………………………… (41)
　第三节　"一带一路"沿线国家始祖文化语篇语域
　　　　　重构及翻译 …………………………………………… (46)
　　一　印度那烂陀寺 …………………………………………… (46)
　　二　伊拉克巴比伦古城遗址 ………………………………… (50)

第四节　基于翻译语境和语篇理论的解释性译文
　　　　　质量评估 ………………………………………… (55)
　　一　语场对比分析 ……………………………………… (56)
　　二　语旨对比分析 ……………………………………… (56)
　　三　语式对比分析 ……………………………………… (59)

第三章　天水大地湾文化描写与解释 …………………… (61)

第一节　天水大地湾文化简述 ……………………………… (61)

第二节　天水大地湾文化语篇语域重构及翻译 …………… (65)
　　一　天水大地湾遗址 …………………………………… (65)
　　二　天水师赵村遗址 …………………………………… (68)
　　三　天水西山坪遗址 …………………………………… (72)

第三节　"一带一路"沿线国家远古文明起源地语篇
　　　　　语域重构及翻译 ………………………………… (74)
　　一　缅甸曼德勒皇宫 …………………………………… (74)
　　二　泰国曼谷皇宫 ……………………………………… (79)

第四节　基于翻译语境和语篇理论的解释性译文
　　　　　质量评估 ………………………………………… (84)
　　一　语场对比分析 ……………………………………… (85)
　　二　语旨对比分析 ……………………………………… (86)
　　三　语式对比分析 ……………………………………… (87)

第四章　天水秦文化描写与解释 …………………………… (89)

第一节　天水秦文化简述 …………………………………… (89)

第二节　天水秦文化语篇语域重构及翻译 ………………… (92)
　　一　天水牧马滩 ………………………………………… (92)
　　二　清水李崖遗址 ……………………………………… (95)
　　三　张家川马家塬战国古墓 …………………………… (98)
　　四　甘谷毛家坪遗址 …………………………………… (102)

第三节　"一带一路"沿线国家人类文明发祥地语篇
　　　　　语域重构及翻译 ………………………………… (107)

一　奥林匹亚考古遗址 …………………………………（107）
　　二　伊朗波斯波利斯遗址 ………………………………（111）
　　三　土耳其以弗所古城遗址 ……………………………（116）
　第四节　基于翻译语境和语篇理论的解释性译文
　　　　　质量评估 ………………………………………（121）
　　一　语场对比分析 ………………………………………（121）
　　二　语旨对比分析 ………………………………………（122）
　　三　语式对比分析 ………………………………………（124）

第五章　天水三国文化描写与解释 ………………………（126）
　第一节　天水三国文化简述 ………………………………（126）
　第二节　天水三国文化语篇语域重构及翻译 ……………（130）
　　一　天水诸葛军垒 ………………………………………（130）
　　二　秦安街亭古战场 ……………………………………（133）
　　三　甘谷姜维墓 …………………………………………（138）
　　四　天水木门道 …………………………………………（143）
　第三节　"一带一路"沿线国家军事文化语篇语域
　　　　　重构及翻译 ……………………………………（148）
　　一　斯里兰卡加勒要塞 …………………………………（148）
　　二　阿曼巴赫莱要塞 ……………………………………（152）
　　三　特洛伊考古遗址 ……………………………………（155）
　第四节　基于翻译语境和语篇理论的解释性译文
　　　　　质量评估 ………………………………………（161）
　　一　语场对比分析 ………………………………………（162）
　　二　语旨对比分析 ………………………………………（163）
　　三　语式对比分析 ………………………………………（165）

第六章　天水石窟文化描写与解释 ………………………（168）
　第一节　天水石窟文化简述 ………………………………（168）
　第二节　天水石窟文化语篇语域重构及翻译 ……………（174）
　　一　天水麦积山石窟 ……………………………………（174）

二　天水仙人崖石窟 …………………………………（179）
　　三　甘谷大像山石窟 …………………………………（187）
　　四　甘谷华盖寺石窟 …………………………………（193）
　　五　武山水帘洞石窟 …………………………………（197）
　　六　武山木梯寺石窟 …………………………………（202）
第三节　"一带一路"沿线国家石窟文化语篇语域
　　　　重构及翻译 ………………………………………（206）
　　一　柬埔寨吴哥石窟 …………………………………（206）
　　二　印度尼西亚婆罗浮屠石窟 ………………………（212）
　　三　斯里兰卡丹布勒石窟寺 …………………………（216）
　　四　斯里兰卡锡吉里耶狮子岩 ………………………（219）
　　五　印度阿旃陀石窟 …………………………………（225）
第四节　基于翻译语境和语篇理论的解释性译文
　　　　质量评估 …………………………………………（231）
　　一　语场对比分析 ……………………………………（231）
　　二　语旨对比分析 ……………………………………（232）
　　三　语式对比分析 ……………………………………（235）
主要参考文献 ……………………………………………（237）
附录　天水"五大文化"补充英语语料 ………………（239）
后记 ………………………………………………………（296）

第一章

总　　论

第一节　天水"五大文化"与"一带一路"沿线国家旅游文化概述

历史上，陆上丝绸之路和海上丝绸之路就是中国同中亚、东南亚、南亚、西亚、东非、欧洲经贸和文化交流的大通道。作为古丝绸之路起点西安"西出长安第一城"的天水，是中华本源文化的重要发祥地之一。她是伏羲、女娲和轩辕黄帝的诞生地，具有8000多年的文明史和地域特色鲜明的"五大文化"。本著按照2004年方志出版社出版的《天水市志》下卷第41编的排列顺序进行描写与解释，依次是：伏羲文化、大地湾文化、秦文化、三国文化、石窟文化。

2013年9月和10月，习近平总书记访问中亚四国和印度尼西亚时，先后提出建设"丝绸之路经济带"和"21世纪海上丝绸之路"的倡议。"一带一路"门户网2016年6月的数据显示，已经有66个国家和地区积极响应和支持这一倡议。名单如下：

（1）中国、蒙古国；

（2）新加坡、马来西亚、印度尼西亚、缅甸、泰国、老挝、柬埔寨、越南、文莱和菲律宾；

（3）伊朗、伊拉克、土耳其、叙利亚、约旦、黎巴嫩、以色列、巴勒斯坦、沙特阿拉伯、也门、阿曼、阿联酋、卡塔尔、科威特、巴林、希腊、塞浦路斯和埃及的西奈半岛；

（4）印度、巴基斯坦、孟加拉、阿富汗、斯里兰卡、马尔代夫、尼泊尔和不丹；

（5）哈萨克斯坦、乌兹别克斯坦、土库曼斯坦、塔吉克斯坦和吉尔吉斯斯坦；

（6）俄罗斯、乌克兰、白俄罗斯、格鲁吉亚、阿塞拜疆、亚美尼亚和摩尔多瓦；

（7）波兰、立陶宛、爱沙尼亚、拉脱维亚、捷克、斯洛伐克、匈牙利、斯洛文尼亚、克罗地亚、波黑、黑山、塞尔维亚、阿尔巴尼亚、罗马尼亚、保加利亚和马其顿。

线路如下：

"丝绸之路经济带"北线：中国—中亚—俄罗斯—欧洲（波罗的海）；中线：中国—中亚—西亚—波斯湾—地中海；南线：中国—东南亚—南亚—印度洋；

"21世纪海上丝绸之路"：从中国沿海港口过南海—印度洋—欧洲；从中国沿海港口过南海—南太平洋；还包括上海、大连、成都、宁波、武汉、合肥、深圳、汕头、青岛、厦门、三亚等城市建设。

2017年1月18日，习近平总书记在联合国日内瓦总部的演讲中证实"已经有100多个国家和国际组织积极响应支持"此倡议。"一带一路"，文化先行。作为"丝绸之路经济带"甘肃黄金段的历史文化名城，天水在入境和出境旅游方面具有巨大的潜能。本著将为更多入境游客了解天水旅游文化架起桥梁，并使广大中国游客在出国前更加了解目的地国家的旅游文化。

第二节　韩礼德语境理论

语境就是使用和理解语言的环境。本著中的语篇重构和翻译均借鉴韩礼德语境理论。该理论是系统功能语法的重要理论之一。马林诺夫斯基（Malinowski）通过对南太平洋上的土著居民的语言进行观察，后于1923年最早提出语境概念并得出结论："如果没有语境，就没有意义。""话语和环境紧密地结合在一起，语言环境对于理解语言来说必不可少。"① 他把语境分成文化语境和情境语境两类。"文化语境"指说话人生活于其中的社会文化背景;"情境语境"指言语行为发生时的具体情景。马林诺夫斯基虽然提出了"语言环境"概念,但是他并未提出一套完整的语境理论,其论述不仅抽象,而且零散。1950 年,弗斯(Firth)继承和发展了这一观点。他吸收了马林诺夫斯基情境语境的概念,把语境切分为"语言因素"和"非语言因素"两类。弗斯的"情境语境"包括参与者的有关特征、参与者的语言行为、参与者的非语言行为,又包括有关的事物和言语行为的影响。他观察到语境的立足点是交际中的话语,界定语境的立足点是语言。一个言语交际系统包括言语交际的主体(发话人和收话人)、话语、信息传递渠道、外部环境等几项基本因素。②

1976 年韩礼德(Halliday)继承了马林诺夫斯基和弗斯的语境理论,对语境因素的种类及其在语言系统中所起的作用进行了深入的研究。他对语境理论最大的贡献是提出了语域理论,将决定语言特征的情景因素归纳为语场、语旨和语式。"语场"即社会行为,也就是正在发生的事件,指正在发生的社会行为的本质、参与者所从事的事情,其中语言是不可或缺的部分;"语旨"即角色结构,指参与者是谁,他们之间是什么样的地位和关系(暂时的或长久的);"语式"即符号构成,也就是语言所起的作用,具体指语言起了什么作用、参与者希望语言起什么作用、语言在语境中的身份及功能等。③ 语域三要素中的任何一项发生改变,都会引起交流意义的改变,从而造成语言的变异,产生不同类型的语境。

---

① Bronislaw Malinowski,"The Problem of Meaning in Primitive Languages", In C. K. Ogden and I. A. Richards (eds.) *The Meaning of Meaning*, London:Rout ledge and Kegan Paul,1923,p. 307.

② John Rupert Firth,"Personality and Language in Society", *The Sociological Review*, Vol. a42, No. 1, January 1950.

③ M. A. K. Haliday and Ruqaiya Hasan, *Cohesion in English*, London:Longman Group Ltd., 1976, p. 56.

第三节　源语语篇与译语语篇语域对比分析

哈蒂姆（Hatim）和梅森（Mason）2001年指出翻译是"在某种社会语境中进行的交际过程"，因而要求译者"不仅具有双语能力，而且要具有双文化视角"。① 廖七一等学者细化这一交际过程包括理解、表达两个阶段，涉及两次交际的过程。第一次交际过程是发生在原文作者和原文读者之间的，然后是译者与译文读者之间的交际过程。译者作为第一个交际阶段（理解）的读者和第二个交际阶段（表达）的作者，实际上是扮演了接受者和制作者两个角色，而这两个阶段的完成都离不开语境分析。从理解到表达，语境分析伴随着翻译的全过程，是达到源语语篇和译语语篇基本"对等"的有力保障。因此翻译的过程就是语境分析的过程。②

为适应新《大学英语课程教学指南》内容在原来通用英语的基础上增加了专门用途英语和跨文化交际的变化，在保证通用英语学习质量的前提下加强旅游英语和跨文化交际学习。合作教师首先把文传学院的120名学生和外国语学院翻译方向的28名学生分别分成14个小组，再把天水地域"五大文化"（伏羲文化、大地湾文化、秦文化、三国文化、石窟文化）中100个景点分成14个模块分发给学生。由文传学院学生完成的汉语语篇主要来自两种途径：借用和原创。部分语篇内容直接借用旅游网站完善的景点介绍材料，对于新开发的、没有任何借鉴资料的景点则自己撰写。为避免天水地域"五大文化"旅游景点翻译的随意性，合作教师指导学生熟悉了源语语篇和译语语篇的语域特点。实例选自天水旅游政务网南郭寺景点介绍并在目的语中寻找到具有相似的语境中起相似作用的英国旅游网站（www.tourist-

---

① Basil Hatim and Ian Mason, *Discourse and the Translator*, Shanghai: Foreign Language Education Press, 2001, p. 223.

② 廖七一等：《当代英国翻译理论》，湖北教育出版社2001年版，第269页。

information-uk.com）伦敦威斯敏斯特教堂介绍。

一 语场对比分析

语场涉及语言交流的目的和主题内容两个方面，在很大程度上决定了语言交流中所使用的词汇，也决定了所使用的语言在语音、语法等方面的特点。哈蒂姆和梅森认为"语篇是一个连贯和衔接的单位，由一个或一个以上的序列组成，而序列又包含彼此相关的成分，它们为共同某一个修辞目的服务"①。为便于具体分析，本著采用哈蒂姆和梅森的语篇分析法将源语和译语语篇内容划分为背景信息、主题信息和附加信息。天水南郭寺语篇结构见表1-1。

表1-1　　　　　　　　天水南郭寺语篇结构分析

序列		内容
背景信息	社会定位	南郭寺为国家4A级旅游景区、省级重点文物保护单位，古树名泉经典。
	名称由来	因地处城郭之南而得名。
	建筑起止年代	始建于南北朝时期。
	地理位置	位于距城2千米的南郊慧音山处。
	社会定位	其寺前临藉水，背负幽林，是市郊最古老的一座梵宫古祠。
	援引名人诗篇	诗圣杜甫行寓留吟："山头南郭寺，水号北流泉。老树空庭得，清渠一邑传。"现成为旅游观光的主要景点之一。
主题信息	观赏内容	南郭寺以古建筑、雕塑、北流泉、邓宝珊将军纪念馆而著称。
	方位与构成	主体建筑依左中右三院横列于山坳台地之上，一字排开。
	景色描绘一	中院的"南山古柏"，树龄约2500年。
	景色描绘二	东院之清泉，千秋不竭，享有"灵湫"之誉。
	景色描绘三	"二妙轩碑"为南郭寺"四绝"之一。碑体长35.6米，高4.36米，清顺治年间，由宋琬主持，集王羲之等晋人书法，镌刻杜甫秦州诗为碑，字妙诗好，故称"二妙"。"二妙轩碑"摹刻精到，自然连贯，气息纯正，美轮美奂，为国内王羲之书法刻石精品。

---

① Basil Hatim and Ian Mason, *Discourse and the Translator*, Shanghai：Shanghai Foreign Language Education Press, 2001, p. 223.

从表 1-1 可以看出，天水南郭寺的语篇内容只有背景信息和主题信息两个序列，没有为游客服务的附加信息序列。强调和突出景区历史文化背景信息、景区地位的介绍，削弱了古树名泉等关键主题信息。伦敦威斯敏斯特教堂的语篇分析见表 1-2。

表 1-2　　　　伦敦威斯敏斯特教堂语篇结构分析

序列		内容
背景信息	地理位置	Westminster Abbey is located in London just to the west of the Palace of Westminster.
	社会功能和历史	The Abbey is a living church where worship still takes place today and it is also the traditional place of coronation and burial site for English monarchs. St. Edward, the confessor's shrine is at the heart of the Abbey Church and is surrounded by the tombs and memorials of many great men and women from British Time.
主题信息	热门看点	More than 1000 years worth of treasures such as paintings, stained glass and textiles are on view to the public within the stunning Gothic architecture of this church.
附加信息	设施和服务	For an additional price there are verger-led tours, guided tours and audio guides available in German, French, Spanish, Italian, Russian, Mandarin Chinese, and Japanese.
	游览指南	Within the Abbey precincts, you can also go to St Margaret's Church, and museum and on certain days to the College Garden.
		For many years Westminster Abbey was the main burial site for royalty although now the royal family burial site is Windsor Castle.
		There is plenty of information for you and there are various kinds of tours available from the personal audio tours available free with all tickets to guided tours for large groups of you.
		There are places to purchase drinks and snacks although they cannot be consumed inside the buildings.
	开放时间	Open from Monday till Saturday throughout the year from 9：30 a.m till 4：45 p.m. On Sundays and religious holidays the Abbey is open for worship only.
	门票价格	Adults -£ 10.00; Under 16s/Students/OAPs - £ 7.00; Family - £ 24.00.

表 1-2 显示，威斯敏斯特教堂语篇内容由背景信息、主题信息和附加信息三个序列组成。重点突出地理环境及服务设施等实用信息的传递，对住宿、交通及开放时间的介绍较多，对风光景色的描述则较少。语篇信息结构依次按照：背景信息（地理位置、社会功能和历

史)—主题信息(热门看点)—附加信息(设施和服务、游览指南等)层层推进,既突出景点的绘画、彩色玻璃和纺织品等关键主题信息又兼顾其他信息,增强了语篇的可接受性,能够实现信息的有效传递。对比分析发现,天水南郭寺和伦敦威斯敏斯特教堂语篇的语场基本相同,但各有所侧重。二者都使用日常用语、标准句型向潜在游客介绍景点的基本信息。

二 语旨对比分析

语旨指交际者之间关系的作用。如交际双方涉及什么人,他们之间的关系如何。从语旨的角度看,南郭寺语篇的交际双方为旅游主管部门、景点的宣传部门和潜在的游客。发话者为旅游主管部门或景区宣传部门。在组织信息时,发话者往往以自身为中心,多从主管部门或官方的角度描写参观感受,如"诗碑摹刻精到,自然连贯,气息纯正,美轮美奂,为国内王羲之书法刻石精品"。总体而言,南郭寺的介绍语篇语体正式,凸显出主管部门或旅游推广部门与游客之间的关系较为疏远,造成宣传推介显得比较生硬,较少顾及游客的个人情感,忽视了游客的游览体验。

威斯敏斯特教堂介绍语篇的交际双方与南郭寺相同,发话者同样为旅游主管部门或旅游推广部门。介绍语篇中反复出现"visitor"一词,如"you can also go to St. Margaret's Church…",在突出组织信息时,威斯敏斯特教堂的旅游推广部门则从潜在的游客角度出发,尽可能多地顾及游客在游览中的个人感受。从权势距离的角度来看,威斯敏斯特教堂的旅游推广部门与潜在游客间的关系较为亲密,发话者尽可能多地为游客提供各种便利的游览信息,如开放时间、门票价格等。

三 语式对比分析

语式指语言交流所采用的具体方式,在很大程度上决定着所使用语言的正式程度和技术性程度。语篇的交流方式主要分为两大类:口语和书面语。从语式的角度来看，南郭寺语篇采用了正式的书面语体，句法表达包括明喻、暗喻、排比等多种修辞方法，如"门前有两株千余年树干直径在两米左右的古国槐，恰似两位将军拱卫在寺门前"。并多用汉语中的华丽四字辞藻如"碑碣遗存、楹联匾额、古树名木、隋塔遗址、杜少陵祠"使游客形成景区优美、朦胧的印象。

威斯敏斯特教堂的介绍语篇虽然也同为书面语体，但其正式程度明显弱于南郭寺语篇。纵览全文，威斯敏斯特教堂语篇虽然大量使用连词"and"连接长句和复杂句，但因多为英语基本词汇，表层结构清晰明了，很少涉及修辞手段，呈现出简明易懂的口语化倾向。潜在游客可以通过跳读或略读的方式轻松找到所需要的各类游览信息。

在熟悉源语和译语在语场、语旨和语式方面的差异后，本著没有简单地把源语语境移植到目的语中而是根据目的语的变化重构语境。为使汉语旅游语篇贴近国外受众思维和阅读习惯、提高译语语篇的可接受性，文传学院学生模仿伦敦旅游语篇对天水旅游景点介绍在语篇结构、信息排列、意义层次、语篇连贯及逻辑修辞等方面进行调整重组。作为跨学科合作学生的交换材料，重构语篇以书面语形式完成。但外国语学院的学生在进行语际转换时以书面语和口语两种形式完成，以满足文传学院学生掌握英语导游词的需求。

第四节 源语语篇的语域重构及翻译

在熟悉源语和译语在不同语场、语旨和语式下的具体语域特点之后，为使汉语旅游语篇贴近国外受众思维和阅读习惯、提高译语语篇的可接受性，文传学院学生参考英国旅游网站伦敦旅游介绍模板，对天水旅游景点介绍在语篇结构、信息排列、意义层次、语篇连贯及逻辑修辞等方面进行调整重组。实例可参见第二章天水伏羲文化描写与解释第二节。

按照威斯敏斯特教堂语篇仿写的南郭寺语篇满足了语境三要素的要求。语场限定语言交际的话题及文类规范。为达到与目的语语场匹配，重构语篇删减了背景信息中景点的社会定位和名人诗篇、保留了地理位置、社会定位和历史信息；主题信息中景点描述特点突出、客观具体；增加了为游客服务的附加信息。译文中更多使用被动语态以及"visit""offer"等过程动词、名词、代词、数词等对景点进行描述，甚少使用形容词以突出景点介绍的客观性。

语旨决定说话情景的适当性。重构语篇更加注重以游客为导向，强调与游客之间的沟通，凸显游客意识，如"游客在本寺可观赏到约2500年树龄的古树"。译文也用"您"或"游客"开头的句子与游客对话交流，如"If you happen to visit the church on April 8th, you will have the opportunity to experience the annual temple fair with thousands of travelers."。同时，增加共享知识拉近与游客的关系。例如，重构语篇中"杜甫"及"朝代"等与本土文化、地域特点有关的专有词汇都提供了更多的语境信息——"Du Fu of the Tang Dynasty（759 AD）"。

语式要求译文交际情景的特点与原文保持一致。重构语篇既保持了书面语特征，如为突出南郭寺古树、清泉和诗碑的特色，重构语篇运用了较长的限定词"约2500年树龄的古树、几千年涓涓流淌永不干涸的清泉，以及用晋朝（公元265—420年）书法家王羲之、王献之书法雕刻的唐朝（公元618—907年）诗人杜甫诗碑等"；同时又呈现口语化倾向，如"如果碰巧在农历四月初八参观本寺将有幸与众游客一起体验南郭寺一年一度的庙会"；译文也遵循了书面语与口语相结合的表达方式。如用分词修饰体现书面语的"towering old trees dated back to more than 2500 years"和尽量使用主动语态表达对话性的"You can appreciate many natural and cultural landscapes here"。

为满足文传学院学生掌握英语导游词的需求，合作教师先推荐选自美国黄石国家公园（参见 www.nps.gov/yell）的目的语样本再分析口语体的特征，最后由外国语学院学生完成重构语篇书面语与口语之间的转换。美国黄石国家公园口语导游词如下：

Tour Guide Speech of Yellowstone National Park

Yellowstone National Park is American's first national park. It was established in 1872. Yellowstone extends through Wyoming, Montana, and Idaho. The park's name is derived from the Yellowstone River, which runs through the park. It's unclear if the name first referred to the sulfurous yellow rocks below the falls of the Grand Canyon of the Yellowstone River or to the sandstone bluffs that border its shores.

Within the massive park boundaries, you can find mountains, rivers, lakes, and some of the most concentrated geothermal activity in the world. The park has 60% of the world's geysers as well as many hot springs and several mud pots. Perhaps the most famous feature of the park is geyser Old Faithful.

You can also see the Grand Canyon of the Yellowstone River, of the world's largest petrified forests, and countless waterfalls. The park is also home to diverse wildlife including grizzly bears, wolves, bisons, and elks. Outdoor recreational is boundless in this iconic national park. Madison and the Yellowstone River are stocked with brown and rainbow trout and mountain whitefish. The many bike trails include an abandoned railroad bed that winds along with the wild Yellowstone River. You can backcountry tramp or hike on the extensive trail system throughout the entire park, or boat on Yellowstone Lake. Stock outfitters lead horse and llama trips into the backcountry.

  T: one of the recreation   R: horse and llama trip

Historic points of interest include Fort Yellowstone, the permanent post of the cavalry when they managed the park in the late 19th century before the National Park Service was established in 1916. Old Faithful Inn, one of the last log hotels in the United States, is an impressive one of seven-story buildings of beautiful rustic architecture.

As the original American national park and icon of the entire national park system, Yellowstone National Park is an American gem with millions of visitors each year. Because of its magnitude and diversity, it is a park that really requires several visits to appreciate all of what offered. Created in 1872 as the first national park in America, it set the standard of entire national park system and is the most iconic park in the country.

转换参照侯维瑞的五大口语体特征：语句松散自由，句子省略不全，词语颇多重复，使用填空词语，借助非语言情况。① 导游词使用了许多简单常用词汇。例如，利用"is""has""see""find"等动词增加情感互动以吸引游客的注意力；出现频率很高的情态动词"can"表达对游客旅游客观条件的允许，获取信任感；形容词"solemn""precious""fantastic"表现出引导者的自豪感；填补词"by the way""you see"能延续交谈；模糊词"let me say"给引导者提供思索的时间；句子结构层面，多用连词"and"和"so"引导并列句或从句突出松散、省略现象如"He was born in 1894 and died in 1968.""it's""isn't"等。经过合作教师校译的实例英语导游词可参见第二章天水伏羲文化描写与解释第二节。

第五节　基于翻译语境和语篇理论的解释性译文质量评估

天水旅游文化翻译不仅数量少、翻译质量低下而且缺少依据连贯方法论施行的系统翻译活动，更缺少一个译文质量的客观评估体系。在针对译文评估、翻译方法论构建等问题的应用翻译研究领域，尽管有朱莉安·豪斯的功能主义语言学模式②，但这些模式关注的仅是译文的语言特征，并未论及影响、制约翻译策略选择的翻译语境问题，同时其操作性也不强。系统功能语言学认为，在构成使用语言的情景语境的各个要素里，只有三个因素对语言的使用产

---

① 侯维瑞编：《英语语体》，上海外语教育出版社1996年版，第28—35页。
② Juliane House, *Translation Quality Assessment: A Model Revisited*, Tübingen: Gunter Narr Verlag, 1997, pp. 1-23.

生直接和重要的影响。① 即语场、语旨和语式三个语域变量，对于使用语言时如何选择语言形式有着直接的、至关重要的影响。

在英译的过程中充分意识到英语旅游文本的语域特点。翻译过程中避免使用生涩难懂的词汇，多使用日常用语；对于一些与本土文化、地域特点有关的专有词汇，要给予进一步补充解释；避免汉语中松散、动态的句子结构，多使用语法正确的标准句法，行文结构需严谨，多体现书面语的特点；加强译文的评价倾向，更多考虑英美国家本地人的阅读习惯，利用不同的句式，如祈使句、强调句等加强文本的呼唤功能；在对景点的描述中谨慎选词，更多使用名词、代词、过程动词、数词等而相对减少形容词的使用，使描述景点的语言更加客观、具体、简单、直白；更多考虑英语旅游文本的"你指向"情感。句子的主位部分，更多地以"您"开头，把读者纳入文本对话。本书将运用韩礼德功能语言学的语域理论对天水"五大文化"及其"一带一路"沿线国家旅游景点描写语料源文与译文从语场、语旨、语式三方面进行对比分析，客观和具体地评判翻译文本的质量。

作为中国古代文化发祥地之一的天水，历代人文荟萃，境内文物古迹众多。深厚的人文历史底蕴形成了以伏羲文化、大地湾文化、秦文化、三国文化、石窟文化为代表的五大特色文化。其一，伏羲是中华民族的始祖，伏羲文化是史前文化的重要组成部分，是中华民族优秀传统文化的源头。天水是伏羲的诞生地和伏羲文化的发祥地，江泽民同志于1992年8月13日视察天水时亲笔题词"羲皇故里"。市内现有一座元代始建、明代重修的全国规模最大、保存最完整的祭奠伏羲的伏羲庙。在距市区17千米的三阳川有伏羲氏创画八卦的卦台山，山上庙内有伏羲塑像和元代时期的八卦盘。伏羲文化博大精深，吸引着国内外无数学者、专家不懈的探索、研究。其二，大地湾遗址位于秦安县境内，是距今8300—4800年的原始社会新石器时代的古村落

---

① 司显柱：《功能语言学与翻译研究——翻译质量评估模式建构》，北京大学出版社2007年版，第6—9页。

遗址。已出土8000多件各类文物及中国最早的原始地画，有最早的"水泥"地面大厅和宫殿等，其规模之大、内涵之丰富，在我国考古史上实属罕见。它较完整地保存了仰韶文化早、中、晚各个时期的文化遗址，具有极高的考古和文化价值，在"二十世纪一百项重大考古发现"中列第12位，影响很大。其三，天水是秦国的发祥地，秦人先祖嬴非子在此牧马有功，于公元前890年被周孝王封邑于秦亭，即今天的天水一带，经200多年的发展壮大，于公元前762年东迁陕西关中一带，开始了统一六国的步伐。秦人在统一六国的过程中，于公元前688年在天水市的清水、甘谷两地建立了邽县和冀县，这是我国历史上最早的县。秦国早期文化遗存主要集中在天水一带。其四，天水在历史上为陇右第一重镇，历来为兵家必争之地。三国时期，天水处于蜀魏交锋的前沿，诸葛亮六出祁山、痛失街亭、智收姜维、计杀张郃等重大战事，都发生在天水，其境内有街亭、天水关、木门道、诸葛军垒等三国古战场遗址。其五，石窟文化。天水堪称丝绸之路东段的"石窟走廊"，全市境内有大小石窟共6处。驰名中外的麦积山石窟是我国四大石窟之一，它始凿于南北朝时期的后秦，距今已有1600多年历史，保存有194个洞窟，荟萃历代的泥塑、石雕造像7000多尊，壁画1000多平方米，是罕见的艺术珍品，素有"东方雕塑馆"之称。还有与麦积山石窟连成一线的甘谷大像山、华盖寺、武山水帘洞、木梯寺、禅殿寺等石窟。①

综上所述，天水"五大文化"地域性特色鲜明、旅游景点众多且各具特色。随着"一带一路"倡议的深入实施，地处丝绸之路黄金段上的天水已成为"一带一路"沿线旅游热点地区。为此，搭建国际性丝绸之路旅游推介营销平台，让天水丝路游越来越受到国内外游客的青睐，是语言工作者的重要任务。

---

① 杨仲杰：《天水旅游景点分布及发展规划的基础研究》，《甘肃科技纵横》2005年第3期。

第二章

天水伏羲文化描写与解释

第一节 天水伏羲文化简述

伏羲文化是黄河流域重要的新石器时代文化,距今五千多年。她是伏羲时代产生的龙文化、玉文化、观天文化、姓氏文化、渔猎文化、太极八卦文化,原始文字与数字文化的总称。

伏羲文化源于天水,但发展到中晚期阶段传播到了整个黄河流域地区。据《帝王世纪》等典籍记载,太昊伏羲生于成纪(今甘肃天水),建都于陈(今河南淮阳)。[①] 伏羲氏族活动范围包括今天的甘、陕、晋、冀、鲁、豫、鄂、川、云、贵等省,其创立和倡导的古文明影响到中原及华北、东南。在伏羲文化资源最集中的甘肃天水、河南淮阳、河北新乐三地保存有规模最大的伏羲文化遗迹:羲皇故里—甘肃天水伏羲庙、羲皇圣里—河北新乐伏羲台、羲皇故都—河南淮阳太昊陵并每年举行各种不同形式的纪念活动。

天水是"羲皇故里",伏羲文化资源丰富。主要由五个方面构成:"羲皇故里"、卦台山和伏羲庙、秦安和甘谷伏羲遗迹、女娲庙、伏羲女娲传说。就旅游角度而言,天水伏羲文化资源属人文旅游资源,既有伏羲庙等文物古迹,又有伏羲祭典等节庆习俗。还有大量的伏羲女娲传说,具备满足各种旅游需求的综合性特质,古远博大,神秘神

---

① (晋)皇甫谧:《帝王世纪》,辽宁教育出版社1997年版,第2—3页。

圣，特色鲜明。①

A Brief Introduction of Fuxi Culture

Fuxi Culture is an important Neolithic culture along the Yellow River Basin, covering a period of more than 5000 years. It is made up of Culture of Dragon, Culture of Jade, Astronomical Culture, Culture of Surname, Culture of Hunting and Fishing, Culture of Taiji Eight Trigrams, and Culture of Original Characters and Figures.

Fuxi Culture originated from Tianshui, a small city of northwest of China, then spreaded to the areas of the Yellow River Basin in middle and late time. According to the records of *the Age of Emperors*, Fuxi was born in Chengji (now called Tianshui) and the capital was founded in Chen (now called Huaiyang in Henan Province). The activities of Fuxi's clans extended to vast provinces, covering Gansu, Shaanxi, Shanxi, Hebei, Shandong, Henan, Hubei, Sichuan, Yunnan, Guizhou and etc. The ancient civilization Fuxi created and advocated had a great influence on central plains, north China and southeast of China. Moreover, the largest-scale Fuxi Culture relics were preserved mainly in places such as Tianshui of Gansu Province, Huaiyang of Henan Province and Xinle of Hebei Province. As a result, three Fuxi Culture relics are developed: Hometown of Legendary Ruler Fuxi-Fuxi Temple, Gansu Tianshui, Holy Land of Fuxi-Fuxi Hill, Hebei Xinle and Onetime Capital of Fuxi-Taihao Mausoleum, Henan Huaiyang. Every year memorial activities in various forms are held in the three places.

Tianshui is called "Hometown of Legendary Ruler Fuxi" with abundant Fuxi Culture resources. Kept the ultimate goal in mind, Fuxi Culture consists of five parts: Birthplace of Fuxi, Guatai Hill and Fuxi Temple,

---

① 刘雁翔等：《天水伏羲文化资源及旅游开发论析》，《天水师范学院学报》2006年第4期。

Fuxi relics in Qin'an County and Gangu County, Nvwa Temple (Nvwa refers to the goddess who patched the holes in the sky with stone blocks) and the legends of Fuxi and Nvwa. Seen from the perspective of travel, Tianshui Fuxi Cuture resources belong to tourist resources of humanity as they not only have culture relics such as Fuxi Temple, but also have some holidays and festivals like Fuxi ceremony. Also there are a great number of legends of Fuxi and Nvwa which obviously can meet the comprehensive needs for various tourists, for the legends are ancient and abundant, holy and mysterious, vivid and distinctive.

第二节 天水伏羲文化语篇语域重构及翻译

一 天水伏羲庙

（一）汉语语篇重构

天水伏羲庙

序列1：背景信息

天水伏羲庙位于天水市秦州区伏羲路110号（景点的地理位置）。是为了纪念上古三帝之一的伏羲所建造的（景点名称由来），始建于明朝（约公元1483—1484年），前后历经九次重修（建筑起止年代），是我国规模最宏大、保存最完整的明代伏羲祭祀建筑群（社会定位）。

序列2：主题信息

游客在庙内可观赏到用各种图案、符号和文字表现的伏羲丰功伟绩。建筑物上的雕塑造型各异、形态逼真，具有极高的艺术价值，虽历经千年嬗变但其质地、颜色、纹理仍然不变。它们图文并茂地介绍着伏羲始创的八卦（代表自然界天地水火山川雷电的象形文字），确定的婚嫁制度，创造的历法，发明的乐器，如何教人类学会打猎、捕鱼、织布、取火以及当时社会生活的变迁（观赏内容）。

序列3：附加信息

游客可以同时免费参观与伏羲庙相连的天水博物馆。博物馆主要介绍天水市从远古到近代的文明发展史，陶器、青铜器比较成体系。博物馆的数字电影将让您详细了解伏羲事迹；如果额外付费，团队游客可以得到汉语或英语的讲解服务；免费为有需要的游客提供拐杖、轮椅等（景点的设施和服务）。

游览完伏羲庙后，游客还可以领略其他周边景点的风采。孔庙、天水民俗博物馆、玉泉观、南郭寺均在1.5千米以内（游览指南/建议）。

游客还可以体验伏羲庙的官方和民间祭祀活动。每年6月22日举办中国天水伏羲文化旅游节，自2014以来海峡两岸"同时异地"举行公祭伏羲活动。太昊伏羲祭祀大典被国务院公布为第一批国家非物质文化遗产名录；每逢农历正月十六伏羲诞辰日，周边群众纷纷前往伏羲庙朝拜祭祀，祈求伏羲保佑来年安康宁寿（游览指南/建议）。

开放时间：9:00—17:30。

门票价格：成人40元；身高1.2米以下儿童、老年人持甘肃省颁发的老年证、现役军人持军官证、残疾人持残疾证免费；60岁以上老人持有效证件、身高1.2米以上大、中、小学生持学生证可购景区优惠票。

交通：市内乘公交1路、13路、14路到城区交警大队站，21路、22路到伏羲庙站，18路外环到秦州区医院站，24路到庆华厂站下可到；或在天水中心广场南侧街道一直向西步行20分钟即可到达；或于市内乘坐出租车，花费约5元。

（二）重构语篇英语书面语介绍

Resort Introduction of Fuxi Temple

Item 1 Background Information

Fuxi Temple is located in No. 110, Fuxi Road, Qinzhou District of Tianshui City (location). It was built to commemorate Fuxi, one of Three Sovereigns in ancient times (name origin). It was first built during 1483 - 1484 AD of the Ming Dynasty and has been rebuilt for nine times (time). It is China's most magnificent, most complete preserved building complex for worshipping Fuxi in the Ming Dynasty (social status).

Item 2 Topic Information

You can watch the great achievements of Fuxi displayed in various patterns, symbols and characters. The sculptures on the building are different in shapes and the lifelike shapes are of great artistic value. Although they have undergone thousands of years of evolution, the quality, color and texture remain unchanged. Most importantly, they introduced both in illustrations and text the Eight Trigrams (also called Bagua, on behalf of the pictographs of heaven and earth, fire and water lightning, mountains and rivers, lightning and thunder in natural world), the marriage systems, the created calendar, the invented musical instruments. Besides, they also introduced that how Fuxi taught people to learn hunting, fishing, weaving, making fire, and reflected the social changes (contents).

Item 3 Additional Information

You are free, at the same time, to visit Tianshui Museum connected with Fuxi Temple. The museum mainly introduces the development time of Tianshui from the far to the modern civilization. Pottery and bronze wares are relatively systematic in the introduction. Digital movies in the museum will allow you to view the details about Fuxi's stories. If extra money is paid, team tourists can get interpretation service in either English or Chinese. In addition, you are provided with free crutches, wheelchairs and so on, if you have any needs (facilities and services).

After visiting Fuxi Temple, tourists can also enjoy the charm of other surrounding attractions: Confucian Temple, Tianshui Folk Museum, Yuquan Taoist Temple and Nanguo Temple, which are all within 1.5 kilometres (guides/advices).

You can also experience the official and folk sacrificial activities of Fuxi Temple. Each year, China Tianshui Fuxi Cultural Tourism Festival is held on

June 22nd. Since 2014, Fuxi Public Memorial Ceremony has been held both in Taiwan and Tianshui, that is to say, at the same time, in different places. So Fuxi worship ceremony has been announced the first batch of national intangible cultural heritages by the State Council. On the birthday of Fuxi, 16th of the first lunar month, people around would flock to Fuxi Temple to worship and pray Fuxi for health and longevity (guides/advices).

Opening Times: From 9 : 00 a. m. till 5 : 30 p. m.

Tickets Prices: RMB 40 for each person. Free for those who are under 1. 2 metres tall, holders of senior citizen card issued by Gansu Province, military officer card holders on service and the disabled card holders. And the over 60-year-old elderly holding valid documents, pupils and college students card holders over 1. 2 metres tall can purchase discount tickets.

Transportation: You can take Bus No. 1, Bus No. 13, and Bus No. 14 to the city Traffic Police Brigade Stop. Or Bus No. 21 and Bus No. 22 to the Fuxi Temple Stop. Or Outer Bus No. 18 to Qinzhou District Hospital Stop. Or Bus No. 24 to the Qinghua Factory Stop. You can also walk westwards for 20 minutes to get there from the south street of Tianshui Central Square. If you do not want to bother, you just pay RMB 5 to reach there by taxi.

(三) 重构语篇英语口语导游词

Tour Guide Speech of Fuxi Temple

Item 1 Background Information

Fuxi Temple is located in No. 110, Fuxi Road, Qinzhou District of Tianshui (location). It was built in honor of Fuxi, one of Three Sovereigns in ancient times (name origin). It was first built in the Ming Dynasty (about 1483-1484 AD) and has been rebuilt for nine times (time). It is China's most magnificent, most complete preserved building complex for worshipping Fuxi in the Ming Dynasty (social status).

Item 2 Topic Information

You can watch the great achievements of Fuxi displayed in various patterns, symbols and characters. The sculptures on the building are different in shapes. Look at the shapes. They are very lifelike. So they are of great artistic value. Although they have undergone thousands of years of evolution, the quality, color and texture remain unchanged. Most importantly, the sculptures explained both in pictures and text the Eight Trigrams (also called Bagua, on behalf of the pictographs of heaven and earth, fire and water lightning, mountains and rivers, lightning and thunder in natural world), the marriage systems, the created calendar, the invented musical instrument. The Eight Trigrams are our China's most extensive and profound culture. Millions of people from home and abroad are fascinated by its charm and essence. Besides, from the sculptures, we can see how people were taught to learn hunting, fishing, weaving, and making a fire. Clearly, the sculptures also reflected the social changes (contents).

Item 3 Additional Information

If you like, you can visit Tianshui Museum which is next to Fuxi Temple. Totally free. The museum mainly introduces the development time of Tianshui from the far to the modern civilization. Form the introduction, we can see that pottery and bronze wares are relatively systematic. Digital movies in the museum will allow you to view the details about Fuxi story. If extra money is paid, team tourists can get interpretation service in either English or Chinese. In addition, if you have any needs, you are provided with free crutches, wheelchairs and so on (facilities and services).

After visiting Fuxi Temple, you can also enjoy the charm of other surrounding attractions: Confucian Temple, Tianshui Folk Museum, Yuquan Taoist Temple and Nanguo Temple. They are all very close to one another, just within 1.5 kilometres (guides/advices).

Dear friends, do you know the sacrificial activities of Fuxi Temple? It is the biggest and most holy ceremony of Fuxi Temple. Each year, China Tianshui Fuxi Cultural Tourism Festival is held on June 22nd. If you are lucky enough to come to Tianshui on that day, you can also witness and enjoy the official and folk sacrificial activities of Fuxi Temple. Since 2014, Fuxi Public Memorial Ceremony has been held both in Taiwan and Tianshui, that is to say, at the same time, in different places. So Fuxi worship ceremony has been announced the first batch of national intangible cultural heritages by the State Council. So on the birthday of Fuxi, 16th, the first lunar month, people around would flock to Fuxi Temple to worship and pray Fuxi for health and longevity (guides/advices).

The temple opens from 9:00 a.m. till 5:30 p.m. The ticket is RMB 40 for each person. Free for those who are under 1.2 metres tall, holders of senior citizen card issued by Gansu Province, military officer card holders on service and the disabled card holders. And the over 60-year-old elderly holding valid documents, pupils and college students card holders over 1.2 metres tall can purchase discount tickets. The transportation is very convenient. You can take Bus No. 1, Bus No. 13 and Bus No. 14 to the city Traffic Police Brigade Stop. Or Bus No. 21 and Bus No. 22 to the Fuxi Temple Stop. Or Outer Bus No. 18 to Qinzhou District Hospital Stop. Or Bus No. 24 to the Qinghua Factory Stop. If you want to wander about Tianshui, you can choose to walk. Just walk westwards for 20 minutes to get there from the south street of Tianshui Central Square. If you do not want to bother, you can just pay RMB 5 to reach there by taxi.

二 天水伏羲庙周边旅游景点

(一) 天水玉泉观

1. 汉语语篇重构

天水玉泉观

序列1：背景信息

天水玉泉观坐落在天水市秦州区城北天靖山麓（景点的地理位置）。因山上泉水晶莹如玉和元代秦州教谕（县掌教学）梁公弼建寺时吟有"山寺北郊，名山玉泉"之句而得名（景点名称由来），始建于元朝（约公元 1299 年）（景点起止年代），为天水市的道教圣地。有"陇东南第一名观"之美誉（社会定位）。

序列 2：主题信息

游客在本观内可以品尝元代道士梁志通用清冽甘美的玉泉之水疗治百姓眼病的明眼泉水。当年的明眼泉已变成如今的八卦井（泉上建有八角攒尖顶亭），一天之中井水成咸、甜、苦三种味道；还可欣赏记述有关道教（全真道）内容、史料价值极为珍贵的"元代四面道流碑"；元代大书法家赵孟頫的四方草书诗碑；树龄在 1000—1500 年的古树，其中悬根露爪、根茎交织、形如女子发辫的"辫柏"最为奇艳（观赏内容）。

序列 3：附加信息

景区免费语音导游系统囊括了景区 15 个景点，有着 10000 多字的讲解词资料，基本上满足了游客游览景点需求（景点的设施和服务）。

离开规模宏大的道教宫观建筑群后，游客还可以参观周边的伏羲庙和文庙等景点（游览指南/建议）。

游客还可以在农历正月初九体验著名的玉泉观庙会，当地人称"朝观"的民俗盛典。相传正月初九是玉皇大帝诞辰，自明代以来玉泉观即有"朝观"民俗。每年农历初八夜间至初九凌晨，来自海内外的万名游客在这里进行"朝观"，拜祭玉皇大帝。朝山时人们习惯身上插一束能消灾免病、带来吉祥的冬青（俗称吉祥草）（游览指南/建议）。

开放时间：8∶00—18∶00（3—11 月）；8∶30—17∶30（12—2 月）。

门票价格：成人 20 元；18 岁以下/学生/退休者 10 元；残疾人/现役军人/1.4 米以下儿童/60 岁以上老人免费。

交通：天水市内乘坐 7 路、24 路、26 路内环、26 路外环到玉泉观站，或乘坐 6 路、10 路、12 路、23 路内环、23 路外环到森美购物广场站，或乘坐18路内环到秦州区人民医院站下车。

2. 重构语篇英语书面语介绍

Resort Introduction of Yuquan Taoist Temple

Item 1 Background Information

Yuquan Taoist Temple is located at the foot of Tianjing Mountain to the north of Qinzhou District of Tianshui City (location). Yuquan Taoist Temple, also named the Jade Spring Taoist Temple, is named so because in it there is a spring whose water is cool, sweet, blue and transparent and also because the verse "On North Mountain Stands the Temple, Jade Spring flows below famous hill" chanted by Liang Gongbi who was mainly in charge of education in Qinzhou of Yuan Dynasty (name origin). It was built in 1299 AD of the Yuan Dynasty (time) and it is regarded as the well-known scenic spot of Taoism (Chinese system of belief). Now it has earned the fame of "the first famous temple of Southeast Gansu" (social status).

Item 2 Topic Information

You can drink the water, coming out of clean and sweet spring, which Taoist priest Liang Zhitong of the Yuan Dynasty used, for curing people's eye diseases. The ancient well for brightening eyes has now become "Bagua" well (the well with an octagonal pinnacle pavilion on it) which would change into salty, sweet and bitter taste within a day. In addition, you can enjoy the precious *The Tetrahedral Daoliu (the spreading order of Taolism) Tablet of the Yuan Dynasty* recording and narrating matters of the Quanzhen Taoism. And the tablets of cursive script (Chinese calligrapher style) written on the square poem tablet by the great calligrapher Zhao Mengfu of the Yuan Dynasty and ancient trees with the age of 1000 to 1500 years, of which the womanlike "pigtail cypress tree" is the most gorgeous one with hanging root, open stems and intertwined roots (contents).

Item 3 Additional Information

Free voice intercom guide system includes 15 scenic spots. And the explanation materials of scenic spots cover more than 10000 words, which basically meet the needs for travellers' visit (facilities and services).

After leaving the huge building complex of Taoism palace, you can also visit Fuxi Temple and the Confucian Temple nearby (guides/advices).

On the ninth day of first lunar month, you will have the chance to experience the famous Yuquan Taoist Temple Fair, also called "Chao Guan" folk festival by the local people. The legend goes that the ninth of first lunar month was the birthday of Jade Emperor. So the folk festival "Chao Guan" in Yuquan Taoist Temple has been inherited since the Ming Dynasty. From the night of the eighth of the first lunar month every year till the early morning of the ninth of the first lunar month, millions of visitors at home and abroad throng to "Chao Guan" (making a pilgrimage to the temple) for worshiping Jade Emperor. When worshiping, people would insert a Chinese holly (commonly known as auspicious grass) on them, which can avoid disease and bring happiness to people (guides/advices).

Opening Times: From March to November, from 8:00 a.m. till 6:00 p.m.; from December to February, from 8:30 a.m. till 5:30 p.m.

Ticket Prices: RMB 20 for adults. RMB 10 for people under 18 years old, students, and retirees. Free for the disabled, soldiers on active service, children under 1.4 metres tall, and the old over 60 years.

Transportation: Take Bus No. 7, Bus No. 24, Bus No. 26 (inner ring) and Bus No. 26 (outer ring) to Yu Quan Taoist Temple Stop. Or take Bus No. 6, Bus No. 10, Bus No. 12, Bus No. 23 (inner ring) and Bus No. 23 (outer ring) to Sen Mei Shopping Plaza Stop. Or take Bus No. 18 (inner ring) to People's Hospital Stop of Qinzhou District.

3. 重构语篇英语口语导游词

Tour Guide Speech of Yuquan Taoist Temple

Item 1 Background Information

The Yuquan Taoist Temple is one of the most famous scenic spots in

Tianshui City (location). It is located at the foot of Tianjing Mountain to the north of Qinzhou District of Tianshui. It is also called the Jade Spring Taoist Temple, named so because in it there is a spring whose water is cool, sweet, blue and transparent and also because the verse "On North Mountain Stands the Temple, Jade Spring flows below famous hill" chanted by Liang Gongbi of the Yuan Dynasty (name origin). It was built in the Yuan Dynasty (1299 AD) (time) and it is regarded as the well-known scenic spot of Taoism. Now it has earned the fame of "the most famous temple of Southeast Gansu" (social status).

Item 2 Topic Information

In Yuquan Taoist Temple, there are a lot worth seeing. Undoubtedly, the first thing you are interested in is the spring water. You must wonder if the water can be drunk. Yes! You are allowed to drink the water coming out of clean and sweet spring. The most magic of water is that Taoist priest Liang Zhitong of the Yuan Dynasty once used it for curing people's eye diseases. More interestingly, the ancient well for brightening eyes has now become "Bagua" well. Why people say that? You have never thought that the water in the spring would change into salty, sweet and bitter taste within a day. In addition, you can enjoy the complete Taosim and precious square tablets with Taoism in the Yuan Dynasty. And the tablets of cursive script (Chinese calligrapher style) written on the square poem tablet by the great calligrapher Zhao Mengfu of the Yuan Dynasty. Next is of course the trees. Look at the ancient trees! How many years are they? Yeah, they are about 1000 to 1500 years. But they still look lush and green. Look at the womanlike "pigtail cypress tree". It is the most gorgeous one among the trees because it has hanging root, open stems and intertwined roots. Amazing! Isn't it (contents)?

Item 3 Additional Information

There are 15 scenic spots in Yuquan Taoist Temple, so free voice intercom guide system is offered to you for clear introduction of the spots. Also, the explanation materials of scenic spots with more than 10000 words are provided to you who want to have a detailed understanding of the spots. Obviously this would basically meet the needs for travellers' visit (facilities and services).

After leaving the huge building complex of Taoism palace, you can also visit Fuxi Temple and Confucian Temple nearby (guides/advices).

Every year a grand Temple Fair is held in Yuquan Taoist Temple. It is on the ninth day of first lunar month. On this day, you will have the chance to experience the famous Yuquan Taoist Temple Fair, also called "Chao Guan" folk festival by the local people. As the legend goes, the ninth of first lunar month was the birthday of Jade Emperor. So the folk festival "Chao Guan" in Yuquan Taoist Temple has been inherited since the Ming Dynasty. From the night of the eighth of the first lunar month every year till the early morning of the ninth of the first lunar month, millions of visitors at home and abroad would throng to Yuquan Taoist Temple to worship Jade Emperor. You can't imagine the magnificent scene as bustling huge crowds of people have to push and shove their way. When worshiping, people would insert a Chinese holly (commonly known as auspicious grass) on them. It is said that a Chinese holly can avoid disease and bring happiness to people (guides/advices).

The temple opens from March to November, from 8:00 a.m. till 6:00 p.m.; from December to February, from 8:30 a.m. till 5:30 p.m. RMB 20 for adults, RMB 10 for people under 18 years old, students, and retirees. Free for the disabled, soldiers on active service, children under 1.4 metres tall and the old over 60 years. You have several options to get there. The transportation is quick and easy. Just take Bus No. 7, Bus No. 24, Bus No. 26 (inner ring) and Bus No. 26 (outer ring) to Yu Quan Taoist Temple Stop. Or take Bus No. 6, Bus No. 10,

Bus No. 12, Bus No. 23 (inner ring) and Bus No. 23 (outer ring) to Sen Mei Shopping Plaza Stop. Or take Bus No. 18 (inner ring) to People's Hospital Stop of Qinzhou District.

(二) 天水文庙

1. 汉语语篇重构

天水文庙

序列 1：背景信息

天水文庙位于甘肃省天水市秦州区中华西路（景点的地理位置），是祭祀孔子的殿堂。作为孔庙的另一名称，"文庙"的叫法起源于唐。唐玄宗年间（公元 739 年）封孔子为文宣王，因此，称孔庙为文宣王庙（景点名称由来）。始建于元朝间（公元 1302 年）（景点起止年代）。它是进行社会宣教、传播儒学的崇圣尊孔之地（社会定位）。

序列 2：主题信息

文庙古建筑中散发出来的传统文化浓郁、博大的气息令游客无法抗拒。可欣赏到孔子塑像、碑廊、千年古柏、清朝道光皇帝公元 1821 年御笔题书的"圣协时中"匾额、一边持笔一边持印的龙纹石刻（观赏内容）。

序列 3：附加信息

文庙外面紧邻文庙商场；东边毗邻天水民俗博物馆（游览指南/建议）。

开放时间：8：00—18：00。

门票价格：免费。

交通：乘坐 1 路、2 路、3 路、4 路到天水市秦州区中心广场下车。

2. 重构语篇英语书面语介绍

Resort Introduction of Tianshui Confucian Temple

Item 1 Background Information

Tianshui Confucian Temple is located on the Zhonghua West Road, Qinzhou District of Tianshui City (location) and also the palace of worshiping Confucius. It is also called Confucian Temple, because Confucius was honored with the title of Lord Wenxuan by Emperor Xuanzong of Tang (739AD). So Confucian Temple can also be called "Temple of Lord Wenxuan" (name origin). It was built in the Yuan Dynasty (1302AD) (time). Confucian Temple has now become the holy land to preach a religion and spread Confucianism (social status).

Item 2 Topic Information

You can not resist the rich and broad atmosphere of the traditional culture emitted from ancient buildings of Confucian Temple. You will never miss enjoying some sights such as the statue of Confucian, corridor of tablets, ancient cypress tree with thousands of years, a Board carrying the inscription "*Shengxieshizhong*" by Emperor Daoguang of the Qing Dynasty and a stone sculpture with dragon line on it (contents).

Item 3 Additional Information

The Confucian Temple is close to Confucious Temple Shopping Mall. The east side is adjacent to Tianshui Folk Museum (guides/advices).

Opening Times: From 8:00 a.m. till 6:00 p.m.

Ticket Prices: Free.

Transportation: Take Bus No. 1, Bus No. 2, Bus No. 3 or Bus No. 4 to Central Square Stop of Qinzhou District.

3. 重构语篇英语口语导游词

Tour Guide Speech of Tianshui Confucian Temple

Item 1 Background Information

Confucian Temple is well-known all over Tianshui. It is located on the Zhonghua West Road, Qinzhou District of Tianshui (location). It is also the palace of worshiping Confucius. It is also called Confucian Temple, originating from the Tang Dynasty when Emperor Xuanzong of Tang (739 AD) appointed Confucius as Lord Wenxuan. So Confucian Temple can also be called "Temple of Lord Wenxuan" (name origin). It was built in the Yuan

Dynasty (1302 AD) (time). Confucian Temple has now become the holy land to preach a religion and spread Confucianism (social status).

Item 2 Topic Information

The atmosphere of traditional culture emitted from ancient buildings of Confucian Temple is so rich and broad that all of you can not resist. Here are some sights that you will never miss, such as the statue of Confucian, corridor of tablets, ancient cypress tree with thousands of years, a Board carrying the inscription "*Shengxieshizhong*" by Emperor Daoguang of the Qing Dynasty and a stone sculpture with dragon line on it (contents).

Item 3 Additional Information

Confucian Temple is close to Confucian Temple Shopping Mall and Tianshui Folk Museum is to the east of it (guides/advices).

The temple is free and opens from 8:00 a.m. till 6:00 p.m. You can take Bus No.1, Bus No.2, Bus No.3 or Bus No.4 to Central Square Stop of Qinzhou District.

(三) 天水民俗博物馆

1. 汉语语篇重构

天水民俗博物馆

序列1：背景信息

天水民俗博物馆位于天水市秦州区民主西路117号（景点的地理位置）。因收藏民俗文物而得名（景点名称由来），2006年在胡氏古民居建筑南宅子基础上建立（景点起止年代），是全面展示明清时期秦州民居民俗文化的殿堂、天水民俗文化的游览胜地、中国古民居的经典样本和国内民俗博物馆的代表（社会定位）。

序列2：主题信息

作为天水市目前保存最为完整的明代民居，始建于明朝时（公元1589年）、为明代"父子乡贤"胡来缙和胡忻宅第的南宅子是本馆最重要的民俗展品。游客在欣赏南宅子古建筑格局和风貌时体验天水民俗文化和民居生活。陈列的2000余件民俗和历史文物展示了明清时期官宦人家的生活场景和历史名人书画、皮影、剪纸、香包、刺绣、生活用具等（观赏内容）。

序列3：附加信息

本馆运用多媒体、三维幻影成像等编创制作的《老天水》和《织锦寄情》三维动画影片更加生动、形象、全面地再现明清时期秦州官宦人家的家居生活场景（景点的设施和服务）。

20人以内讲解收费30元，20人以上每增加1人增收讲解费1.5元；每天限量发行参观券1000张，团体参观需提前预约；入馆参观者在服务中心寄存行李；馆内为需要的游客免费配备拐杖（景点的设施和服务）。

天水民俗博物馆西边毗邻文庙和文庙商场（游览指南/建议）。

开放时间：8：30—18：00。

门票价格：10元/人。春节初一到初五免费。

交通：乘坐1路、2路、3路、4路到天水市秦州区中心广场下车。

2. 重构语篇英语书面语介绍

Resort Introduction of Tianshui Folk Museum

Item 1 Background Information

The museum is located at No. 117 Minzhu West Road, Qinzhou District (location). It was named so because of the types of its cultural relics collection (name origin). The museum, established in 2006 on the basis of Hu's Folk Residences, fully demonstrates an art palace of dwelling, folk custom and culture in Qinzhou District within the Ming–Qing Dynasties, takes a role as a hot tourist attraction of Tianshui folk custom and culture, and also represents a classic sample of China's ancient residences and a representative of China's national folk arts museums (social status).

Item 2 Topic Information

As the most completely preserved residential building of the Ming Dynasty currently in Tianshui, the South Residence built in the Ming Dynasty

(1589AD) by Hu Laijin and Hu Xin, called "father-son country worthies", is the most important folk custom exhibits of the museum. You can experience the folk custom, culture and life of local people when enjoying the architecture pattern, style and features of the South Residence. Its more than 2000 folk custom and historic relics on display not only demonstrate the real life scenarios of official families in the Ming-Qing Dynasties, but also exhibit historic calligraphy and paintings from famous people, shadow play, papercut, sachet, embroidery, daily necessities etc. (contents).

Item 3 Additional Information

The two 3D-animated films, *Ancient Tianshui* and *Brocade Valentine* created and compiled by the museum through multi-media and 3D holographic projection technology, represent the real life scenarios of official families in the Ming-Qing Dynasties more vividly, more lively and more comprehensively.

The explanation fee is RMB 30 for people less than 20; RMB 1.5 extra money will be charged whenever one more person added for people over 20. Only 1000 tickets are limited sold every day and team tour tickets need to be booked in advance. Tourists entering the museum have to store their luggages at the service centre. Also free walking sticks are provided for those who need (facilities and services).

The west of Tianshui Folk Museum is adjacent to Confucian Temple and Confucian Temple Shopping Mall (guides/advices).

Opening Times: From 8 : 30 a. m. till 6 : 00 p. m.

Ticket Prices: RMB 10 for each person. Free from Chinese New Year's day to the fifth day.

Transportation: Take Bus No. 1, Bus No. 2, Bus No. 3 or Bus No. 4 to Central Square Stop of Qinzhou District.

3. 重构语篇英语口语导游词

Tour Guide Speech of Tianshui Folk Museum

Item 1 Background Information

Hello, everyone! Today I will show you around a famous scenic spot. Here we are. Now I will introduce it in details. The museum is located at No. 117 Minzhu West Road, Qinzhou District (location). It was named so because many folk cultural relics were collected here (name origin). The museum was established in 2006 based on the Hu's Folk Residences (time). It fully demonstrates an art palace of local dwellers, folk custom and culture in Qinzhou District within the Ming-Qing Dynasties. And now it has taken a role as a hot tourist attraction of Tianshui folk custom and culture. Most importantly, Folk Museum also represents a classic sample of China's ancient residences and a representative of China's national folk arts museums (social status).

Item 2 Topic Information

Look at the pictures. They are very old and precious. See the house? It is called South Residence. As the most completely preserved residential building of the Ming Dynasty currently in Tianshui, the South Residence was built in the Ming Dynasty (1589AD) by Hu Laijin and Hu Xin called "father and son county sages". Of course, it is the most important folk custom exhibits of the museum. When you enjoy the architecture pattern, style and features of the South Residence, you can also experience the folk custom, the culture and the life of local people. Now let's move to the next display window. Look at these folk customs and historic relics. Marvelous! There are about more than 2000 folk custom and historic relics on display. They demonstrate not only the real life scenarios of official families in the Ming – Qing Dynasties, but also the exhibit historic calligraphy and paintings from famous people, shadow play, paper cut, sachet, embroidery, daily necessities etc. (contents).

Item 3 Additional Information

Dear tourists! You will be amazed by the modernest technology used in the museum. There are two 3D-animated films, *Ancient Tianshui* and *Brocade Valentine*. They were created and compiled by the museum through multi-media and 3D holographic projection technology. The films represent the real life scenarios of official families in the Ming-Qing Dynasties more vividly, more lively and more comprehensively (facilities and services).

The explanation fee is RMB 30 for people less than 20; RMB 1.5 extra money will be charged whenever one more person added for people over 20. Only 1000 tickets are limited to sell every day. Besides, if a team tour want to visit, they need to book tickets in advance. Oh, by the way, if entering the museum, you have to store your luggage at the service center. If people are handicapped, free walking sticks are provided (facilities and services).

The west of Tianshui Folk Museum is next to Confucian Temple and Confucian Temple Shopping Mall (guides/advices).

The museum opens from 8:30 a.m. till 6:00 p.m. RMB 10 for each person. Free from Chinese New Year's day to the fifth day of the first lunar month. You need to take Bus No. 1, Bus No. 2, Bus No. 3 or Bus No. 4 to Central Square Stop of Qinzhou District.

（四）天水南郭寺

1. 汉语语篇重构

天水南郭寺

序列1：背景信息

天水南郭寺位于距城2千米的南郊慧音山处（景点的地理位置）。因地处城郭之南而得名（景点名称由来），始建于南北朝（公元420—589年）时期（建筑起止年代），是市郊最古老的一座梵宫古祠（社会定位）。

序列2：主题信息

游客在本寺可观赏到约2500年树龄的古树，几千年涓涓流淌永不干涸的清泉以及用晋朝（公元265—420年）书法家王羲之、王献之书法雕刻的唐朝（公元618—907年）诗人杜甫的诗"二妙轩碑"等自然人文景观（观赏内容）。

序列3：附加信息

如果额外付费，团队游客可以得到汉语或英语的讲解服务；免费为有需要的游客提供拐杖、轮椅等（景点的设施和服务）。

除核心区南郭寺外，游客还可以参观邓宝珊将军纪念馆和成纪博物馆等人文景观（游览指南/建议）。

夏天到南郭寺旅游是最好的选择。景区内南苑山庄的大型观景台可让您将天水市的全景尽收眼底（游览指南/建议）。

如果碰巧在农历四月初八参观本寺，您将有幸与众游客一起体验南郭寺一年一度的庙会（游览指南/建议）。

开放时间：8：00—18：00。

门票价格：成人20元；18岁以下/学生/退休者10元；残疾人/现役军人/1.4米以下儿童/60岁以上老人免费。

交通：天水市中心乘26路、9路公交车可直达。

2. 重构语篇英语书面语介绍

Resort Introduction of Nanguo Temple

Item 1 Background Information

Nanguo Temple is located in the southern suburbs of Huiyin Mountain, only 2 kilometres away from the heart of Tianshui city (location). The temple got its name for being in the south of the city (name origin) and was first built during the Northern and Southern Dynasties (420-589AD) (time), also is the oldest Buddhist temple on the outskirts of Tianshui (social status).

Item 2 Topic Information

You can appreciate many natural and cultural landscapes here. Among them there are towering old trees which can date back to more than 2500 years ago, a spring flowing for thousands of years without drying even in dried-up seasons and "the Stele of Ermiaoxuan" which was carved into the poem of the famous poet Du Fu of the Tang Dynasty (759AD), whose sculptors copied calligraphy from famous calligraphers Wang Xizhi and Wang Xianzhi of the Jin Dynasty (265–420 AD). Both the great calligrapher's calligraphy and the great poet's poems are combined together, for which it is named "Ermiao" (contents).

Item 3 Additional Information

You can be provided with guided tours in Chinese or English for extra pay. Free crutches and wheelchairs are also provided for those who are in need (facilities and services).

Other cultural landscapes of Deng Baoshan Memorial (1894–1968, a patriotic general of modern China) and Cheng Ji Museum (a nongovernmental museum to collect and display over 5000 important cultural relics of Tianshui) can also be visited (guides/advices).

Summer is the most pleasant season to visit Nanguo Temple as a large viewing platform within Nanyuan Mountain Villa offers fantastic panoramic views of Tianshui (guides/advices).

If you happen to visit the temple on April 8th of the lunar calendar, you will have the opportunity to experience the annual temple fair with thousands of travelers (guides/advices).

Opening Times: From 8:00 a.m. till 6:00 p.m.

Ticket Prices: Admission is RMB 20 for adults, RMB 10 for Under 18s/students/OAPs, or free for the disabled/Chinese serving soldiers/children below 1.4 metres and the senior citizens over 60.

Transportation: Bus No. 26 and Bus No. 9 are available to take travelers from downtown to the temple.

3. 重构语篇英语口语导游词

Tour Guide Speech of Nanguo Temple

Item 1 Background Information

Nanguo Temple is the oldest Buddhist temple in the outskirts of Tianshui (social status). It was first established during the Northern and Southern Dynasties (420－589AD). The temple's name is derived from its location in the southern suburbs (name origin).

Item 2 Topic Information

Within the solemn temple, you can find many natural and cultural landscapes. The temple has many towering ancient trees which have been over 2500 years old, a fantastic spring which has been flowering for thousands of years, even never stops flowing water in dried-up seasons. And most impressively, you are able to enjoy our great poet Du Fu's famous poems on poem tablets. Du Fu was of the Tang Dynasty. You see, the calligraphy works are so beautiful, aren't they? Do you know whose handwritings are they? Yeah, they came from the greatest calligraphers of the Jin Dynasty, Wang Xizhi and Wang Xianzhi, who are father and son (contents).

Item 3 Additional Information

If you pay extra money, you can get extra services. Let me say, you can get a tour guide serving you in English or in Chinese (facilities and services).

Apart from Nanguo Temple, you can also see Deng Baoshan Memorial, who was a patriotic general in China. He was born in 1894 and died in 1968. Ok, here we are—Cheng Ji Museum. It was established by a president of Cheng Ji Biological Pharmaceutical Industry. In the museum, over 5000 precious cultural relics of Tianshui are displayed. You will gasp in amazement when seeing them (guides/advices).

As we all know, the weather is very pleasant in Tianshui, especially in summer. So we suggest that you come to visit Nanguo Temple in this season. There is a mountain villa called Nanyuan in Nanguo Temple. You can have a beautifully panoramic view of Tianshui when you stand on the large viewing platform (guides/advices).

April 8th of the lunar calendar is a special day when the annual temple fair is held here. The fair is bustling and interesting. If you are lucky to come on that day, you will surely experience the joy and excitement together with thousands of travelers (guides/advices).

The temple opens from Monday to Sunday throughout the year from 8:00 a.m. till 6:00 p.m. Admission is RMB 20 for adults, RMB 10 for Under 18s/students/OAPs or free for the disabled, Chinese serving soldiers, children below 1.4 metres and the senior citizens over 60. However, it's very convenient to get there as it is only 2 kilometres away from the city centre. So you can either take Bus 26 or Bus 9 to get there directly, even can walk there if you like. By the way, the easiest and quickest way to get there, of course, is to take a taxi.

三 天水卦台山

(一) 汉语语篇重构

天水卦台山

序列1：背景信息

天水卦台山位于天水市北30千米处的三阳川境内（景点的地理位置）。因山上有伏羲创绘八卦（代表自然界"天、地、水、火、山、雷、风、泽"八种自然现象符号）的画卦台而得名（景点名称由来），从隋朝（公元581—618年）开始建造庙宇（景点起止年代），为海内外华人弘扬伏羲文化、探索八卦奥秘的文化主题园（社会定位）。

序列2：主题信息

登上卦台山，游客将发现为伏羲创造八卦提供灵感的"龙马洞"和"分心石"奇观。相传对面山洞中的云雾深处有一匹两翼振动的龙马腾空而起与渭河中呈太极图形的分心石相映，伏羲不禁灵机触动立即在卦台山上画出了八卦文字。另外不要错过观赏卦台山下现存直径 64 厘米、厚约 10 厘米的木制雕刻"伏羲六十四卦二十八宿全图"（观赏内容）。

序列 3：附加信息

游客可以多次体验卦台山民间祭祀伏羲活动。自官祭伏羲移至天水市后，卦台山遂成为民间祭祀伏羲的中心。农历正月十六日、二月十五日、五月十三日（龙的诞辰日）为祭祀日并举行声势浩大的祭祀活动。卦台山民间祭祀伏羲活动也被列为"中国天水伏羲文化旅游节"重要活动内容之一（游览指南/建议）。

开放时间：8：00—17：40。

门票价格：15 元/人。

交通：乘坐公交 303 路（麦积公交站至石佛镇）、公交 304 路（麦积公交站至中滩镇）、公交 305 路（麦积公交站至渭南镇）、公交 306 路（中滩至中滩环川）均可到达景区。

（二）重构语篇英语书面语介绍

Resort Introduction of Guatai Hill

Item 1 Background Information

Tianshui Guatai Hill is located in Sanyangchuan, 30 kilometres to the north of Tianshui (location). It was named for the reason that there are eight terraces with which Fuxi created Eight Trigrams (or called Bagua), eight symbols representing eight natural phenomena: sky, earth, water, fire, mountain, thunder, wind, lake (name origin). The temple started to be built from the Sui Dynasty (581–618AD) (time). Tianshui Guatai Hill has now become a cultural theme park for all Chinese people, either at home or abroad, to promote Fuxi culture and explore the profound mystery of Eight Trigrams (social status).

Item 2 Topic Information

Climbing the hill, you can see two marvelous spectacles – the Longma

Cave and the Fenxinshi Stone (the stone is divided from the center), from which Fuxi acquired inspiration and created Eight Trigrams. According to the legend, there was a legendary animal, called Longma with dragon-head and horse-body living in the opposite cave, spreading its wings to fly out of the cave encircled by cloud and mist, thus making an echo with the Fenxinshi Stone with the shape of Taiji in the Wei River. Capturing such a marvelous view, Fuxi could not help but have an inspiration and drew Eight Trigrams at once on Guatai Hill. You are also advised not to miss the opportunity to enjoy the existing full wooden sculpture— "The Panorama of Fuxi's Sixty-four Trigrams and Twenty-eight Constellations" —at the foot of the hill, with 64 centimetres in diametre and about 10 centimetres thick (contents).

Item 3 Additional Information

You can participate in folk activities of worshiping Fuxi in Guatai Hill many times. Since the official worshiping activities have been transferred to Tianshui, the Guatai Hill has become the center for worshiping Fuxi civilly. On 16th January, 15th February, and 13th May (birthday of the dragon) of Chinese lunar calendar every year, there will be many grand worshiping activities held in the area. The Guatai Hill folk worshiping activity of Fuxi has become one of the important activities in "China Tianshui Fuxi Cultural Tourism Festival" (guides/advices).

Opening Times: From 8:00 a.m. till 5:40 p.m.

Ticket Prices: RMB 15 for each person.

Transportation: You can take Bus No. 303 (from Maiji Bus Stop to Shifo County), Bus No. 304 (from Maiji Bus Stop to Zhongtan County) or Bus No. 306 (from Zhongtan to Huanchuan of Zhongtan) to get to Guatai Hill.

(三) 重构语篇英语口语导游词

Tour Guide Speech of Guatai Hill

Item 1 Background Information

Located in Sanyangchuan, 30 kilometres to the north of Tianshui city, the Guatai Hill is high with tall cypress and surrounding the Wei River with its 1,363 metres high above the sea level and comparative height of 170 metres (location). It was named for the reason that there are eight terraces with which Fuxi created Eight Trigrams (or called Bagua), eight symbols representing eight natural phenomena: sky, earth, water, fire, mountain, thunder, wind, lake (name origin). The temple started to be built from the Sui Dynasty (581-618AD) (time). Tianshui Guatai Hill has now become a cultural theme park for all Chinese people, either at home or abroad, to promote Fuxi culture and explore the profound mystery of Eight Trigrams (social status).

Item 2 Topic Information

At the center of the hill there are several bottomlands, forming a shape of Taiji, or called Supreme Ultimate. On the hill there is a terrace where Fuxi created Bagua, or called Eight Trigrams. Across the river is the Cave of Misty Longma, and Longma is a legendary animal in ancient China, with dragon-head and horse-body. When cloud and mist encircles the Longma Cave on the hill, it seems that Longma is coming out, flying with spread wings, which obviously presents a mysterious view (contents).

Item 3 Additional Information

Dear friends! There are many interesting legends about Guatai Hill. It is said that Fuxi, one of the three great emperors in the time of China, came to realize the Eight Trigrams during the period of his practicing here, and then the name of the mountain came out. According to the modern archaeology, during the period of Yangshao Culture five or six thousand years ago, ancient people had been living and working there and they created early civilization of China. Legend has it that Fuxi, ruler of great antiquity in China, created Bagua, or called Eight Trigrams, with eight kinds of symbols representing eight kinds of natural phenomenon. There are looks of Taiji and Longma in Guatai Hill. In order to commemorate Fuxi, many temples were built from 1517 AD in the Ming Dynasty, with only the main gate, theatre, meridian gate, drum tower, west hall there and main hall of Fuxi being preserved now. At the center of the main hall there is a statue of Fuxi wholly covered with gold foil and wearing leaves, on the right there is a statue of Longma spreading the wings to fly with a fancy look, on the left there is a picture of Eight Trigrams which is carried on the back of Longma coming out of river (facilities and services).

Guatai Hill is famous for its unique dragon-head appearance. With the Wei River in its west and Sanyangchuan (a small town) in its east, Guatai Hill is surrounded by others as if it is embraced by someone. Sanyangchuan, in appearance of Taiji, is divided by the Wei River in a shape of S, while Guatai Hill and Daoliu Mountain are respectively on each side of the Wei River just like the two points of Taiji (facilities and services).

The ticket is cheap, only 15 Yuan for one person. Also the transportation is easy and quick. There are three buses heading for Guatai Hill. You can take Bus No. 303 (from Maiji Bus Stop to Shifo County), Bus No. 304 (from Maiji Bus Stop to Zhongtan County) or Bus No. 306 (from Zhongtan to Huanchuan of Zhongtan) to get to Guatai Hill.

四 秦安女娲庙

(一) 汉语语篇重构

秦安女娲庙

序列1：背景信息

秦安女娲庙地处甘肃省天水市秦安县城50千米的陇城镇龙泉山上（景点的地理位置）。因相传为女娲出生之地而得名（景点名称由来），可追溯到秦朝（公元前221—公元前207年），距今已有2000多年的历史（建筑起止年代），是弘扬女娲文化、全球华夏儿女祭祀人文初祖女娲的圣地（社会定位）。

序列2：主题信息

游客在本庙可随处发现女娲的生活遗迹和传说。大殿正中的女娲塑像生动再现了女娲"抟土造人""炼石补天"的情景。她坐在水边，掘起一团黄泥，掺和了水，仿照自己映在水中的容貌，捏成一个个小人的形状。陇城北门内有一口冬夏不干竭的泉水，相传女娲抟黄土造人时即用此泉水。传说盘古开天用四根"不周山"大柱子支撑天地，共工与颛顼争夺帝位将不周山撞倒，天地裂了一条大缝，女娲在高山上架起神火，炼了36501块五彩石把天的裂缝补了起来，砍大鳌腿支撑天，从此天地就永久牢固了。游客还能够触摸女娲补天时剩下的五彩石（观赏内容）。

序列3：附加信息

如果额外付费，团队游客可以得到汉语或英语的讲解服务。景点免费为有需要的游客提供拐杖、轮椅等（景点的设施和服务）。

除女娲祠外，游客还可以参观位于陇城镇东南约2千米的风沟女娲洞和仅5千米距离的大地湾遗址、街亭古战场遗址（游览指南/建议）。

如果游客在农历正月十五（相传是女娲娘娘生日）这天参观本庙将有幸体验天水市政府主持的公祭女娲大典，秦安女娲祭典仪式于2011年列入国家级非物质文化遗产保护名录（游览指南/建议）。

女娲因建立了婚姻制度被人类作为婚姻之神来崇拜。每到农历正月十五日的元宵之夜，青年夫妇都要用纸剪一对鸳鸯，捧着去到女娲祠上香，意在女娲为媒，天地为证，海枯石烂，永不变心（游览指南/建议）。

开放时间：8：00—18：00。

门票价格：10元/人。

交通：天水长途汽车站有发往秦安陇城方向的汽车。

（二）重构语篇英语书面语介绍

Resort Introduction of Nvwa Temple

Item 1 Background Information

Qin'an Nvwa Temple is located on the Longquan Mountain, 50 kilometres away from Qin'an County of Tianshui, Gansu Province (location). It got the name as the legend goes that it was the birthplace of Nvwa (name origin). The time can be dated back to the Qing Dynasty (221BC-207BC) and has a long history of over 2000 years (time). Qin'an Nvwa Temple is the holy place to promote Nvwa Culture and also a sacred place for the global Chinese people to worship our ancestor Nvwa (social status).

Item 2 Topic Information

Here and there you can find the relics of life and legends of Nvwa. In the middle of the hall stands the statue of goddess Nvwa which vividly shows the scenes of Nvwa "created men by moulding yellow clay" and "melted down rocks to patch the sky". She sat at the edge of the water, picking up a lump of clay, adding some water, and molding clay figurines according to herself reflected in the water. Inside the north gate of Longcheng there is a spring which never dry up in winter and summer. The legend says that goddess Nvwa used the spring water when making men. It is said that Pangu held the heaven and the earth with four "Buzhoushan" (name of a mountain) pillars when splitting heaven and earth apart. When fighting for the position of emperor, Gong Gong and Zhuan Xu knocked the Buzhoushan over, making the heaven and the earth split open. Goddess Nvwa set up divine fire, melted 36501 five-colored rocks to patch the big hole, chopped the legs of huge legendary green sea turtle to hold the heaven. From then on, the heaven and the earth have been secure and firm once and for all.

Item 3 Additional Information

If extra money is paid, team tourists can be provided with explanation service in Chinese or English. Also walking sticks and wheelchairs are offered free if any of you need them (facilities and services).

Apart from Nvwa Temple, you are able to visit the Nvwa Cave about 2 kilometres southeast to the town, the Relics of Jieting Ancient Battle and Dadiwan Relics only 5 kilometres away (guides/advices).

If you happen to visit Nvwa Temple on the fifteenth day of lunar year (the legend goes that the day was the birthday of goddess Nvwa), you will be able to experience the Public Memorial Ceremony of Nvwa hosted by Tianshui municipal government. Blessedly, Qin'an Nvwa Memorial Ceremony was listed on the list of China's national intangible cultural heritage protection in 2011 (guides/advices).

Nvwa, as the goddess of human marriage, is worshiped by people in that she established the marriage system. On the night of Lantern Festival (the final event of Chinese New year), the fifteenth of the first month of lunar year, young couples would cut a pair of mandarin ducks in paper, then go to the Nvwa temple to incense with it, which means they will never change in the presence of Nvwa-the matchmaker-with heaven and earth as the witness (guides/advices).

Opening Times: From 8:00 a.m. till 6:00 p.m.

Ticket Prices: RMB 10 for each person.

Transportation: Take any buses heading for Longcheng of Qin'an from Tianshui Long-distance Bus Station.

(三) 重构语篇英语口语导游词

Tour Guide Speech of Nvwa Temple

Item 1 Background Information

Hello! Today we will visit an interesting scenic spot, Qin'an Nvwa Temple. I bet all of you must be interested in it. Nvwa, as called, is the China's goddess. Here we are. Qin'an Nvwa Temple is located on the Longquan Mountain, 50 kilometres away from Qin'an County, Tianshui, Gansu Province (location). Why dose it get this name? Because the legend goes that it was the birthplace of Nvwa (name origin). The time can be dated back to the Qing Dynasty (221BC-207BC) and it has a very long history about over 2000 years (time). Now Qin'an Nvwa Temple is the holy place to promote Nvwa Culture and also a sacred place for the global Chinese people to worship our ancestor, Nvwa (social status).

Item 2 Topic Information

Once you go into the temple, you will never miss finding the relics of life and legends of Nvwa. Look at the statue in the middle of the hall. Huge and beautiful, right? It is just the goddess Nvwa. What is she doing then? OK! The statue of Nvwa vividly reproduces the scenes of Nvwa "created men by moulding yellow clay" and "melted down rocks to patch the sky". She was sitting at the edge of the water, picking up a lump of clay, adding some water, and molding small clay figurines according to herself reflected in the water. Marvelous! We are all her offspring. Next, I will show you another spot. Inside the north gate of Longcheng there is a spring which never dry up in winter and summer. The legend says that Goddess Nvwa used the spring water to make men. Let me tell everyone a very interesting story. It is said that Pangu held the heaven and the earth with four "Buzhoushan" pillars when splitting heaven and earth apart. When fighting for the position of emperor, Gong Gong and Zhuan Xu knocked the Buzhoushan over. As a result, the heaven and the earth split open. Later Goddess Nvwa set up divine fire, melted 36501 five-colored rocks to patch the big hole, cut the legs of huge legendary green sea turtle to hold the heaven. From then on, the heaven and the earth have been secure and firm forever (contents).

Item 3 Additional Information

If you pay extra money, you can be provided with explanation service in Chinese or English. Also if any visitor need walking sticks or wheelchairs, they will be offered free (facilities and services).

Apart from Nvwa Temple, you are able to visit the Nvwa Cave about 2 kilometres southeast to the town, the Relics of Jieting Ancient Battle and Dadiwan Relics only 5 kilometres away (guides/advices).

Another pleasant thing needed to know. If you happen to visit Nvwa Temple on the fifteenth day of lunar year (the legend goes that the day was the birthday of Goddess Nvwa), you will be able to experience the Public Memorial Ceremony of Nvwa hosted by Tianshui municipal government. Blessedly, Qin'an Nvwa Memorial Ceremony was listed on the list of China's national intangible cultural heritage protection in 2011 (guides/advices).

Nvwa, as the goddess of human marriage, is worshiped by people in that she established the marriage system. On the night of Lantern Festival (the final event of Chinese New Year), the fifteenth of the first month of lunar year, young couples would cut a pair of mandarin ducks in paper, then go to the Nvwa temple to incense with it, which means they will never change in the presence of Nvwa-the matchmaker-with heaven and earth as the witness (guides/advices).

The temple opens from 8∶00 a.m. till 6∶00 p.m. The ticket costs RMB 10 for each person. You can take any buses heading for Longcheng of Qin'an from Tianshui Long-distance Bus Station.

第三节 "一带一路"沿线国家始祖文化语篇语域重构及翻译

一 印度那烂陀寺

（一）汉语语篇重构

印度那烂陀寺

序列1：背景信息

印度那烂陀寺坐落在今印度拉查基尔北方约11千米处的巴达加欧（景点的地理位置）。因当地森林水池中有条名叫那烂陀的神龙而得名（景点名称由来），公元5世纪由笈多王朝的帝日王始建，公元12世纪因遭到伊斯兰教教徒的侵略而毁灭（建筑起止年代），为古代印度规模宏大之佛教寺院及佛教最高学府和学术中心，唐朝（公元618—907年）高僧玄奘法师曾在此地留学（社会定位）。

序列 2：主题信息

在往日上万人的佛教大学中，游客看到的只是寺庙和佛学院遗留下的古迹，包括窣堵坡（坟冢）、舍利塔、寺庙（僧房学舍）以及重要的墙画、石刻、金属器物等艺术作品（观赏内容）。

序列 3：附加信息

如果额外付费，游客可以得到当地导游的汉语或英语的讲解服务，还可以在景区内体验能洗去罪孽的温泉洗身（景点的设施和服务）。

除佛塔外，游客还可以参观遗址对面的博物馆，陈列有从遗址中挖掘出的佛像、铜盘和印章等（游览指南/建议）。

那烂陀寺是玄奘西天取经的终极目的地，就是《西游记》中所描写的西天大雷音寺。3 千米处的玄奘纪念堂是中国政府在 1957 年捐款 30 万元人民币建造的以纪念这位中印文化交流的先驱（游览指南/建议）。

开放时间：9：00—18：00。

门票价格：100 卢比/人。

交通：景点位于王舍城外 10 多千米处，建议包车或自驾前往。

（二）重构语篇英语书面语介绍

Resort Introduction of Nalanda Temple in India

Item 1 Background Information

Nalanda Temple is located at the present-day Baragaon, 11 kilometres to the north of Rajgir, India (location). It got the name because there was a dragon god called Nalanda in the pool of local forest (name origin). It was built by King Skandagupta of the Gupta Dynasty in the 5th century and destroyed by Islamic disciples aggression in the 12th century (time). In ancient India, it was the grandest Buddha Temple and the top universities as well as the academic centre of Buddhist learning, so that the eminent monk Xuanzang of the Tang Dynasty (618-907 AD) studied here (social status).

Item 2 Topic Information

In the Buddhist universities where once millions of people studied, now you can only see the archaeological remains of a monastic and scholastic institution including stupas, shrines, viharas (residential and educational buildings) and important art works in stucco, stone and metal (contents).

Item 3 Additional Information

If extra money is paid, a local guide will provide you with the service of explanation in Chinese or English. Also you can experience the hot spring in the scenic spot, which is said to wash away people's sins (facilities and services).

Apart form Nalanda Temple, you can also visit the museum opposite to the relics. Statue of Buddha, copper coils and seals excavated in the relics are displayed in it (guides/advices).

Nalanda Temple, the ultimate destination for Xuanzang (Tang Dynasty Buddhist monk and translator) to go westwards to India to obtain Buddhist's scriptures, is also the Big Leiyin Temple depicted in *Journey to the West*. The memorial Hall, 3 kilometres away, was built by the Chinese government in 1957 with RMB 300 thousand donation in order to commemorate the pioneer of cultural exchange between China and India (guides/services).

Opening Times: From 9:00 a.m. till 6:00 p.m.

Ticket Prices: 100 rupees for one person.

Transportation: As Nalanda Temple is 10 kilometres far away from Rajagaha, you are strongly advised to hire a car or drive a car to get there.

(三) 重构语篇英语口语导游词

Tour Guide Speech of Nalanda Temple in India

Item 1 Background Information

Dear friends! I feel horned to be your guide today. I will take everyone to visit Nalanda Temple and give you a detailed explanation. OK, let's start. Nalanda Temple is located at the present-day Baragaon, 11 kilometres to the north of Rajgir, India. It is very famous around India (location). It was named after a dragon god called Nalanda in the pool of local forest (name origin). It was built by King Skandagupta of the Gupta Dynasty in the 5th century and destroyed by Islamic disciples aggression in the 12th century (time). In ancient India, it was the grandest Buddha Temple and the top universities as well as the academic centre of Buddhist learning. And China's eminent monk Xuanzang of the Tang Dynasty (618-907AD) used to study here (social status).

Item 2 Topic Information

Once millions of people thronged to the Buddhist university to study, but now you can only see the archaeological remains of a monastic and scholastic institution. There are stupas, shrines, viharas (residential and educational buildings) and important art works in stucco, stone and metal (contents).

Item 3 Additional Information

If extra money is paid, you can hire a local guide to explain in Chinese or English. Also you can experience the hot spring in the scenic spot. It is said that it can wash away people's sins. Interesting! Isn't it (facilities and services)?

Apart form Nalanda Temple, you can also visit the museum just across from the relics. You will enjoy the statue of Buddha, copper coils and seals excavated in the relics (guides/services).

Nalanda Temple is not only the ultimate destination for Xuanzang (Tang Dynasty Buddhist monk and translator) to go westwards to India to obtain Buddhist's scriptures, but also the Big Leiyin Temple depicted in *Journey to the West*. The memorial Hall, 3 kilometres away, was built by the Chinese government in 1957 with RMB 300 thousand donation in order to commemorate him, the pioneer of cultural exchange between China and

India (guides/services).

The temple opens from 9:00 a.m. till 6:00 p.m. The ticket price is 100 rupees for one person. As Nalanda Temple is 10 kilometres far away from Rajagaha, you are strongly advised to hire a car or drive a car to get there.

二 伊拉克巴比伦古城遗址

（一）汉语语篇重构

伊拉克巴比伦古城遗址

序列1：背景信息

巴比伦古城遗址坐落在伊拉克首都巴格达以南约90千米的幼发拉底河右岸（景点的地理位置）。在巴比伦语中，"巴比伦"就是"神之门"的意思。巴比伦的主要城门都是以神的名字命名的。其中最重要的伊什塔尔门，得名于古代巴比伦（景点名称由来），古城大约始建于公元前3000年。现古城遗址为新巴比伦王国国王尼布甲尼撒二世在位时期建造，它自公元前4世纪末逐渐衰落，公元2世纪沦为一片废墟（建筑起止年代），是世界著名古城遗址和人类文明的发祥地之一，是与古代中国、印度、埃及齐名的人类文明发祥地（社会定位）。

序列2：主题信息

游客在遗址不仅可以看到20世纪五六十年代根据史书记载复制建造的部分城墙和建筑（绘有雄狮、公牛及神龙图案的蓝色伊斯塔尔城门原件完整收藏在德国贝加蒙博物馆，刻写在城门内小广场墙上顶部的《汉谟拉比法典》浮雕原件收藏于法国卢浮宫博物馆），而且还可以体验有2600年历史的砖制甬路真实古迹，欣赏用巨大岩块雕琢而成的雄狮足踏人的巨石雕刻。狮身长约3米，高约2米，宽近1.5米，巍然屹立在一块长方形的石座上，强有力的狮爪下踩着一个石头人。它象征着古代巴比伦人不畏强暴、勇于斗争的英雄气概（观赏内容）。

序列 3：附加信息

城内博物馆陈列着出土的巴比伦文物，和根据出土文物复制成的巴比伦古城"空中花园"、巴别塔全貌的巨大模型，及高近 2 米的黑色闪绿岩的石碑。碑的上半部为精致的浮雕，刻着太阳神将权标授予汉穆拉比的情景，下半部是用楔形文字刻记了巴比伦王国国王汉穆拉比（约公元前 1792—公元前 1750 年）领导制定的世界上第一部法典《汉穆拉比法典》的全文，法典共 282 条。石碑的原件现存于巴黎卢浮宫博物馆内。如果额外付费，游客可以得到当地导游的汉语或英语讲解服务（景点的设施和服务）。

除古城外，游客还可以参观在巴比伦遗址和巴格达市内仿古重建的宁马克神庙和空中花园（游览指南/建议）。

2015 年伊拉克正式向联合国教科文组织申请将巴比伦古城遗址列入世界遗产名录以使其得到更好的保护（游览指南/建议）。

开放时间：全天。

门票价格：免费。

交通：从巴格达租车前往。

（二）重构语篇英语书面语介绍

Resort Introduction of Babylon Ancient City Ruins

Item 1 Background Information

Babylon Ancient City Ruins, on the right bank of Euphrates River, is about 90 kilometres south to Baghdad, the capital of Iraq (location). In Babylonian language, "Babylon" refers to "Gateway of the Gods". As a result, each main gate of the city was granted a Babylon God's name, with the most important one being the Ishtar Gate, whose name was acquired in ancient Babylon (name origin). Early Babylon city was built in about 3000 BC. The Babylon city with the present city ruins was built in the period when King Nebucha-dnezzar II was on the throne, went downhill gradually from the end of 4th century BC and finally became ruins in 2nd century AD (time). The Babylon Ancient City Ruins is one of the famous ancient city relics and one of the birthplaces of human civilization, with the same position as those of other three ones such as ancient China, ancient India and ancient Egypt (social status).

Item 2 Topic Information

In the attraction, you can see the partial city walls and buildings reconstructed in the 50s-60s of 20th century based on time records. The complete original blue Ishtar city gate, with sphinx, bull and fairy dragon patterns on it, is collected in Pergamon Museum of Germany. The original relief sculpture of the Code of Hammurabi, which was carved in the top part of the wall of the small square within the Ishtar city gate, is collected in Louvre Museum of France. You can also experience the real relic of the brick paved path of 2600 years old and enjoy the Babylon sphinx statue sculptured by a huge rock mass, with its body of about 3 metres in length, around 2 metres in height and nearly 1.5 metres in width, stands out majestically on a big rectangular block of stone base with a stone man under the mighty lion's claws, symbolizing the heroic spirit of ancient Babylonians with fearlessness to powerful enemy and bravery of fighting (contents).

Item 3 Additional Information

Besides the unearthed cultural relics displayed in city museums, a huge full appearance model of the Hanging Gardens and Babel Tower—replicas of the ancient Babylon city duplicated based on unearthed relics, and a black diorite—a stone made tablet of about 2 metres in height, are available for you to view. The stone tablet was carved with delicate relief sculpture on its top half, showing the spectacle when the chief Sun God Shamash granted the kingship token to Hammurabi. While on its lower half it was engraved in cuneiform that the full content, 282 laws in total, of the Code of Hammurabi—the world's first law code made under the leadership of Hammurabi (1792BC-1750BC), the King of the Babylon Kingdom. The original stone tablet is preserved in Louvre Museum of France. The one displayed in the site is a reproduced one. If paying extraly, you can get Chinese or English tourist guiding service from a local interpreter (facilities and services).

Besides the Babylon Ancient City Ruins, Ninmakh God's Temple on the Babylon relics and the Hanging Gardens of ancient Babylon in the city of Bagdad - rebuilt based on the old ones - are available for you to view (guides/advices).

In 2015, Iraq Government made a formal application to United Nations Educational, Scientific, and Cultural Organization (UNESCO) for placing Babylon Ancient City Ruins on the World Heritage List so as to protect it better (guides/advices).

Opening Times: The whole day.

Ticket Prices: Free.

Transportation: By Taxi from Baghdad.

(三) 重构语篇英语口语导游词

Tour Guide Speech of Babylon Ancient City Ruins

Item 1 Background Information

Dear friends! I am so happy to be your guide. Today I will take everyone of you to visit the one of the most famous ruins in the world, Babylon Ancient City Ruins. Babylon Ancient City Ruins is located on the right bank of Euphrates River, about 90 kilometres south to Baghdad, the capital of Iraq (location). In Babylonian language, "Babylon" means "Gateway of the Gods". So you will know that each main gate of the city was granted a Babylon God's name (name origin). Among the gates, the most important one is the Ishtar Gate, whose name was acquired in ancient Babylon. Early Babylon city was built in about 3000 BC. And the Babylon city with the present city ruins was built in the period when King Nebuchadnezzar II was on the throne. But it went downhill gradually from the end of 4th century BC and finally became ruins in 2nd century AD (time). Do you know how great the Babylon Ancient City Ruins is? It has been recognized as one of the famous ancient city relics and one of the birthplaces of human civilization. It has gained the same position as those of other three ones such as ancient China, ancient India and ancient Egypt (social status).

Item 2 Topic Information

There are some impressive sights that you will never miss. You can not only see the partial city walls and buildings reconstructed in the 50s–60s of 20th century based on time records, experience the real relic of the brick paved path of 2600 years old, but also enjoy the Babylon sphinx statue sculptured by a huge rock mass. The statue has a body of about 3 metres in length, around 2 metres in height and nearly 1.5 metres in width, stands out majestically on a big rectangular block of stone base with a stone man under the mighty lion's claws. It also symbolizes the heroic spirit of ancient Babylonians with fearlessness to powerful enemy and bravery of fighting (contents).

Item 3 Additional Information

Besides the unearthed cultural relics displayed in city museums, a huge full appearance model of the Hanging Gardens and Babel Tower—replicas of the ancient Babylon city duplicated based on unearthed relics, and a black diorite—a stone made tablet of about 2 metres in height, are available for you to view. You must be amazed by the wisdom and skills of ancient people when seeing them. On the stone tablet's top half, it was carved with delicate relief sculpture, showing vividly the scene when the chief Sun God Shamash granted the kingship token to Hammurabi. On the lower half, it was engraved in cuneiform with the full content, 282 laws in total, of the Code of Hammurabi—the world's first law code made under the leadership of Hammurabi (1792BC–1750BC), namely the King of the Babylon Kingdom. The original stone tablet is preserved in Louvre Museum of France. The one displayed in the site is a reproduced one. If you pay extra money, you can get Chinese or English tourist guiding service from a local interpreter (facilities and services).

Besides the Babylon Ancient City Ruins in Babylon, Iraq, you can also enjoy seeing Ninmakh God's Temple on the relics and the Hanging Gardens of ancient Babylon in the city of Bagdad, which was rebuilt based on the old ones (guides/advices).

In 2015, Iraq Government made a formal application to United Nations Educational, Scientific, and Cultural Organization (UNESCO) for placing Babylon Ancient City Ruins on the World Heritage List so as to protect it better (guides/advices).

The ancient city opens the whole day. You can visit freely and take Taxi from Baghdad to get there.

第四节　基于翻译语境和语篇理论的解释性译文质量评估

天水旅游文化翻译不仅数量少、翻译质量低下而且缺少依据连贯方法论施行的系统翻译活动，更缺少一个译文质量的客观评估体系。在针对译文评估、翻译方法论构建等问题的应用翻译研究领域，尽管有朱莉安·豪斯的功能主义语言学模式①，但这些模式关注的仅是译文的语言特征，并未论及影响、制约翻译策略选择的翻译语境问题，同时其操作性也不强。系统功能语言学认为，在构成使用语言的情景语境的各个要素里，只有三个因素对语言的使用产生直接和重要的影响。② 即语场、语旨和语式三个语域变量，对于使用语言时如何选择语言形式有着直接的、至关重要的影响。本著运用韩礼德功能语言学的语域理论对天水伏羲文化及"一带一路"沿线国家始祖文化源文

---

① Juliane House, *Translation Quality Assessment: A Model Revisited*, Tübingen: Gunter Narr Verlag, 1997, pp.1-23.

② 司显柱:《功能语言学与翻译研究——翻译质量评估模式建构》，北京大学出版社2007年版，第6—9页。

与译文从语场、语旨、语式三方面进行对比分析,客观和具体地评判翻译文本的质量。

一 语场对比分析

语场是关于言语活动的主题或焦点。根据这一情景参数,语用场景一般分为技术场景和日常场景两类,不同场景的语言表现出各自不同的特征。九组语料分别来自天水伏羲庙及其周边旅游景点天水玉泉观、天水文庙、天水民俗博物馆、天水南郭寺、天水卦台山、秦安女娲庙、印度那烂陀寺、伊拉克巴比伦古城遗址。就语场参数而言,采用哈蒂姆和梅森的语篇分析法[①]重构源语语境为背景信息、主题信息和附加信息,与英国旅游网站的语篇结构相比,两者显示出相同的语言特征。重构语篇的主题都相同,都是对景点进行描述和宣传,普遍使用日常用语、标准句法,向潜在的游客提供旅游景点的三类基本信息:包括景点位置、名称由来、起止年代和社会地位等背景信息;观赏内容等主体信息;景点设施与服务、游览指南或建议、气候、当地风土人情、旅游特色项目、开放时间、门票、交通等附加信息。两者均属于呼唤型文本,描述旅游体验,目的都是吸引潜在游客来旅游。

从九组重构语境语料可以看出,天水伏羲文化及"一带一路"沿线国家始祖文化语场特征是相同的。旅游景点的描写都使用日常用语而非技术用语,避免生涩难懂,便于读者阅读,有利于对景点进行宣传介绍。描写多使用标准句法和过程动词。

二 语旨对比分析

语旨是反映言语交际行为的双方,在权势关系、接触密度和亲切程度等方面的情景参数,主要用来区分正式和非正式情景两类。非正式情景中,交际双方一般地位平等,经常见面,关系亲密,语言上常

---

① Basil Hatim and Ian Mason, *Discourse and the Translator*, Shanghai: Shanghai Foreign Language Education Press, 2001, p. 223.

用带有感情色彩的词语、口头用语,使用典型语气;而正式情景里,交际者之间在权势方面是不对等的,接触稀少,关系疏远,语言在形式上,多使用中性词语、正式用语和非常规语气。① 就语旨参数而言,天水伏羲文化及"一带一路"沿线国家始祖文化在语旨方面的评价潜势都较强,在态度资源的利用上都倾向于"鉴赏资源",在情感资源方面均以"你指向"情感为主。例句如下。

(1)源语:作为天水市目前保存最为完整的明代民居,始建于明朝时(公元1589年)、为明代"父子乡贤"胡来缙和胡忻宅第的南宅子是本馆最重要的民俗展品。

译语:As the most completely preserved residential building of the Ming Dynasty currently in Tianshui, the South Residence built in the Ming Dynasty (1589 AD) by Hu Laijin and Hu Xin, called "father – son country worthies", is the most important folk custom exhibit of the museum.

语料多使用夸张的和具有劝导性的词汇如"保存最为完整的"(the most completely preserved)、"最重要的"(the most important)并结合鉴赏性词汇"famous""beautiful"等。

(2)源语:从天水中心广场南侧街道一直向西步行20分钟即可到达。

译语:Just walk westwards for 20 minutes to get there from the south street of Tianshui Central Square.

多用祈使句来实现呼唤功能。游客直接从祈使句的核心动词成分开始理解,按照不同的句子语境去体会祈使句的功能指向,更能成功完成交际目的。

(3)源语:天水伏羲庙……始建于明朝(约公元1483—1484年),前后历经九次重修。

---

① Suzanne Eggins, *An Introduction to Systemic Functional Linguistics*, London: Pinter, 1994, p. 78.

译语：It was first built during 1483-1484 AD of the Ming Dynasty and has been rebuilt for nine times.

汉语为主动语态可译作被动语态。源语中的词类、句型和语态等进行转换使译文更符合目标语的表述方式、方法和习惯。

（4）源语：游客在本观内可以品尝元代道士梁志通用清冽甘美的玉泉之水疗治百姓眼病的明眼泉水。当年的明眼泉已变成如今的八卦井（泉上建有八角攒尖顶亭），一天之中井水成咸、甜、苦三种味道；还可欣赏记述有关道教（全真道）内容、史料价值极为珍贵的"元代四面道流碑"；元代大书法家赵孟頫的四方草书诗碑；树龄在1000—1500年的古树，其中悬根露爪、根茎交织、形如女子发辫的"辫柏"最为奇艳。

译语：You can drink the water, coming out of clean and sweet spring, which Taoist priest Liang Zhitong of the Yuan Dynasty used, for curing people's eye diseases. The ancient well for brightening eyes has now become "Bagua" well (the well with an octagonal pinnacle pavilion on it) which would change into salty, sweet and bitter taste within a day. In addition, you can enjoy the precious *The Tetrahedral Daoliu (the spreading order of Taolism) Tablet of the Yuan Dynasty* recording and narrating matters of the Quanzhen Taoism. And the tablets of cursive script (Chinese calligrapher style) written on the square poem tablet by the great calligrapher Zhao Mengfu of the Yuan Dynasty and ancient trees with the age of 1000 to 1500 years, of which the womanlike "pigtail cypress tree" is the most gorgeous one with hanging root, open stems and intertwined roots.

从态度资源上看，九组语料多使用名词、代词、过程动词、数字等来描述景点。分清主从句进行组合，根据需要利用连词、分词、介词、不定式、定语从句、独立结构等把汉语短句连成长句。

（5）源语：如果碰巧在农历四月初八参观本寺，您将有幸与众游客一起体验南郭寺一年一度的庙会。

译语：If you happen to visit the temple on April 8th of the lunar calendar, you will have the opportunity to experience the annual temple fair with thousands of travelers.

"你指向"的大量使用增强了文本的对话性,九组语料多把"您"用作主位,让读者直接参与对话中。描写也更加直白、简单。

三 语式对比分析

语式是描述语言与情景在空间和人际距离方面关系的参数。据埃金斯,这一情景变量主要用来区分口语和书面语的言语特征。口语依赖语境,句子结构松散、动态,使用日常词汇,句子的语法不标准,词汇化密度低。书面语不依赖语境,多使用纲要式结构的句子,使用"声望"词汇,句子语法标准,词汇化密度高。当然,这是对位于语式连续体两极,即典型口语和书面语言辞特征的概括,而实际话语中的多数是介于两极之间,也就是说往往既有口语体又有书面语体特征,差异只是多寡大小而已,即混合语体。[①] 示例如下。

源语:游客在本寺可观赏到约 2500 年树龄的古树,几千年涓涓流淌、永不干涸的清泉以及用晋朝(公元 265—420 年)书法家王羲之、王献之书法雕刻的唐朝(公元 618—907 年)诗人杜甫的诗"二妙轩碑"等自然人文景观。

书面语介绍:You can appreciate many natural and cultural landscapes here. Among them there are towering old trees which can date back to more than 2500 years ago, a spring flowing for thousands of years without drying even in dried-up seasons and "the Stele of Ermiaoxuan" which was carved into the poem of the famous poet Du Fu of the Tang Dynasty (759AD), whose sculptors copied calligraphy from famous calligraphers Wang Xizhi and Wang Xianzhi of the Jin Dynasty (265–420 AD). Both the great calligrapher's calligraphy and the great poet's poems are combined together,

---

[①] Suzanne Eggins, *An Introduction to Systemic Functional Linguistics*, London: Pinter, 1994, p. 78.

for which it is named "Ermiao".

口语导游词：Within the solemn temple, you can find many natural and cultural landscapes. The temple has many towering ancient trees which have been over 2500 years old, a fantastic spring which has been flowering for thousands of years, even never stops flowing water in dried-up seasons. And most impressively, you are able to enjoy our great poet Du Fu's famous poems on poem tablets. Du Fu was of the Tang Dynasty. You see, the calligraphy works are so beautiful, aren't they? Do you know whose handwritings are they? Yeah, they came from the greatest calligraphers of the Jin Dynasty, Wang Xizhi and Wang Xianzhi, who were father and son.

九组语料均是介于口语和书面语两极之间的混合语体，既包含口语特点又包含书面语特点。汉语重构语境的口语倾向通过英语书面语介绍和口语导游词转换更加清晰。

九组语料中除了"二妙轩""八卦"等少数短语的翻译属于隐性翻译之外，基本上是属于显性翻译的语篇。虽然通过分析发现，语篇中出现了少数的信息不匹配和错误，但是正如豪斯在其翻译评估模式的阐释中指出的，"少数的不匹配与错误的出现是不可避免的"[1]。因此，九组语料的译文中的不匹配现象不会影响语篇的概念功能、人际功能及语篇的质量。

---

[1] Juliane House, *Translation Quality Assessment: A Model Revisited*, Tübingen: Gunter Narr Verlag, 1997, pp.1-23.

第三章

天水大地湾文化描写与解释

第一节 天水大地湾文化简述

天水大地湾文化是中国黄河中游已知最早的新石器时代文化，主要分布在渭河流域、关中及丹江上游地区，存在于约公元前6000年至公元前5000年。距今约7800年前的大地湾文化遗址所展示的天水远古文明，存在的时间跨度约3000年，内容异常丰富。其在原始建筑、艺术、农业起源、文字和宗教等多方面均是悠久、博大和先进的中华文明的典型代表，是中华文明火花的最初闪现。主要遗迹有天水大地湾遗址、天水师赵村遗址、天水西山坪遗址。

1958年，天水大地湾遗址被发现于天水市秦安县城东北45千米处的五营乡邵店村。该文化以文化类型多、延续时间长、历史渊源早、技艺水平高、分布面积广、面貌保存好而备受考古界关注。该文化包含五个文化期，距今约4800—7800年，延续3000余年。第一期即前仰韶文化，距今约7300—7800年，它是迄今为止渭河流域最早的新石器文化。这批最早开发陇原的先民创造发明了我国最早的彩陶，同时种植生产了我国第一批粮食品种——黍。第二期即仰韶文化早期，距今约5900—6500年。这里发掘出可称为"陇原第一村"的较完整的原始氏族村落。出土了一批绚丽夺目的彩陶，如著名的人面鲵鱼瓶，通高32厘米，口径4.5厘米，人头形口塑有清秀的五官、整齐的刘海、微鼓的鼻翼、尖圆的下颌，其面呈鸭蛋形，双耳有穿孔，口目镂空，显得生趣盎然。瓶身以优美的弧线为轮廓，由弧线三角形和柳叶纹组成流畅的图案,造型优美,动人心弦。第三期即仰韶文化中期,距今约 5600—5900 年。彩陶艺术达到鼎盛阶段,生动活泼的线条、变化无穷的图案、造型与彩绘的完美结合,无不体现出原始艺术大师们的精湛技艺以及对生活的热爱。第四期仰韶文化晚期,距今约 4900—5500 年。此时的聚落由于农业的发展、人口的剧增,迅速扩展到整个遗址,山坡中轴线分布着数座大型原始殿堂式建筑,周围为密集的部落或氏族。本期还发现了白灰地面上绘制的我国最早的地画,神秘而古朴。第五期即常山下层文化,距今约 4800—4900 年。这是仰韶文化向齐家文化过渡性质的遗存。

天水师赵村与西山坪遗址是位于渭河上游的保存较好、发掘规模较大的史前时期聚落遗址,文化层厚,遗迹多,遗物丰富。其文化内涵包括史前时期诸多文化遗存,有大地湾一期文化,师赵村第一期(新文化遗存)、第二期(半坡类型)、第三期(庙底沟类型)、第四期(石岭下类型)、第五期(马家窑类型)、第六期(新文化遗存)和第七期(齐家文化)等文化遗存,还有西周、秦汉和隋唐时期墓葬。在相距不远的两处遗址中,发现这么多不同时期的古文化遗存和历史时期墓葬,在我国考古发掘中尚属首次。

由于大地湾一期文化早于中原仰韶文化的典型代表半坡文化千年以上,两者在文化原貌上又有沿袭承传的密切关系。因而,她上开中原仰韶文化之先河,下启陇右马家窑齐家文化之滥觞,对探索中华文明的线索和原生面貌,揭示陇右与天水古代文化的考古编年和文化序列都具有极为重要的价值。

Part one A Brief Introduction of Dadiwan Culture

Dadiwan Culture stands for the historic relics of Dadiwan. In 1958, the relics were found in the east to the Shaodian Village, 45 kilometres northeast to Qin'an County of Tianshui City. The culture of Dadiwan is characterized by its diversity of culture, long period, early historic origin, advanced arts, vast spread of distribution and its good preservation, so it arouses the archeologists' wide concern.

Dadiwan Culture consists of five phases of culture and it has a time of about 4800 years to 7800 years, which has lasted approximately 3000 years. The first phase is called Pre-Yangshao Culture with a time of around 7300 to 7800 years and it is the earliest Neolithic along the Wei River. The ancestors who first exploited the field invented the earliest Chinese painted pottery and grew the first grain crop-millet. The second phase is called Early Yangshao Culture, lasting around 6500 years or 5900 years. Here the well preserved primitive village called "the First Village of Gansu Province" was unearthed, and a great deal of painted potteries were uncovered, among which there was a famous fish bottle with human face on it. The bottle is 32 centimetres high and 4.5 centimetres wide. Also it has a good-looking, goose-egged shape of face with neat fringes of hair, slightly flared wing of nose, pointed and round jaw, punched ears and fretwork eyes and mouth, which makes it vivid and lifelike. The body of bottle is outlined with beautiful curves, and the exquisite and deeply moving patterns on it are triangles with pitch arc and lines of willow leaves. The third phase is called Middle Yangshao Culture, covering a period of 400 years from 5900 BC to 5600 BC. During the time, the pottery arts reached its peak with vivid lines, variable patterns and perfect combination of shapes and colored patterns. All of these reflected the magnificent skills and the love of life of the old artists. The fourth period is Late Yangshao Culture which covered a time of 4900 years to 5500 years. With the development of agriculture and the vast increase of population, the settlements at this time rapidly extended to the whole relics with several large scale primitive palace style constructions scattered on the slope and densely populated tribes or clans dotted around them. Also some mysterious and simple floor paintings drawn on the black and white floor were found during this period. The fifth period is also named Lower Changshan Culture with a long time of 4800 years to 4900 years. This period was a historical remain from Yangshao Culture to Qijia Culture.

Tianshui Shi-Zhao and Xishanping ruins are relatively two well preserved prehistoric settlement ruins with relatively big unearthed scale in the upper reaches of the Wei River, with profound cultural development, multiple remains and plentiful relics. Their cultural connotations contain various cultural remains of pre-historic age, including the first stage of Dadiwan Culture, the first stage (new cultural relics) of Shi-Zhao Village Culture, the second stage (Banpo remains) of Shi-Zhao Village Culture, the third stage (Miaodigou remains) of Shi-Zhao Village Culture, the fourth stage (Shilingxia remains) of Shi-Zhao Village Culture, the fifth stage (Majiayao remains) of Shi-Zhao Village Culture, the sixth stage (new cultural survival) of Shi-Zhao Village Culture and the seventh stage (Qijia culture) of Shi-Zhao Village Culture etc., and also including tombs in the periods of West Zhou Dynasty, Qin-Han Dynasties and Sui-Tang Dynasties. It is the first time in China's archaeological and excavation history that so many ancient cultural relics and tombs from different historic periods could be found in so close two historic ruins.

Since the first stage of Dadiwan Culture was 1000 years earlier than Banpo Culture—the typical representative of Yangshao Culture in Central Plains, the two cultures, based on original cultural nature, have a close relationship by the way of cultural inheritance and transmission. Therefore, Dadiwan Culture not only set a precedent for Yangshao Culture, but also was an original source of Longyou Majiayao Culture and Qijia Culture. As a result, Dadiwan Culture is of very important value for people to explore the clue of Chinese civilization and its primary nature, and disclose the archaeological annals and time series of Tianshui ancient culture.

第二节　天水大地湾文化语篇语域重构及翻译

一　天水大地湾遗址

（一）汉语语篇重构

天水大地湾遗址

序列1：背景信息

天水大地湾遗址位于甘肃省秦安县城东北45千米处的五营乡邵店村（景点的地理位置）。因当年挖掘遗址现场在小河的转弯处而得名（景点名称由来），存在于公元前6000年至公元前5000年（景点起止年代），是中国西北地区考古发现中最早的新石器文化（社会定位）。

序列2：主题信息

游客能观赏到中国最早的旱作农作物标本、最早的彩陶、最早的文字雏形、最早的宫殿式建筑、最早的"混凝土"地面和最早的绘画六项中国考古之最而闻名遐迩（观赏内容）。

序列3：附加信息

如果额外付费，团队游客可以得到汉语的讲解服务。景区还免费为有需要的游客提供拐杖、轮椅等（景点的设施和服务）。

大地湾博物馆展示遗址出土的文物和历史遗迹介绍；遗址复原区能看到8000年前中国人生活的房屋建筑和食材；大地湾殿堂遗址拥有中国最早的殿堂式建筑（游览指南/建议）。

除古建筑群外，游客还可以参观位于陇城镇南门的女娲庙、镇东南约2千米的风沟女娲洞和仅5千米距离的街亭古战场遗址、秦安兴国寺、泰山庙（游览指南/建议）。

春天桃花盛开的时候是参观原始村落的最美季节。在大地湾仰韶文化中发现有35座陶窑，是甘肃考古发掘中最多的（游览指南/建议）。

开放时间：8∶00—17∶00。

门票价格：成人14元；18岁以下/学生/退休者7元；残疾人/现役军人/1.4米以下儿童/60岁以上老人免费。

交通：在天水市汽车总站乘五营乡方向的长途汽车。

（二）重构语篇英语书面语介绍

Resort Introduction of Dadiwan Relics

Item 1 Background Information

Dadiwan Relics is located primarily in east Shaodian Village, 45 kilometres northeast to Qin'an County of Tianshui City in Gansu Province of China (location). It was named so because the spot of relics was just at the turning when the relics was unearthed (name origin). The relics lasted from 6000 BC to 5000 BC (time) and were the first Neolithic culture found by the archaeologists in northwest area of China (social status).

Item 2 Topic Information

Visitors can appreciate six artifacts that broke Chinese archeological records. These finds are the earliest crop specimens of dry farming, the earliest painted potteries, the earliest Chinese character writings, the earliest palace style constructions, the earliest concrete floors in China and the earliest painting drawings in the world (contents).

Item 3 Additional Information

If additional money is paid, team tourists can be commentated in Chinese. Walking sticks and wheelchairs are also provided free if people need (facilities and services).

The Museum of Dadiwan displays the cultural artifacts excavated in relics and the introduction of historical relics. In Restoration Area, the construction of houses and foods of ancient Chinese living 8000 years ago can be seen. The relics of Dadiwan palace has the earliest palace style of construction in China (guides/advices).

Apart from groups of old buildings, you can also visit Xingguo Temple of Qin'an County and the Taishan Temple (guides/advices).

The best season to visit the primitive tribes is spring when peach blossoms will be blooming (guides/advices).

Opening Times: From 8:00 a.m. till 5:00 p.m.

Ticket Prices: RMB 14 for adults. RMB 7 for pupils under 18 years old or people who have retired. Free for the disabled/soldiers on active service/children under 1.4 metres high/senior citizens above 60 years old.

Transportation: Take coaches heading for Wuying Town from Tianshui Coach Station.

(三) 重构语篇英语口语导游词

Tour Guide Speech of Dadiwan Relics

Item 1 Background Information

The Relics of Dadiwan is located primarily in east Shaodian Village, Wuying Town, 45 kilometres northeast to Qin'an County of Tianshui, Gansu Province, China (location). Why is it named so? Because the spot of relics was just at the turning place when unearthed (name origin). The relics existed from 6000 BC to 5000 BC (time) and were the first Neolithic culture found by the archaeologists in northwest of China (social status).

Item 2 Topic Information

Visitors can appreciate six artifacts that broke Chinese archeological records. These finds are the earliest crop specimens of dry farming, the earliest painted potteries, the earliest Chinese character writings, the earliest palace style constructions, the earliest concrete floors in China and the earliest painting drawings in the world (contents).

Item 3 Additional Information

If you pay additional money, you can get interpretation service in Chinese. If you need walking sticks and wheelchairs, you will get them free (facilities and services).

The Museum of Dadiwan displays the cultural artifacts excavated in relics and the introduction of historical relics. In Restoration Area, you can see the construction of houses and foods on which ancient Chinese lived 8000 years ago. The relics of Dadiwan palace has the earliest palace style of construction in China (tour guides/advices).

Apart from groups of old buildings, you can also visit Xingguo Temple of Qin'an County and Taishan Temple (tour guides/advices).

The best season for visitors to visit the primitive tribes is spring when peach blossoms will be blooming (tour guides/advices).

The relics opens from 8∶00 a. m. till 5∶00 p. m. all year around.

The ticket Prices: RMB 14 for adults. RMB 7 for pupils under 18 years old or people who have retired. Free for the disabled/soldiers on active service/children under 1.4 metres high/senior citizens above 60 years old. You can take any coaches heading for Wuying Town from Tianshui Coach Station.

二 天水师赵村遗址

(一) 汉语语篇重构

天水师赵村遗址

序列1：背景信息

天水师赵村遗址位于甘肃省天水市秦州区太京镇师赵村（景点的地理位置）。因在师家崖、赵家崖两村首先发现而得名（景点名称由来），存在于公元前5300年至公元前4900年，其间约经历了400年（景点起止年代），以早期齐家文化为主，是迄今为止在渭河流域发掘的内容丰富、规模最大的一处聚落遗址（社会定位）。

序列2：主题信息

通过1981年至1989年多次发掘师赵村遗址，出土了2000多件重要文物，其中现藏于中国社会科学院考古研究所的人像彩陶罐价值极高。游客能观赏到房址、圆形窖穴、半地穴式房址、横穴窖址、圆形灰坑等遗迹及石器和陶器等遗物（观赏内容）。

序列 3：附加信息

天水市博物馆收藏有该遗址的部分修复文物（游览指南/建议）。

游客在师赵村遗址可以参观 6 座保存较好的陶窑，其中有 2 座较先进的浅穴平底式窑和横穴窑（游览指南/建议）。

景区周边可以购买天水花牛苹果和天水大樱桃（游览指南/建议）。

除师赵村遗址外，游客还可以体验每年农历三月二十八日举办的佛公桥庙会，参观佛公桥寺院并游览传说中《西游记》中的高老庄；附近西山坪遗址也能顺道游览（游览指南/建议）。

开放时间：全天。

门票价格：免费。

交通：在天水市南湖汽车站乘坐 14 路公交车。

（二）重构语篇英语书面语介绍

Resort Introduction of Tianshui Shi-Zhao Village Ruins

Item 1 Background Information

Tianshui Shi-Zhao Village Ruins is situated in Shi Village and Zhao Village, Taijing Town, Qinzhou District, Tianshui, Gansu Province (location). It was named for the reason that the Ruins was found originally from both Shijiaya Village and Zhaojiaya Village, and then was given a combination name (name origin). The original settlement, taking the Early Qijia Culture as its main culture, went through approximately 400 years of time from 5300 BC to 4900 BC (time). So far, Tianshui Shi-Zhao Village Ruins is the biggest settlement ruin with rich contents unearthed in the reaches of the Wei River (social status).

Item 2 Topic Information

During the years from 1981 to 1989, experiencing many times of excavation, there were over 2000 important relics unearthed from Tianshui Shi-Zhao Village Ruins, of which a Pottery Jar with Human-face Relief currently collected in the Institute of Archaeology, Chinese Academy of Social Sciences, has very high value. At the ruins, you can see its remains such as house sites, round storage pits, semi-subterranean house sites, crosswise pit sites and round ash pits etc., and also you can see some of its relics like stoneware and pottery (contents).

Item 3 Additional Information

There are some repaired relics of the Village Ruins preserved in the Tianshui Museum (guides/advices).

You can see six a bit better reserved pottery kilns, with two of which being the relatively advanced, shallow caved and flat-bottomed crosswise ones (guides/advices).

Around the spot, you can buy the famous "Tianshui Huaniu Apples" and Tianshui Large Cherries (guides/advices).

Besides viewing Shi-Zhao Village Ruins, you can experience Fogongqiao Temple Fair in every 28th March of Chinese lunar calendar, visit Fogongqiao Temple and the legendary "Gaolaozhuang" described in the book *Journey to the West*. You can call by Xishanping Ruins on your way (guides/advices).

Opening Times: The whole day.

Ticket Prices: Free.

Transportation: Take Bus No.14 at Tianshui Nanhu Bus Station directly to the site.

（三）重构语篇英语口语导游词

Tour Guide Speech of Tianshui Shi-Zhao Village Ruins

Item 1 Background Information

Dear friends! Let me take everyone to see around Tianshui Shi-Zhao Village Ruins today. Tianshui Shi-Zhao Village Ruins is located between Shi and Zhao Villages, Taijing Town, Qinzhou District, Tianshui City, Gansu Province (location). The reason why it is named so is that the ruins were found originally in both Shijiaya Village and Zhaojiaya Village, and then was given a combination name (name origin). The original settlement took the Early Qijia Culture as its main culture and went through about 400 years of time from 5300 BC to 4900 BC (time). Up till now, Tianshui Shi-Zhao Village Ruins has been the biggest settlement ruin with rich contents unearthed in reaches of the Wei River (social status).

Item 2 Topic Information

During the years from 1981 to 1989, experiencing many times of excavation, over 2000 important relics were unearthed from Tianshui Shi-Zhao Village Ruins. Among the relics, a Pottery Jar with Human-face Relies has very high value and is currently collected in Institute of Archaeology, Chinese Academy of Social Sciences. At the ruins, you can see its remains, such as house sites, round storage pits, semi-subterranean house sites, crosswise pit sites and round ash pits etc., and also you can see some of its relics like stoneware and pottery (contents).

Item 3 Additional Information

Some repaired relics of the Village Ruins are now preserved in the Tianshui Museum (guides/advices).

Six better reserved pottery kilns can be seen here. Of them, there are two pottery kilns which are relatively advanced. One is shallow caved and flat-bottomed, the other is crosswise (guides/advices).

Near the spot, you can buy famous "Tianshui Huaniu Apples" and large cherries grown in Tianshui (guides/advices).

Apart form Shi-Zhao Village Ruins, you can experience Fogongqiao Temple Fair in every 28th March of Chinese lunar calendar, and visit Fogongqiao Temple and the legendary "Gaolaozhuang" described in the book *Journey to the West*. Oh, by the way, you can also visit Xishanping Ruins on your way if you like (guides/advices).

The relics opens full day. You can take Bus No. 14 at Tianshui Nanhu Bus Station directly to the site and visit it freely.

三 天水西山坪遗址

(一) 汉语语篇重构

天水西山坪遗址

序列1：背景信息

天水西山坪遗址位于甘肃省天水市秦州区太京镇西山坪村（景点的地理位置）。因遗址分布在西山坪台而得名（景点名称由来），建于公元前2300年前后（景点起止年代），证明了早在4300多年前，天水已经存在农业多样化（社会定位）。

序列2：主题信息

西山坪遗址出土的原始农业遗存包括砾石打制或磨制石器以及陶片、陶罐等陶器均收藏在天水市博物馆或陕西博物馆；游客在遗址能观赏到暴露的灰层、灰坑、墓葬和白灰面居址等遗迹（观赏内容）。

序列3：附加信息

天水市博物馆收藏有该遗址的部分修复文物（游览指南/建议）。

景区周边可以购买天水花牛苹果和天水大樱桃（游览指南/建议）。

除西山坪遗址外，您还可以参观附近的师赵村遗址；体验每年农历三月二十八日举办的佛公桥庙会、参观佛公桥寺院并游览传说中《西游记》中的高老庄（游览指南/建议）。

开放时间：全天。

门票价格：免费。

交通：在天水市南湖汽车站乘坐14路公交车。

(二) 重构语篇英语书面语介绍

Resort Introduction of Tianshui Xishanping Relics

Item 1 Background Information

Tianshui Xishanping Relics is situated in Xishanping Village of Taijing Town, Qinzhou District in Tianshui, Gansu Province (location). It was named for the reason that the Relics was distributed at the tableland of Xishanping (origin). Built in around 2300 BC (time), it has been turned out that Tianshui has developed the diversity of agriculture as early time as 4300 years ago (social status).

Item 2 Topic Information

Some remains of primitive agriculture, including stone artifacts chipped and polished with gravel, pottery, pots etc. unearthed in Xishanping Relics, are collected in the Tianshui Museum or the Museum of Shaanxi. You can watch the exposure of ash layer, pits, tombs and ruins of the residence painted with white lime (contents).

Item 3 Additional Information

Partial restored cultural relics are collected in the Tianshui Museum (guides/advices).

The famous "Tianshui Huaniu Apples" and Tianshui Large Cherries can be bought near the scenic spot (guides/advices).

Apart from Xishanping Relics, you can also visit Shi-Zhao Village Ruins nearby, experience Fogongqiao Temple fair in every 28th March of Chinese lunar calendar, visit Fogongqiao Temple and the legendary "Gaolaozhuang" described in the book *Journey to the West* (guides/advices).

Opening Times: The whole day.

Ticket Prices: Free.

Transportation: Take Bus No. 14 at Tianshui Nanhu Bus Station to get there.

(三) 重构语篇英语口语导游词

Tour Guide Speech of Tianshui Xishanping Relics

Item 1 Background Information

Dear friends! Today we will go to visit Tianshui Xishanping Relics. It is located in Xishanping Village of Taijing Town, Qinzhou District in Tianshui City, Gansu Province (location). The reason for such a name is that the Relics was distributed at the tableland of Xishanping (name origin). It was built in around 2300 BC (time) and it has been proved that Tianshui developed the diversity of agriculture as early time as 4300 years ago (social status).

Item 2 Topic Information

There are a great number of remains of primitive agriculture unearthed in the site. There are stone artifacts chipped and polished with gravel, pottery, pots etc. and they are all collected in the Tianshui Museum or the Museum of Shaanxi. You can see the exposure of ash layer, pits, tombs and ruins of the residence painted with white lime (contents).

Item 3 Additional Information

In the Tianshui Museum, some restored cultural relics are collected (guides/advices).

Do you know the special local products in Tianshui? Yeah, they are the famous "Tianshui Huaniu Apples" and Tianshui Large Cherries. You can buy them near the scenic spot (guides/advice).

Besides Xishanping Relics, you can also visit Shi-Zhao Village Ruins nearby, experience Fogongqiao Temple fair in every 28th March of Chinese lunar calendar, visit Fogongqiao Temple and the legendary "Gaolaozhuang" described in the book *Journey to the West* (guides/advices).

The relics opens the whole day. You can take Bus No. 14 at Tianshui Nanhu Bus Station directly to the site.

第三节 "一带一路"沿线国家远古文明起源地语篇语域重构及翻译

一 缅甸曼德勒皇宫

(一) 汉语语篇重构

缅甸曼德勒皇宫

序列1：背景信息

曼德勒皇宫位于缅甸曼德勒的市中心（景点的地理位置）。作为缅甸最后一个王朝，贡榜王朝（公元 1752—1885 年）的宫殿因皇宫所在地而得名（景点名称由来），1857 年由敏东王所建，1859 年竣工。第二次世界大战时被火烧毁，1989 年至 1996 年 9 月重建、竣工并对公众开放（建筑起止年代），是缅甸历史上保存最完整的皇城（社会定位）。

序列 2：主题信息

金瓦红墙的建筑群、高达 9 米的城墙、塔楼、宽 60 米的护城河都会让游客印象深刻；复建的 89 个主要大殿，包括皇帝上朝召见群臣的大殿、居室、嫔妃居住的一大片后宫；层层向上、越上越小的蒲甘建筑风格；均由缅甸特有的珍贵树种柚木建造而成的 104 座殿宇（观赏内容）。

序列 3：附加信息

游客可登上皇宫内高 33 米的瞭望塔鸟瞰整个皇宫及曼德勒市的景色；也可参观古代缅甸文化博物馆，缅甸国王用过的物品、少量家私、相片、佛教艺术等，是唯一可以了解缅甸历史的地方；有当地汉语、英语导游服务（景点的设施与服务）。

游客除游览曼德勒皇宫外，周边景点也不容错过。距其约 2.9 千米处的曼德勒山是看日落和俯瞰曼德勒的好地方；以"天下最大的书"著称于世、约 2.4 千米处的曼德勒碑林佛塔，300 余座塔中都有一方刻满经文的石碑，相传这些经文是当年唐僧西天取经的全部诗经（游览指南/建议）。

皇宫亦是缅甸新人喜爱的婚纱摄影背景地（游览指南/建议）。

开放时间：7：30—17：30。

门票价格：皇宫不收门票，但外国游客入境需购买曼德勒通票，10 基亚/张，有效期 5 日。

交通：游客可骑自行车一同游览曼德勒山周边景点；或乘坐人力三轮车，往返约 4000 基亚；或乘摩的，往返约 10000 基亚。

(二) 重构语篇英语书面语介绍

Resort Introduction of Mandalay Palace

Item 1 Background Information

The Mandalay Palace is situated in the heart of Mandalay City, Myanmar (Burma) (location). As the last royal palace of the last Burmese monarchy, Konbaung Dynasty (1752–1885 AD), which was named for the place of its location (name origin). The palace was constructed by King Mindon, starting from 1857 and was completed in 1859. It was destroyed by fire during the World War II, but was reconstructed from 1989 to September 1996, and reopened to public after completion (time). It is the most completely preserved royal palace in Myanmar (Burma) time (social status).

Item 2 Topic Information

Visitors will be impressed by its building complex with golden tiles and red walls, 9 metres height of palace wall, towers, and 60 metres width of palace city moat. There are 89 reconstructed main halls to see, including the one where the King held court and summoned all of officials, King's bedroom, and an imperial harem for the concubines of a monarch to live. The palace building presents a strong Pugam style—upward, a layer of more than one layer, the overall looks like the Pugam pagoda. A total of original 104 large and small palace temple buildings were all built by the precious species of teak wood endemic in Myanmar (Burma) (contents).

Item 3 Additional information

Visitors can climb to the watch tower of 33 metres in height to get a bird's eye view of the landscape of the palace and Mandalay city. You can also look around Mandalay Cultural Museum, where the King used items, small furniture, photographs and Buddhist art etc. are displayed. The museum is the only place in Myanmar (Burma) for you to learn about Myanmar's (Burma's) history. Both Chinese and English tour guide services are available on site (facilities and services).

Besides Mandalay Palace, other tourist attractions should not be missed. Mandalay Hill, only 2.9 kilometres away from the city, is a resort to watch the sunset and overlook landscape of the whole city. Mandalay forest of pagoda steles, about 2.4 kilometres away from the city, has a huge stone book, known as "the world's largest book" in Myanmar (Burma). There are more than 300 towers there with a stone tablet in each, on which scriptures were carved in full. According to legend, these Buddhist scriptures were the complete ones acquired by Monk Xuanzang of the Tang Dynasty from ancient India (guides/advices).

Mandalay Palace is also the favorite background place for newly-wed Burmese couples to take wedding photographies (guides/advices).

Opening Times: From 7:30 a.m. till 5:30 p.m.

Ticket Prices: Free for the natives, but foreign tourists have to buy Mandalay Pass, 10 Kyat for one ticket, valid for 5 days.

Transportation: Visitors can ride to Mandalay Hill, or ride tricycles to get there, the return fare of which costs 4000 Kyat, or take a motorcycle to go there, the return ticket of which is about 10000 Kyat.

(三) 重构语篇英语口语导游词

Tour Guide Speech of Mandalay Palace

Item 1 Background Information

Dear visitors! This is the Mandalay Palace. It is situated in the heart of Mandalay City, Myanmar (Burma) (location). As the last royal palace of the last Burmese monarchy, Konbaung Dynasty (1752-1885 AD), which was named for its place of its location (name origin). The palace was constructed by King Mindon, started in 1857 and was completed in 1859. Unfortunately, it was destroyed by fire during the World War II. Then from 1989 to September 1996, it was reconstructed and reopened to public (time). Now it is the most completely preserved royal palace in Myanmar (Burma) time (social status).

Item 2 Topic Information

There are some beautiful scenes that you will never miss. First, you will be impressed by its building complex with golden tiles and red walls, 9-metre palace walls in height, towers, and a 60 metres palace city moat in width. Also there are 89 reconstructed main halls to see, including the one where the King held court and summoned all officials, King's bedroom, and an imperial harem for the concubines of a monarch to live. You may have noticed that the palace building has a special style. It is called Pugam style. You see? Upward, a layer by another, the overall looks like the Pugam pagoda. Finally, let me show you the original 104 large and small palace temple buildings. Observe the materials of buildings carefully. Yeah! They are the precious species of teak wood endemic in Myanmar (Burma) (contents).

Item 3 Additional information

If you want to view the landscape of the palace and Mandalay city, you can climb to the watch tower which is 33 metres high to get a bird's eye view of them. You can also look around Mandalay Cultural Museum, where the King used items, small furniture, photographs and Buddhist art are displayed. By the way, I have to tell everyone that the museum is the only place in Myanmar (Burma) for you to learn about Myanmar's (Burma's) history. Also I want to remind you that both Chinese and English tour guide services are available on site (facilities and services).

There are also other gorgeous tourist attractions all around Mandalay Palace, so I strongly suggest that you should not miss. First is the Mandalay Hill which is only 2.9 kilometres away from the city. It is a resort to watch the sunset and overlook landscape of the whole city. Another is Mandalay forest of pagoda steles which is about 2.4 kilometres away from the city. Here is a huge stone book, well-known as "the world's largest book" in Myanmar (Burma). Last, there are more than 300 towers. So many! And there stands a stone tablet in each tower, on which scriptures were carved in full. The legend goes that these Buddhist scriptures were the complete ones Monk Xuanzang of the Tang Dynasty acquired from ancient India (guides/advices).

Mandalay Palace is also the favorite background place for newly-wed Burmese couples to take wedding photographies (guides/advices).

The palace opens from 7:30 a.m. till 5:30 p.m. The ticket is free for the natives, but foreign tourists have to buy Mandalay Pass, 10 Kyat for one ticket, valid for 5 days. You can ride to Mandalay Hill or ride tricycles to get there, the return fare of which costs 4000 Kyat. Or you can take a motorcycle to go there, the return ticket of which is about 10000 Kyat.

二 泰国曼谷皇宫

(一) 汉语语篇重构

泰国曼谷皇宫

序列1：背景信息

泰国皇宫位于首都曼谷市中心湄南河畔（景点的地理位置）。因曾一直是皇室居所（现已搬迁）而得名（景点名称由来），始建于拉玛一世时期的1782年（建筑起止年代），是历代王宫中保存最完美、规模最大、最有民族特色的王宫，现仅用于举行加冕典礼、宫廷庆祝等仪式（社会定位）。

序列2：主题信息

金碧辉煌的22座宫殿建筑群，汇集了泰国建筑、装饰、雕刻、绘画等民族特色的精华，主要建筑物有节基宫、律实宫、阿玛林宫和玉佛寺。游客在国王接受各国使节递交国书的节基宫可参观王室的藏骨堂和武器博物馆；在国王、王后、太后等皇室成员举行丧礼的律实宫里可观赏拉玛一世国王时代制造的御座、御床和其他一流的艺术品；在举行国王加冕礼的阿玛林宫中可看到国王加冕坐的椅子（观赏内容）。

序列3：附加信息

游客参观时要求穿着整齐，禁止穿无袖T恤、背心、露脐装、透视装、任何短裤、破洞乞丐裤、紧身裤、裙裤、迷你裙、拖鞋，如果衣服不合格，入口有免费衣服供游客借用。免费租用的服装押金每件200铢，不找零，归还时原金额退回（景点的设施与服务）。

检票处景区中文游览图有详细的介绍；只有一处免费饮水地点，不卖饮料；售票处有中文语音导游机出租（200铢/2小时）；景点有汉语、英语导游服务（景点的设施与服务）。

进玉佛寺内部参观要脱鞋、脱帽，不能穿短裤、短裙，不能拍照，不能喧哗；走出玉佛寺不能再返回，其他区域可以往返（游览指南/建议）。

皇宫内的皇家警卫队约11点举行交接仪式。游客可以和上岗卫兵合影但要注意礼节（游览指南/建议）。

开放时间：8：30—16：30，午间不休；售票截止时间是15：30；有皇室仪式时闭馆。

门票价格：500铢。含王宫内的皇室装饰博物馆和玉佛寺门票（仅当日有效），以及王宫外的柚木宫门票（7日内有效）。

交通：乘公交船至大象路（N9）码头；或乘1、3、25、44、47、53、60、82、91等多路公交车可到达景点附近。

（二）重构语篇英语书面语介绍

Resort Introduction of Grand Palace in Bangkok

Item 1 Background Information

The Grand Palace is located in the heart of Bangkok, Thailand, on the south bank of Mekong River (location). The palace was named so because it used to be the official residence of royal family (name origin). But now they have already moved out. The palace was constructed in 1792 of King Rama Ⅰ (Buddha Yodfa Chulaloke) period (time). The Grand Palace is the best preserved, the biggest in size and the most distinctively national-featured royal palace of all in Thailand time. This palace is now only used for holding some ceremonies such as coronation ceremony and court celebration etc. (social status).

Item 2 Topic Information

The resplendent palace is a building complex of 22 palaces, having condensed the national-featured essence of Thai architecture, decoration, engraving art, drawing and so on. There are many buildings in the palace, namely Hakri Maha Prasad, Dusit Maha Prasad, Amarin Winitchai Hall and Wat Phra Kaeo. You can look around royal family's ossuary and weapon arms museum in Hakri Maha Prasad, where the King accepts credentials presented by diplomatic envoys of other countries. You can enjoy the sight of the throne and royal bed made in King Rama I time as well as other first class works of art in Dusit Maha Prasad, where royal family members like the king, queen and empress dowager hold funeral ceremonies. You can also see the chair where the King seated in his coronation ceremony in Amarin Winitchai Hall, where King's coronation ceremony was held (contents).

Item 3 Additional Information

When entering the palace, you are asked to get well dressed, without wearing sleeveless T-shirts, vests, bare-midriffs, see-through clothing, any shorts, ripped jeans, briefs, pantskirts, miniskirts and slippers. If your clothes are not up to standard, you can borrow some for free. However, you need pay deposit THB 200 for each with no change. When given back, you can get refund in full (facilities and services).

There are tourist maps in Chinese with detailed tour introductions for scenic spots at check-in point. There is only one point for free water to drink, no other drinks for sale. You can hire Chinese voice guide machines at the ticket office at the rate of THB 200 per 2 hours. There are both Chinese and English tour guide services available on the site (facilities and services).

You have to take off your shoes and caps, without wearing shorts and miniskirts, without taking photos and making loud noises after entering Wat

Phra Kaeo. No returning is permitted after coming out of Wat Phra Kaeo, but in other areas, you can go in and out freely (guides/advices).

The Royal Guard of the palace holds handover ceremony at 11∶00 a.m. every day. You can take photos together with the guard on duty, but you should be in a good manner (guides/advices).

Opening Times: From 8∶30 a.m. till 4∶30 p.m. No lunch break, ticket sale until 3∶30 p.m. The palace closes when there are royal activities.

Ticket Prices: THB 500, including the door tickets for the Royal Decoration Museum and Wat Phra Kaeo inside the palace (only valid for one day), also including the door ticket for Vimanmek Teak Mansion outside the palace (valid for 7 days).

Transportation: Take public boat to Pier Tha Chang (N9), or take public bus No.1, 3, 25, 44, 47, 53, 60, 82, 91 to the site's vicinity area.

(三)重构语篇英语口语导游词

Tour Guide Speech of Grand Palace in Bangkok

Item 1 Background Information

Dear friends! Today I will take everyone of you to see a famous palace-the Grand Palace in Bangkok. The location is very convenient, just in the heart of Bangkok, Thailand, on the south bank of Mekong River (location). Why is the palace so well-known? Because it used to be the official residence of royal family (but now they have already moved out) (name origin). The palace was constructed in 1792 of King Rama Ⅰ (Buddha Yodfa Chulaloke) period (time). Long long ago, isn't it? You never know that the Grand Palace is the best preserved, the biggest in size and the most distinctively national-featured royal palace of all times in Thailand. This palace is now only used for holding some ceremonies such as coronation ceremony and court celebration etc. (social status).

Item 2 Topic Information

The resplendent palace is a building complex of 22 palaces. And it has condensed the national-featured essence of Thai architecture, decoration, engraving art, drawing and so on. The main buildings in the palace are Hakri Maha Prasad, Dusit Maha Prasad, Amarin Winitchai Hall and Wat Phra Kaeo. You can look around royal family's ossuary and weapon arms museum in Hakri Maha Prasad. I have to remind everyone, Hakri Maha Prasad used to be the palace where the King accepted credentials presented by diplomatic envoys of other countries. Now let's come to another important palace-Dusit Maha Prasad. Here you can enjoy the sight of the throne and royal bed made in King Rama Ⅰ time as well as other first class works of art. Also here is the sacred place where royal family members like the king, queen and queen mother hold funeral ceremonies. OK! Here we are! This is Amarin Winitchai Hall. You can also enjoy the chair where the King seated in his coronation ceremony in Amarin Winitchai Hall where King's coronation ceremony was held (contents).

Item 3 Additional Information

There are some taboos you must bear in mind when you enter the palace. You are supposed to get well dressed, without wearing sleeveless T-shirts, vests, bare-midriffs, see-through clothing, any shorts, ripped jeans, briefs, pantskirts, miniskirts and slippers. If your clothes are not up to standard, you can borrow some for free. Of course, you need to pay deposit THB 200 for each with no change. When given back, you can get refund in full. So for those who would like to visit the Grand Palace in Bangkok, please do remember these (facilities and services).

If Chinese tourists go to visit the palace, you will be happy to find that there are tourist maps in Chinese with detailed tour introductions for scenic spots at check-in point. But there is only one place to drink free water, no other drinks for sale. You can hire Chinese voice guide machines at the ticket office at the rate of THB 200 per 2 hours. There are both Chinese and English tour guide services available on the site (facilities and services).

I have to remind everyone of one thing again. When you enter Wat Phra Kaeo, you must take off your shoes and caps, without wearing shorts and miniskirts, without taking photos and making loud noises. Once you come out of Wat Phra Kaeo, you are not allowed to return. But in other areas, you can go in and out freely (guides/advices).

One exciting thing for you! Usually the Royal Guard of the palace holds handover ceremony at 11:00 a.m. every day. So you will have the chance to take photos together with the guards on duty. Want to try? But you should pay attention to the good manner (guides/advices).

Opening Times: From 8:30 a.m. till 4:30 p.m. No lunch break, ticket sale until 3:30 p.m. The palace closes when there are royal activities.

Ticket Prices: THB 500, including the door tickets for the Royal Decoration Museum and Wat Phra Kaeo inside the palace (only valid for one day), also including the door ticket for Vimanmek Teak Mansion outside the palace (valid for 7 days).

Transportation: Take public boat to Pier Tha Chang (N9), or take public bus No. 1, 3, 25, 44, 47, 53, 60, 82, 91 to the site's vicinity area.

第四节　基于翻译语境和语篇理论的解释性译文质量评估

天水旅游文化翻译不仅数量少、翻译质量低下而且缺少依据连贯方法论施行的系统翻译活动，更缺少一个译文质量的客观评估体系。在针对译文评估、翻译方法论构建等问题的应用翻译研究领域，尽管有朱莉安·豪斯的功能主义语言学模式[1]，但这些模式关注的仅是译

---

[1] Juliane House, *Translation Quality Assessment: A Model Revisited*, Tübingen: Gunter Narr Verlag, 1997, pp. 1–23.

文的语言特征，并未论及影响、制约翻译策略选择的翻译语境问题，同时其操作性也不强。系统功能语言学认为，在构成使用语言的情景语境的各个要素里，只有三个因素对语言的使用产生直接和重要的影响。[①] 即语场、语旨和语式三个语域变量，对于使用语言时如何选择语言形式有着直接的、至关重要的影响。本著运用韩礼德功能语言学的语域理论对天水大地湾文化及"一带一路"沿线国家远古文明起源地源文与译文从语场、语旨、语式三方面进行对比分析，客观和具体地评判翻译文本的质量。

一 语场对比分析

语场是关于言语活动的主题或焦点。根据这一情景参数，语用场景一般分为技术场景和日常场景两类，不同场景的语言表现出各自不同的特征。五组语料分别来自天水大地湾遗址、天水师赵村遗址、天水西山坪遗址、缅甸曼德勒皇宫、泰国曼谷皇宫。就语场参数而言，采用哈蒂姆和梅森的语篇分析法[②] 重构源语语境为背景信息、主题信息和附加信息，与英国旅游网站的语篇结构相比，两者显示出相同的语言特征。重构语篇的主题都相同，都是对景点进行描述和宣传，普遍使用日常用语、标准句法，向潜在的游客提供旅游景点的三类基本信息：包括景点位置、名称由来、起止年代和社会地位等背景信息；观赏内容等主体信息；景点设施与服务、游览指南或建议、气候、当地风土人情、旅游特色项目、开放时间、门票、交通等附加信息。两者均属于呼唤型文本，描述旅游体验，目的都是吸引潜在游客来旅游。

从五组重构语境语料可以看出，天水大地湾文化及"一带一路"沿线国家远古文明起源地语场特征是相同的。旅游景点的描写都使用

[①] 司显柱：《功能语言学与翻译研究——翻译质量评估模式建构》，北京大学出版社2007年版，第6—9页。

[②] Basil Hatim and Ian Mason, *Discourse and the Translator*, Shanghai：Shanghai Foreign Language Education Press, 2001, p.223.

日常用语而非技术术语,避免生涩难懂,便于读者阅读,有利于对景点进行宣传介绍。描写多使用标准句法和过程动词。

二 语旨对比分析

语旨是反映言语交际行为的双方,在权势关系、接触密度和亲切程度等方面的情景参数,主要用来区分正式和非正式情景两类。非正式情景中,交际双方一般地位平等,经常见面,关系亲密,语言上常用带有感情色彩的词语、口头用语,使用典型语气;而正式情景里,交际者之间在权势方面是不对等的,接触稀少,关系疏远,语言在形式上,多使用中性词语、正式用语和非常规语气。[①] 就语旨参数而言,天水大地湾文化及"一带一路"沿线国家远古文明起源地在语旨方面的评价潜势都较强,在态度资源的利用上都倾向于"鉴赏资源",在情感资源方面均以"你指向"情感为主。例句如下。

(1) 源语:大地湾殿堂遗址拥有中国最早的殿堂式建筑。

译语:The relics of Dadiwan palace has the earliest palace style of construction in China.

语料多使用夸张的和具有劝导性的词汇的如"最早的"(the earliest)并结合鉴赏性词汇"famous""beautiful"等。

(2) 源语:在天水市汽车总站乘五营乡方向的长途汽车。

译语:Take coaches heading for Wuying Town from Tianshui Coach Station.

多用祈使句来实现呼唤功能。游客直接从祈使句的核心动词成分开始理解,按照不同的句子语境去体会祈使句的功能指向,更能成功完成交际目的。

(3) 源语:如果额外付费,团队游客可以得到汉语的讲解服务。

译语:If additional money is paid, team tourists can be commentated in

---

① Suzanne Eggins, *An Introduction to Systemic Functional Linguistics*, London: Pinter, 1994, p. 78.

Chinese.

汉语为主动语态可译作被动语态。源语中的词类、句型和语态等进行转换使译文更符合目标语的表述方式、方法和习惯。

(4) 源语：西山坪遗址出土的原始农业遗存包括砾石打制或磨制石器以及陶片、陶罐等陶器均收藏在天水市博物馆或陕西博物馆；游客在遗址能观赏到暴露的灰层、灰坑、墓葬和白灰面居址等遗迹。

译语：Some remains of primitive agriculture, including stone artifacts chipped and polished with gravel, pottery, pots etc. unearthed in Xishanping Relics, are collected in the Tianshui Museum or the Museum of Shaanxi. You can watch the exposure of ash layer, pits, tombs and ruins of the residence painted with white lime.

从态度资源上看，五组语料多使用名词、代词、过程动词、数字等来描述景点。分清主从句进行组合，根据需要利用连词、分词、介词、不定式、定语从句、独立结构等把汉语短句连成长句。

(5) 源语：除西山坪遗址外，您还可以参观附近的师赵村遗址。

译语：Apart form Xishanping Relics, you can also visit Shi-Zhao Village Ruins nearby.

"你指向"的大量使用增强了文本的对话性，五组语料多把"您"用作主位，让读者直接参与对话中。描写也更加直白、简单。

三 语式对比分析

语式是描述语言与情景在空间和人际距离方面关系的参数。据埃金斯，这一情景变量主要用来区分口语和书面语的言语特征。口语依赖语境，句子结构松散、动态，使用日常词汇，句子的语法不标准，词汇化密度低。书面语不依赖语境，多使用纲要式结构的句子，使用"声望"词汇，句子语法标准，词汇化密度高。当然，这是对位于语式连续体两极，即典型口语和书面语言辞特征的概括，而实际话语中的多数是介于两极之间，也就是说往往既有口语体又有书面语体特征,差异只是多寡大小而已,即混合语体。① 示例如下。

源语:如果额外付费,团队游客可以得到汉语的讲解服务。景区还免费为有需要的游客提供拐杖、轮椅等。

书面语介绍:If additional money is paid, team tourists can be commentated in Chinese. Walking sticks and wheelchairs are also provided free if people need.

口语导游词:If you pay additional money, you can get interpretation service in Chinese. If you need walking sticks and wheelchairs, you will get them free.

五组语料均是介于口语和书面语两极之间的混合语体,既包含口语特点又包含书面语特点。汉语重构语境的口语倾向通过英语书面语介绍和口语导游词转换更加清晰。

五组语料中除了"西游记"等少数短语的翻译属于隐性翻译之外,基本上是属于显性翻译的语篇。虽然通过分析发现,语篇中出现了少数的信息不匹配和错误,但是正如豪斯在其翻译评估模式的阐释中指出的,"少数的不匹配与错误的出现是不可避免的"②。因此,五组语料的译文中的不匹配现象不会影响语篇的概念功能、人际功能及语篇的质量。

---

① Suzanne Eggins, *An Introduction to Systemic Functional Linguistics*, London: Pinter, 1994, p. 78.

② Juliane House, *Translation Quality Assessment: A Model Revisited*, Tübingen: Gunter Narr Verlag, 1997, pp. 1–23.

第四章

天水秦文化描写与解释

第一节 天水秦文化简述

据《史记·秦本纪》记载，秦人、秦族、秦文化的形成与发展，经过了悠久而漫长的发展过程。秦人以西垂即今天水一带为根据地，经14代历时约300年的艰辛历程，终于创建了伟大的秦国。

广义的秦文化指伴随秦人兴起、建国和统一的过程，而由其创造、发展并不断得到扩充的物质文化与精神文化的总和。秦早期文化是秦人经过漫长的起源而形成自为的民族之后，由其在陇右天水地区创造和发展起来的一种地域文化，亦可称天水秦文化。天水秦文化是秦文化发展史上的最早阶段和源头所在，积淀和蕴藏着秦文化的种种原始基因和本质要素。该文化形成于先秦时期。最初，它属于一种地域文化，与之同时的还有齐文化、鲁文化、赵文化等不少列国文化。后来，伴随秦国的崛起和扫灭六国，进而完成统一中国的伟业，秦文化也就由地域文化上升为曾一度统治中国的主流文化和强势文化。[①]

天水秦文化是早期秦人入主中原之前，兼取西戎游牧文化和中原华夏文化的优点而形成的一种带有鲜明地域特色的地方文化。秦人族出东夷，经夏末商初、商末和周公东征后三次西迁，终于由定居东方变为定居于陇右天水一带。在商末至西周长达300多年的时间里，秦人完成了由边陲小族到重新兴起、崛起建国的历史进程。秦人的起源

---

① 雍际春：《秦文化与秦早期文化概念新探》，《西安财经学院学报》2007年第4期。

与发展经历了中原—天水—关中的运动轨迹,其文化也有一个华夏化—戎化—回归华夏文化的发展历程。它具有强烈的兼容性和博大的开放性,具有鲜明的功利色彩和进取精神,也有典型的尚武精神和质朴无华的风格;它以华戎交汇、农牧并举为特征。天水秦文化既是秦人东向、一统天下的秦文化的活水源头和文化优势所在,也是天水地域文化形成的标志。①

A Brief Introduction of Qin Culture

According to the time record in the "Qin Dynasty in Historical Records" of *Records of the Historian* (or *Shiji*), the formation and development of Qin people, the Qin nationality, and Qin culture experienced a long standing and long lasting developing process. Holding Xichui (modern as Tianshui) as their base area, through 14 generations' great efforts and more than 300 years of hard developing time, Qin people finally established their own great Qin State.

Broad sense of Qin Culture refers to the totality of material culture and spiritual culture which were created, developed and continuously expanded by Qin people in all over the process of their springing up and also in the entire course when they established their state, and then reunited the whole China. Early Qin Culture was created and developed by Qin people in Longyou Tianshui area as a regional culture (also called Tianshui Qin Culture) after their own nationality was formed through a long lasting originally growing up period. Tianshui Qin Culture was the earliest stage and original source of Qin Culture in its developing time, accumulating and being pregnant with various original genes and essential elements for the latter. Tianshui Qin Culture was formed in Pre-Qin Period. Originally it was only a regional culture, the same as other states cultures at that time such as Qi Culture, Lu Culture, and Zhao Culture. With the abrupt rise of Qin and

---

① 雍际春:《论天水秦文化的形成及其特点》,《天水师范学院学报》2000年第4期。

extinction of the other six states, the great reunification cause of China was completed, therefore, Qin Culture naturally rose from a regional one to a mainstream and strong one, once in a dominating position in China.

Tianshui Qin Culture was a regional culture with distinct region features, which was formed through Qin people's combining and absorbing the advantages of both Xirong Nomadic Culture and Huaxia Culture (or Chinese Culture) in Central Plains before they dominated the central plains of China at the Early Stage of Qin. Originally, Qin people were from Dongyi, areas in the Lower Reaches of the Yellow River. After three times of movements towards West in Late Xia Dynasty to Early Shang Dynasty, Late Shang Dynasty and after Duke Zhou's Conquest of the East respectively, Qin people finally settled in Longyou Tianshui area. Over 300 years from Late Shang Dynasty to Western Zhou Dynasty, Qin people completed their historic development process by turning themselves from a remote small nationality to a re-springing up and then an abrupt rising one and establishing their own state. Origination and development of Qin people experienced a motion trail-from Central Plains, to Tianshui, and then to Guanzhong, while their culture also experienced a developing process-from Huaxia fusion, to Rong fusion, and finally returning to Huaxia Culture. Qin Culture contains strong compatibility and broad openness, abounds in a strong utilitarian overtone and pioneering spirit, as well as possesses typical warrior spirit and simplicity style. Qin Culture is also characterized in intersection of both Huaxia and Rong Cultures and simultaneous development of both agricultural and nomadic civilizations. Tianshui Qin Culture was not only a live source and cultural advantage of Qin Culture that Qin people's eastwards moving and country reunifying ambition, but was also an indicating symbol of the formation of Tianshui regional culture.

第二节　天水秦文化语篇语域重构及翻译

一　天水牧马滩

（一）汉语语篇重构

天水牧马滩

序列1：背景信息

天水牧马滩位于麦积山以东20千米、石门景区西面10千米处（景点的地理位置）。因传说秦始皇（公元前259—公元前210年）的祖先嬴非子（？—公元前858年）在此地为周孝王（？—公元前886年）牧马而得名（景点名称由来）。非子牧马开始于公元前889年，至公元前886年获封秦地结束（建筑起止年代）。从嬴非子之后，经12代到秦始皇称帝，牧马滩一直是秦国（公元前770—公元前206年）战马繁育基地（社会定位）。

序列2：主题信息

20世纪80年代以来在天水牧马滩考古发掘出的战国时期（公元前476—公元前221年）考古实物秦简、木板地图、纸张等珍贵文物都收藏在甘肃省博物馆，游客在森林公园里只能看见8匹自远而近奔腾而来姿态迥异的白色石马和石马最前方一个驮在龟背上刻有"牧马滩"三个大字的石碑。8匹白马和黑底白字的石碑在青灰色的树林中分外显眼（观赏内容）。

序列3：附加信息

作为通往石门景区后山的必经之路，游客还可以游览距离10千米的石门景区和20千米的麦积山石窟等自然石窟景观（游览指南/建议）。

牧马滩四面环山，有草地和小溪。游客能看到放牛人在放牛。适合户外活动，可以烧烤也可以露营（游览指南/建议）。

开放时间：9：00—18：00。

门票价格: 10 元/人。

交通: 在火车站西面的麦积大酒店的入口处乘 34 路到达贾河,在贾河转乘 37 路公交到仙人崖下,再乘坐"天水—利桥"或"天水—党川"的县级班车到达牧马滩。

(二) 重构语篇英语书面语介绍

Resort Introduction of Pastureland of Grazing Horses

Item 1 Background Information

The Pastureland of Grazing Horses which is located about 20 kilometres east to Maiji Mountain and 10 kilometres west to Stone Gate (location) is said to be the place where the forefather of the Qin people, Yingfeizi (? – 858BC), herded horses for King Xiao of the Zhou Dynasty's emperor (? – 886BC) (name origin). The horse herding began in 889BC and ended in 886BC when he was granted a place of land in Qin City (time). And from Yingfeizi until Emperor Qinshihuang became the founding emperor of the Qin Dynasty after 12 generations, the Pastureland of Grazing Horses had always been the base of cultivating warhorses (social status).

Item 2 Topic Information

Since 1980s, precious archaeological objects such as bamboo slips of the Qin State, board map, paper etc., during Warring States Period (476 BC-221 BC), excavated in Tianshui Pastureland of Grazing Horses, have been collected in Gansu Province Museum. In the forest park, you can only see eight white stone horses with varied shapes galloping from far to near and a stone tablet carved *The Pastureland of Grazing Horses* beared on a turtle's back in front of stone horses. The eight white horses and a stone tablet exceptionally stand out among the gray woods (contents).

Item 3 Additional Information

As the Pastureland of Grazing Horses is also the road that one has to take to the back mountain of Stone Gate, you can also visit the natural scenic spots of Stone Gate, 10 kilometres away, and the Grottoes of Maiji

Mountain, 20 kilometres away (guides/advices).

The Pastureland of Grazing Horses is surrounded with mountains, vast green grass and clear streams. Cowherds can be seen to graze cattle. It is very suitable for you to have outdoor activities, such as barbecue and camping (guides/advices).

Opening Times: From 9∶00 a.m. till 6∶00 p.m.

Ticket Prices: RMB 10 for each person.

Transportation: Take Bus No. 34, which stops at the entrance of Maiji Grand Hotel, west to Tianshui Railway Station, to get to Jiahe, then transfer Bus No. 37 to get to the Immortal Cliff, finally take "Tianshui-Liqiao" or "Tianshui-Dangchuan" county shuttles to get to the Pastureland of Grazing Horses.

（三）重构语篇英语口语导游词

Tour Guide Speech of Pastureland of Grazing Horses

Item 1　Background Information

Hello! Everyone! Today I will show you around the Pastureland of Grazing Horses. It is located about 20 kilometres east to Maiji Mountain and 10 kilometres west to Stone Gate (location). It is the place where Qin people, Yingfeizi, herded horses for King Xiao of Zhou (name origin). His horse herding only lasted for three years (time), from then until Emperor Qinshihuang became the emperor, the Pastureland of Grazing Horses had been the base of cultivating warhorses (social status).

Item 2　Topic Information

Since 1980s, many precious archaeological objects such as bamboo slips of the Qin State, board map and paper, excavated in Pastureland of Grazing Horses are collected in Gansu Province Museum. If you are in the forest park, you can only see eight white stone horses with varied shapes. These eight white horses and a stone tablet exceptionally stand out among gray woods (contents).

Item 3 Additional Information

Do you know the Pastureland of Grazing Horses is also the road you have to take to go to the back mountain of Stone Gate? You can also visit the natural scenic spots of Stone Gate. It is only 10 kilometres away near. Or you can go to the Grottoes of Maiji Mountain if you like. It is 20 kilometres away from here (guides/advices).

The Pastureland of Grazing Horses is surrounded with mountains, vast green grass and clear streams. Cowherds can be seen to graze cattle. It is very suitable for you to have some outdoor activities, such as barbecue and camping (guides/advices).

The park opens from 9∶00 a.m. till 6∶00 p.m. The ticket costs RMB 10 for each person. You can take No. 34 Bus, which stops at the entrance of Maiji Grand Hotel, west to Tianshui Railway Station, to get to Jiahe, then transfer No. 37 Bus to get to the Immortal Cliff, finally take "Tianshui-Liqiao" or "Tianshui-Dangchuan" county shuttles to get to the Pastureland of Grazing Horses.

二 清水李崖遗址

（一）汉语语篇重构

清水李崖遗址

序列1：背景信息

清水李崖遗址位于天水市清水县城北侧樊河西岸和牛头河北岸交汇处的台地上（景点的地理位置）。因20世纪60年代首先发现于永清镇李崖村而得名（景点名称由来），存在于西周（公元前1046—公元前771年），历史跨度至少在5000年以上（建筑起止年代），是秦朝（公元前221—公元前207年）祖先秦非子封邑地（社会定位）。

序列2：主题信息

游客可在清水县博物馆目睹李崖遗址中出土的文物。有寺洼文化（中国西北地区的青铜时代文化，因最初发现于甘肃临洮寺洼山而得名）时期的马鞍口形褐色陶罐、双耳乳状鬲、三足单耳夹砂罐，周代饮酒用的铜觯和宋代的陪葬品灰陶塔形罐。游客在残留的古城中能发现灰坑、窖穴、城墙、壕沟等遗迹（观赏内容）。

序列3：附加信息

游客还可参观也位于李崖村的轩辕窑（轩辕指黄帝，古代传说中的中华民族人文始祖之一），相传轩辕母亲曾携轩辕帝居住在此窑。窑内有齐家文化陶片遗存（游览指南/建议）。

开放时间：全天。

门票价格：免费。

交通：从清水县城向西北步行1千米左右就可到李崖古城遗址的古城塬遗址。

（二）重构语篇英语书面语介绍

Resort Introduction of Liya Relics

Item 1 Background Information

Tianshui Liya Relics is located at a tableland, on the junction of west bank of Fan River and north bank of Niutou River, north side of Qingshui County of Tianshui (location). It got the name because it was initially found in Liya Village of Yongqing Town in 1960s (name origin). It had already existed in Western Zhou Dynasty (1046 BC – 771 BC), covering a long time of over 5000 years (time) and it is also the place where the ancestor Qinfeizi of the Qin Dynasty was granted the territory (social status).

Item 2 Topic Information

You can see the cultural relics unearthed in Liya Relics of Qingshui County Museum. Among them there are saddle-shaped brown pottery during the Period of Siwa Culture (Bronze Age Culture of northwest China, named after the fact that it was found at Lintao Siwa of Gansu Province), a two-eared pottery tripod (an ancient cooking tripod with hollow legs), and a three-feet single ear clip sand tank. Also there are bronze drinking goblets in the Zhou Dynasty and funerary objects, namely the gray tower-shaped pottery in the Song Dynasty. You can find pits, storage pits, city walls, trenches and other relics in the remains of old town (contents).

Item 3 Additional Information

You can also enjoy Xuanyuan Cave (Xuanyuan refers to Huangdi who was one of legend ancestors of Chinese nation in ancient myth). The legend goes that Xuanyuan's mother used to live with him in it. Pottery remains of Qijia Culture were found here (guides/advices).

Opening Times: The whole day.

Ticket Prices: Free.

Transportation: From Qingshui County, only about 1 kilometre's walk northwestwards can get to Liya Relics.

(三) 重构语篇英语口语导游词

Tour Guide Speech of Liya Relics

Item 1 Background Information

Hello! Everyone! I am happy to be your guide today. I will explain Tianshui Liya Relics to everyone. It is located at a tableland, on the junction of west bank of Fan River and north bank of Niutou River, north side of Qingshui County of Tianshui (location). Why it got the name? Because it was initially found in Liya Village of Yongqing Town in 1960s (name origin). The relics had already existed as long ago as in Western Zhou Dynasty (1046 BC-771 BC), so it has a long time of over 5000 years (time). It is also the place where the ancestor Qinfeizi of the Qin Dynasty was granted the territory (social status).

Item 2 Topic Information

You can see some cultural objects unearthed in Liya Relics of Qingshui County Museum. Typical ones are saddle-shaped brown pottery during the Period of Siwa Culture (Bronze Age Culture of northwest China, named so because it was found at Lintao Siwa of Gansu Province), a two-eared pottery tripod (an ancient cooking tripod with hollow legs), and a three-feet single ear clip sand tank. Also there are bronze drinking goblets in Western Zhou Dynasty and funerary objects, namely the gray tower-shaped pottery in the Song Dynasty are typical as well. Dear friends! Can you find some other remains? Yes! There are pits, storage pits, city walls, trenches and other relics in the remains of old town (contents).

Item 3 Additional Information

Very exciting thing is that you can also enjoy Xuanyuan Cave (a kind of cave dwelling on the Loess Plateau in northwest China). Who is Xuanyuan? You must be very interested in it. OK, let me tell you. He is said to be the first emperor of China. Chinese people call him Huangdi, and the first legend of our five ancient legends. The legend goes that Xuanyuan's mother used to live with him in it. Pottery remains of Qijia Culture were found here (guides/advices).

You can visit the relics at anytime freely. It's very convenient to go there. If you set out from Qingshui County, you just walk northwestwards about 1 kilometre and then will get to Liya Relics.

三 张家川马家塬战国古墓

(一) 汉语语篇重构

张家川马家塬战国古墓

序列1: 背景信息

马家塬遗址位于甘肃省张家川回族自治县距县城17千米的木河乡桃园村马家塬（景点的地理位置）。因首先发现于张家川马家塬而得名（景点名称由来），距今约2300年（建筑起止年代），该遗址带有较为浓厚的北方、西亚少数民族风格和秦文化特色，对研究秦和西戎（我国古代对西部各族的泛称，这里具体指以张家川陇山周围地区为中心发展起来的少数民族文化）的关系，北方、西亚古代民族史，中国古代中外民族文化交流、民族融合、冶金技术、古代科技史具有重要价值（社会定位）。

序列 2：主题信息

2006 年在马家塬遗址出土的车辆和车马饰件等 1600 余件实物均收藏在张家川回族自治县博物馆。游客在遗址地面随处可见属于常山、齐家文化类型的横篮纹泥质红陶片和夹砂红陶片，断崖上还有大量的灰坑和房屋遗迹（观赏内容）。

序列 3：附加信息

游客可以在张家川回族自治县民族博物馆参观马家塬墓葬展区，透过玻璃陈列柜目睹车辆、车马饰件、青铜器和琉璃器。其中 2000 多年前的马车用金、银、铜、锡、漆、宝石及料珠等诸多材料装饰；"青铜茧形壶"颈部铸有一圈贝文，器腹为瓜棱形，瓜棱内间饰以蟠螭纹，腹部两面有衔环兽头，椭圆形圈足，圈足铸以拧绳纹，底部阳铸大篆铭文"鞅又"；"连珠纹釉陶杯"的出土将丝绸之路的开通年代提前 200 余年。这件釉陶杯通体饰淡蓝色釉，腹下部装饰七层连珠纹，敞口小平底。该类器物为地中海文明的器形，为中西文化交流的产物，该类器物应属早期玻璃器（游览指南/建议）。

开放时间：全天。

门票价格：免费。

交通：在张家川县城乘车到木河乡桃园村。

（二）重构语篇英语书面语介绍

Resort Introduction of Majiayuan Ancient Tombs in Warring States

Item 1 Background Information

The Relics of Majiayuan is located at Majiayuan of Taoyuan Village in Muhe County, 17 kilometres away from Zhangjiachuan Hui Autonomous County, Tianshui City, Gansu Province (location). The name derived from the Majiayuan found in Zhangjiachuan (name origin). It has an old history of about 2300 years (time). Majiayuan Ancient Tombs have very typical styles of North China and Western Asia minority nationality and characteristic of Qin Culture. This will be of great value to the study of the relationship between Qin and Xirong (a common name of the ancient western tribes, here refers to the minority nationality developed around Zhangjiachuan Longshan as the center), the study of the ancient Ethnic history of North China and Western Asia minority nationality, cultural exchanges between Chinese and foreign people in ancient China, national amalgamation, technology of metallurgy, and the history of ancient science and technology (social status).

Item 2 Topic Information

Over 1600 objects including vehicles and decorations of carriages and horses, excavated in Majiayuan in 2006, are collected in the Museum of Zhangjiachuan Hui Autonomous County. Mud-textured red pottery and sand-textured red pottery of Changshan and Qijia Culture category can be seen everywhere in the relics. And a large number of pits and house sites can also be seen on the bluff (contents).

Item 3 Additional Information

You can visit the exhibition at the ethic museum of Majiayuan tombs in Zhangjiachuan Hui Autonoumous County. Through the glass cabinet, vehicles, accessories of vehicles, bronze and colored glass utensils can be seen. Among them, carriages and horses, made 2000 years ago, are decorated with various materials such as gold, silver, bronze, tin, paint, gem and pearls, and so on. There is a "bronze cocoon shaped pot" with a circle of Buddist scripts in the neck, a melon shape in the abdomen, PanChi pattern within the abdomen, a ringed beast head on both sides of abdomen, oval round feet, round feet casted in the rope lines, and "Yangyou" casted at the bottom in ancient seal character. An excavated cup called "Lianzhu Glazed Pottery Cup" made the year of opening the Silk Route 200 years ahead. This light blue pottery has seven layers of string of peals pattern, with its mouth open and its bottom flat. The pottery belongs to the type of Mediterranean civilization and also the product of cultural commuication between China and foreign countries. In addition, it is widely acknowledged as the early glass utensil (guides/services).

Opening Times: The whole day.

Ticket Prices: Free.

Transportation: Take any buses heading for Taoyuan Village of Muhe Town from Zhangjiachuan County.

(三) 重构语篇英语口语导游词

Tour Guide Speech of Majiayuan Ancient Tombs in Warring States

Item 1 Background Information

Hello! Everyone! Today we are going to visit an old place-Majiayuan Ancient Tombs in Warring Sates. The relics of Majiayuan is located at Majiayuan of Taoyuan Village in Muhe County. It is in Zhangjiachuan Hui Autonomous County, Gansu Province (location). Why is it called so? Because it was found in Majiayuan of Zhangjiachuan (name origin). Now it has a 2300 years history (time). An unusual characteristic of Majiayuan Ancient Tombs is that it has very typical styles of North China and Western Asia minority nationality and characteristic of Qin Culture. And this will be very important to study the relationship between Qin and Xirong (a common name of the ancient western tribes, here refers to the minority nationality around Zhangjiachuan Longshan), the ancient ethnic history of North China and Western Asia minority nationality, cultural exchanges between Chinese and foreign people in ancient China, national amalgamation, technology of metallurgy, as well as the history of ancient science and technology (social status).

Item 2 Topic Information

Over 1600 objects were excavated in Majiayuan in 2006, including vehicles and decorations of carriages and horses. Amazing! Aren't they? They are all collected in the Museum of Zhangjiachuan Hui Autonomous County. You can see mud-textured red pottery and sand-textured red pottery of Changshan and Qijia Culture category everywhere in the relics. And also you can see a large number of pits and house sites on the bluff (contents).

Item 3 Additional Information

You can visit Majiayuan tombs exhibit in Zhangjiachuan Hui Autonoumous County Museum. Through the glass cabinet, you can see vehicles, accessories of vehicles, bronze and colored glass utensils. You can also enjoy carriages and horses which were made 2000 years ago. You see? They are decorated with various materials such as gold, silver, bronze, tin, paint, gem and pearls, and so on. Very beautiful! Right? There are two precious cultural objects that you need to know. One is the "bronze cocoon shaped pot". Look at the patterns on it. There is a circle of Buddist scripts in the neck, a melon shape in the abdomen, PanChi pattern within the abdomen, a ringed beast head on both sides of abdomen, oval round feet, round feet casted in the rope lines, and "Yangyou" casted at the bottom in ancient seal character. The other is "Lianzhu Glazed Pottery Cup". You will never know that the unearth of the cup made the year of opening the Silk Route 200 years ahead. Why is it called Lianzhu glazed Pottery cup? Watch carefully! This light blue pottery was decorated with seven layers of string of peals pattern. Its mouth is open and its bottom is flat. One thing you must know is that the pottery belongs to the type of Mediterranean civilization. Also it is the product of cultural communication between China and foreign countries. In addition, it is widely acknowledged as the early glass utensil (guides/services).

You can visit the relics at anytime freely. Take any buses heading for Taoyuan Village of Muhe Town from Zhangjiachuan County.

四 甘谷毛家坪遗址

（一）汉语语篇重构

甘谷毛家坪遗址

序列1：背景信息

毛家坪遗址位于甘肃省天水市甘谷县磐安镇毛家坪村渭河南岸的

台地（景点的地理位置），因1947年首先发现于磐安镇毛家坪村而得名（景点名称由来）。它从西周（公元前1046—公元前771年）延续到战国（公元前475—公元前221年），距今约2700年（建筑起止年代），为秦人西迁的初始地，确认了秦国（公元前770—公元前206年）最早设立的古冀县县治所在，印证了当地民间"华夏第一县"的说法（社会定位）。

序列2：主题信息

2013年以来遗址共发掘到三种文化遗存：以彩陶为特征的仰韶文化石岭下类型遗存，以绳纹灰陶为代表的周秦文化遗存，以夹砂红褐陶为特征的西戎文化遗存。出土实物均收藏在甘谷县博物馆。遗址沟西、沟东区主要为墓葬区。分布区内除一处以展厅形式被保护起来的车马坑可供游客远观外，其余被开挖过的遗址已经保护性回填。游客能清晰地看到保存比较完整的战车车厢、车轮、车辕、车轭等构件，驾车的两匹骏马的骨架，两马中间摆放的长约3米的长矛（观赏内容）。

序列3：附加信息

除毛家坪遗址外，游客还可以参观磐安镇内五甲坪遗址、刘家墩各期文化遗址等（游览指南/建议）。

您如果在农历正月十五参观毛家坪遗址，还可以体验著名的"磐安高台"。这种具有浓郁地方特色的民俗文化是将面目姣好的孩童画上戏妆，穿好戏服，固定在铁架子上面，周围被装饰成相符的环境，造型奇特，生动传神，然后众人将铁架子固定在大型方桌上抬起移动，故名"高台"（游览指南/建议）。

游客还可以在素称"甘谷辣椒之乡"的磐安购买和品尝各种芳香浓郁、香味适口的辣椒（游览指南/建议）。

开放时间：全天。

门票价格：免费。

交通：在天水长途汽车站乘坐甘谷磐安方向县级班车。

（二）重构语篇英语书面语介绍

Resort Introduction of Maojiaping Relics

Item 1 Background Information

Maojiaping Relics is located at a tableland, on the south bank of the Wei River in Maojiaping Village of Pan'an Town, Gangu county, Tianshui City, Gansu Province (location). It got the name for the reason that it was found in Maojiaping Village of Pan'an County (name origin). It has a very long history, approximately more than 2700 years, covering the period from the Western Zhou Dynasty (1046 BC – 771 BC) until Warring States Period (475 BC–221 BC) (time). Maojiaping Relics was the initial place before Qin people moved westwards. Also it confirms that the Qin Dyanasty (770 BC–206 BC) was the earliest established county and testifies the folk saying "the first Chinese county" (social status).

Item 2 Topic Information

Three kinds of cultural relics were excavated since 2013. The first one is the Yangshao Culture of Shiling type remains characterized by colored pottery, the second one is Zhou-Qin cultural relics represented by Jomon pottery, and the third one is Xirong cultural relics featured by red sandy brown pottery. All unearthed cultural relics were collected in Gangu Museum. West Ditch Relics and East Ditch Relics are mainly the burial areas. In addition to one pit of carriages and horses protected in the form of window display in the distribution area, the other remains excavated have been backfilled. So you can clearly see the well completely protected carriages of chariots' components such as wheels, shafts, yokes, two fine horses skeletons and a 3 metres long spear placed between the two horses (contents).

Item 3 Additional Information

Apart from Maojiaping Relics, you can also visit Wujiaping Relics, Liujiadun Relics of different periods in Pan'an County (guides/advice).

If you come to Maojiaping Relics on the 15th day of the first lunar month, you will have the chance to experience the famous "Pan'an Gaotai", a folk culture with strong local features. "Gaotai" is so called because fairly good-looking children wearing costumes are usually painted makeup, fixed on a metal frame with peculiar poses, dressed up on the basis of the surrounding environment, lively and vivid, then lifted up by the crowds from the large square table fixed on the metal (guides/advices).

Also you can buy and taste pepper with a variety of aroma and flavor in the town of Pan'an called "hometown of Gangu pepper" (guides/advices).

Opening Times: The whole day.

Ticket prices: Free.

Transportation: Take any buses heading for Pan'an Town, Gangu County from Tianshui Long-distance Bus Station.

(三) 重构语篇英语口语导游词

Tour Guide Speech of Maojiaping Relics

Item 1 Background Information

Dear friends! Today I will take everyone to visit a small scenic spot, Maojiaping Relics. It is located at a tableland, on the south bank of the Wei River in Maojiaping Village of Pan'an Town (location). This name comes from Maojiaping Village of Pan'an County (name origin). It has a more than 2700 years history, from the Western Zhou Dynasty to Warring States Period (time). Maojiaping Relics was the place before Qin people moved westwards first. Also it helped confirm the Qin Dynasty as the earliest established country and also "the first Chinese county" wording (social status).

Item 2 Topic Information

There are three kinds of cultural relics excavated since 2013. The first one is Yangshao Culture of Shiling type which remains color pottery, the second one is Zhou-Qin Cultural relics with Jomon pottery and the last one is Xirong Cultural relics with red sandy brown pottery. All the unearthed objects are collected in Gangu museum. There are mainly two parts of burial areas, West Ditch Relics and East Ditch Relics. Besides one pit of carriages and horses in the distribution area, the other remains excavated have been backfilled. So everyone of you can see clearly the well completely protected carriages of chariots' wheels, some shafts, yokes, also two fine horses skeletons and a 3 metres long spear between two horses (contents).

Item 3 Additional Information

Besides Maojiaping Relics, there are other places I can recommend to you—Wujiaping Relics and Liujiadun Relics of different periods in Pan'an County. Also, if you come here on the 15th of the first lunar month, you will have the chance to experience the famous "Pan'an Gaotai", a folk culture with strong local features. Do you know why is it called "Gaotai"? Because good-looking children wearing costumes are usually painted makeup, fixed on a metal frame with peculiar poses. Moreover, they are dressed up in accordance with lively and vivid surrounding environment and then lifted up by crowds (guides/advices).

By the way, you can buy and taste pepper with a variety of aroma and flavor in the town of Pan'an called "hometown of Gangu pepper" (guides/advices).

You can visit the relics any time freely. Take any buses heading for Pan'an Town, Gangu County from Tianshui Long-distance Bus Station.

第三节 "一带一路"沿线国家人类文明发祥地语篇语域重构及翻译

一 奥林匹亚考古遗址

（一）汉语语篇重构

奥林匹亚考古遗址

序列1：背景信息

奥林匹亚考古遗址位于希腊雅典阿提卡大区伯罗奔尼撒半岛的山谷（景点的地理位置），得名于希腊传说中诸神会聚的奥林波斯山（景点名称由来）。其始于公元前2000—公元前1600年（景点起止年代），从公元前8世纪至4世纪末因举办祭祀宙斯主神的体育盛典而闻名于世，是奥林匹克运动会的发祥地，为古希腊宗教圣地和举行奥林匹克运动会之处。1989年联合国教科文组织将奥林匹亚的考古遗迹作为文化遗产列入《世界遗产名录》（社会定位）。

序列2：主题信息

作为宗教仪式和体育运动的混合体，该遗址主要包括神庙和运动场两部分。游客除了参观神域内的主要建筑宙斯神庙、赫拉神庙以外，还能领略到至今仍保持原貌的专供奥运会使用的各种体育设施（观赏内容）。

序列3：附加信息

景点内的博物馆出售手工复制的仿博物馆藏品陶器、金属制品、民俗娃娃、皮革制品、天然海绵、橄榄皂及各种珠宝饰品（景点的设施和服务）。

除杰出的希腊建筑群外，游客还可以游览卫城博物馆、帕特农神庙、伊瑞克提翁神庙等景点（游览指南/建议）。

如果有幸在奥运年圣火采集日参观该遗址，您将目睹圣火点燃全过程（游览指南/建议）。

景区附近的饮食既有地方特色又便宜。除食品连锁店外还有经济实惠的街头餐馆,希腊大餐和土耳其美食应有尽有(游览指南/建议)。

最好的旅游时间是夏秋两季,可欣赏露天音乐和戏剧表演。由于四季分明、温差很大的气候特点,服装配备应适宜(游览指南/建议)。

开放时间:4月至10月8:00—19:30;11月至次年3月8:30—15:00。

门票价格:成人6欧元,优惠价3欧元。考古博物馆和遗址通票:成人9欧元,优惠价5欧元。持有效雅典卫城套票者可免费游览。

交通:搭乘地铁二号线至卫城站即可到达。

(二) 重构语篇英语书面语介绍

Resort Introduction of Archaeological Site of Olympia

Item 1 Background Information

Archaeological Site of Olympia is located in a valley in the Peloponnesus of Attica Region in Athens, Greece (location). The legend is named after Olympus Mons where the gods got together (name origin). It started from 2000 BC - 1600 BC (time) and became famous all over the world for holding the sports festival by Lord Jose from 8 Century BC to 4 Century BC. So it is the birthplace of the Olympic Games and the Ancient Greek religious shrine and the place for holding Olympic Games. It was inscribed on the world heritage list by UNESCO in 1989 (social status).

Item 2 Topic Information

As a mixture of religion ritual and sports, this archaeological site mainly consists of temples and playgrounds. Tourists can not only visit the main building such as Temple of Zeus and Hera Temple, but enjoy every original facility that was specially used for Olympic Games as well (contents).

Item 3 Additional Information

The museum in the archaeological site sells the replicas of museum collections such as metal work, folk dolls, natural sponges, olive soups and various jewelry (facilities and services).

Besides the outstanding Greek architecture complex, tourists can also visit the Acropolis Museum, Parthenon Temple, the Erechtheion etc. (guides/advices).

If tourists happen to visit the archaeological site on the collection day of Olympic torch, they will be able to witness the whole process of Olympic torch's igniting (guides/advices).

The food and drink around the archaeological site are not only cheap but have local characteristics as well. Apart from the food chain stores and economical street restaurants, there are Greek feast and Turkish cuisine everywhere (guides/advices).

The best time for tourists to visit this archaeological site is summer and autumn when they can enjoy open air music and comedy shows. Tourists should be aware of wearing proper clothes because of the four distinctive seasons and large temperature difference there (guides/advices).

Opening Times: From April to October, from 8:00 a.m. till 7:30 p.m., from November to next March, from 8:30 a.m. till 3:00 p.m.

Ticket prices: EUR 6/3 for adults. Archaeology Museum and Sites through ticket: EUR 9/5 for adults. Free for ticket holders who have the valid Athens Acropolis ticket package.

Transportation: Take subway Line 2 to Acropolis Stop.

(三) 重构语篇英语口语导游词

Tour Guide Speech of Archaeological Site of Olympia

Item 1 Background Information

Dear friends! Today I will show you around a well-known place—Archaeological Site of Olympia. Have you ever heard about it? It is located in a valley in the Peloponnesus of Attica Region in Athens, Greece (location). The legend is named after Olympus Mons where the gods got together. It started from 2000 BC-1600 BC (time) and became famous all over the world because the sports festival was held from 8 Century BC to 4 Century BC. So it is the birthplace of the Olympic Games. Also it was the religious shrine of Ancient Greece and the place of holding the Olympic Games (social status).

Item 2 Topic Information

As a mixture of religion ritual and sports, this archaeological site mainly consists of temple hierons and playgrounds. So tourists can not only visit the main building such as Temple of Zeus and Hera Temple, but enjoy sports facilities as well. Why is that? Because all the facilities used for Olympic Games still preserve the original forms (contents).

Item 3 Additional Information

The museum in the archaeological site sells the replicas of museum collections such as metal work, folk dolls, natural sponges, olive soups and various jewelry (facilities and services).

Besides the outstanding Greek architecture complex, there are plenty of scenic spots for you to enjoy. You can visit the Acropolis Museum, Parthenon Temple, the Erechtheion etc. (guides/advices).

If tourists happen to visit the archaeological site on the collection day of Olympic torch, they will be very lucky. Why? Because they will be able to witness the whole process of Olympic torch's igniting (guides/advices).

Around the archaeological site, the food and drink are not only cheap but have local characteristics as well. Apart from the food chain stores and economical street restaurants, there are Greek feasts and Turkish cuisine everywhere (guides/services).

When is the best time to visit archaeological site of Olympia? OK, let me tell you. The best time for tourists to visit this archaeological site are summer and autumn, because they can enjoy open air music and comedy shows. But you have to bear one thing in mind: wearing proper clothes as the four seasons are distinctive and the difference in temperature is large there (guides/advices).

The Relics opens from 8:00 a.m. till 7:30 p.m. during April to October and opens from 8:30 a.m. till 3:00 p.m. during November to next March. EUR 6/3 for adults. Archaeology Museum and Sites through ticket: EUR 9/5 for adults. Free for ticket holders who have the valid Athens Acropolis ticket package. You can take subway Line 2 to Acropolis Stop.

二 伊朗波斯波利斯遗址

(一) 汉语语篇重构

伊朗波斯波利斯遗址

序列1：背景信息

波斯波利斯位于伊朗法尔斯省设拉子市东北51千米扎格罗斯山区盆地中（景点的地理位置）。因希腊语的"波利斯"与英语的Palace相同，"波利斯"在希腊语中意思是"都城"，从而得名"波斯之都"（景点名称由来）。建于大流士一世时期（公元前522—公元前486年）（景点起止年代），是中亚古代文明的一个独特的证明。1979年联合国教科文组织将其作为文化遗产列入《世界遗产名录》（社会定位）。

序列2：主题信息

游客可以欣赏波斯波利斯宏伟的石头建筑和精美的石刻艺术特色。主要遗迹有刻有进贡者画像的台阶浮雕；万国门上的人首翼兽（人面、牛身、鸟翅）石雕；觐见大厅高18米的公牛雕饰柱头和对称的狮子斗牛浮雕；百柱大殿身材相连呈卧姿的双头马柱头等（观赏内容）。

序列3：附加信息

景区门口免费寄存大件行李和三脚架；景点都有英语说明（景点的设施和服务）。

波斯波利斯入口大道两边种植的2500棵树是巴列维国王在1971年为庆祝波斯帝国建国2500周年专门从国外购买的（游览指南/建议）。

景区内没有树荫，5—10月游览一定要做好防晒措施。景区内无处买水和食物，需要自己准备（游览指南/建议）。

最好的游览时间是下午。下午前往可游玩到日落时分，此时日落下的波斯波利斯非常漂亮（游览指南/建议）。

游客可以先游览和波斯波利斯相距不远的波斯帝陵等景点（游览指南/建议）。

开放时间：4月至10月8：00—18：00；11月至次年3月7：30—17：00。伊朗的重大节日不开放。

门票价格：每人20里亚尔。

交通：没有公共交通直达波斯波利斯，可以从设拉子卡兰蒂什客运站外搭乘萨瓦里或小巴到马夫达沙特镇（人均1.1万里亚尔），然后打车前往波斯波利斯（5万里亚尔）。

（二）重构语篇英语书面语介绍

Resort Introduction of Persepolis Relics

Item 1 Background Information

The Ancient Relic of Persepolis is situated in the basin area of Zagros Mountains, 51 kilometres northeast to Shiraz City, Fars Province, Iran (location). Persepolis in Greek language means "metro city", with the same meaning as "palace" in English, therefore, it was given a name "Persian City" (name origin). Persepolis, built in the period of Darius I of Persia (522 BC-486 BC) (time), is an unique example of Central Asian ancient civilization. In 1979, as a cultural relic, it was listed into the World Heritage List by UNESCO (social status).

Item 2 Topic Information

You can enjoy the magnificent stone buildings and the delicate stone-carving arts of unique features in Persepolis. The relics mainly includes: (1) a stepping relief sculpture carved with tributaries' portraits; (2) the Gate of All Nations engraved with stone-carving mythological creatures (of human's face, bull's body and bird's wings); (3) an Apadana (Audience Hall) with 18 metres high of column heads carved with stone relief of bulls and a symmetrical stone relief of "a lion fighting against a bull"; (4) the Hall of A Hundred Columns with column heads each carved with a dual-headed and body-linked horse in prone position (contents).

Item 3 Additional Information

At the entrance of the scenic spot, there is a baggage depository for storing big luggages and camera tripods, with free of charge. Scenic spot introduction in English is provided in every scenic site (facilities and services).

The 2500 trees grown on both sides of the main entrance road were bought exclusively by the King Pahlavi from abroad in 1971 for celebrating the 2500th anniversary of Persian Empire (guides/advices).

As there are no tree shades in the scenic spot, you have to take necessary measures to protect yourselves from sunburn when touring there from May to October. There is no drinking water and food available, therefore you must get ready by yourselves (guides/advices).

The best time to visit is in the afternoon as you can stay until sunset time when Persepolis is especially beautiful under sunset (guides/advices).

You can also visit other attractions such as Naqshi Rostam at first, which are not far from Persepolis (guides/advices).

Opening Times: From 8:00 a.m.till 6:00 p.m. from April to October; from 7:30 a.m. till 5:00 p.m. from November to next March; closed during big national festivals of Iran.

Ticket prices: 20 Rial for each person.

Transportation: There is no public transport available directly to Persepolis. You can take Savari or mini-bus from Karandish Bus Terminal to Marvdasht Town, with average ticket fee of 1,000 Rial per person, then you can take a taxi to Persepolis with ticket fee of 50,000 Rial per person.

(三) 重构语篇英语口语导游词

Tour Guide Speech of Persepolis Relics

Dear friends! Here is the Persepolis Relics, a famous scenic spot in the world. The Ancient Relic of Persepolis is located in the basin area of Zagros Mountains which is 51 kilometres northeast to Shiraz City, Fars Province, Iran (location). Persepolis in Greek language means "metro city" and it has the same meaning as "palace" in English. That's why it was given a name "Persian City" (name origin). Persepolis was built in the period of Darius Ⅰ of Persia (522 BC-486 BC) (time) and now it is an unique example of Central Asian ancient civilization. As a cultural relic, it was listed into the World Heritage List by UNESCO in 1979 (social status).

Item 2 Topic Information

In Persepolis Relics, there are some amazing things to see. You can enjoy the magnificent stone buildings and the delicate stone-carving arts of unique features. The relics mainly includes the following. First, the stepping relief sculpture which was carved with tributaries' portraits. Second, the Gate of All Nations which was engraved with stone-carving mythological creatures (of human's face, bull's body and bird's wings). Just imagine! Very interesting, isn't it? Third, an Apadana (Audience Hall) with 18 metres high of column heads which were carved with stone relief of bulls and a symmetrical stone relief of "a lion fighting against a bull". The last one is the Palace of A Hundred Columns, see that? The column heads each as carved with a dual-headed and body-linked horse in prone position (contents).

Item 3 Additional Information

If you take big baggage with you and if you wouldn't like to tour with it, you can go to the entrance of the scenic spot. There is a baggage depository for storing big luggage and camera tripods. You don't have to pay, it's free! Besides, scenic spot introduction in English is available in every scenic site (facilities and services).

Look at these trees! They are so many and beautiful. Do you want to know the story about them? OK, let me tell you. There are 2500 trees in all and they are grown on both sides of the main entrance road. They were bought exclusively by the King Pahlavi from abroad in 1971 in order to celebrate the 2500th anniversary of Persian Empire. Meaningful, right (guides/advices)?

In the scenic spot, there are no tree shades, so you have to take necessary measures to protect yourselves from sunburn, especially when you visit it from May to October. Also, there is no drinking water and food available, so you must get ready by yourselves (guides/advices).

When is the best time to visit it in a day? Yeah, the best time is in the afternoon. You can leave for Persepolis Relics in the afternoon and stay there until sunset time. Persepolis is especially beautiful under sunset (guides/advices).

You can also visit other attractions like Naqshi Rostam and so on first. Because they are not far from Persepolis (guides/advices).

The relics open from 8 : 00 a. m. till 6 : 00 p. m. from April to October; from 7 : 30 a. m. till 5 : 00 p. m. from November to next March; close during big national festivals of Iran. 20 Rial for each person. There is no public transport available directly to Persepolis. You can take Savari or minibus from Karandish Bus Terminal to Marvdasht Town. with average ticket fee of 1,1000 Rial per person, then you can take a taxi to Persepolis with ticket fee of 50,000 Rial per person.

三 土耳其以弗所古城遗址

(一) 汉语语篇重构

土耳其以弗所古城遗址

序列1：背景信息

以弗所古城位于土耳其伊兹密尔市南边大约50千米的塞尔丘克小镇（景点的地理位置）。因古城所在地得名（景点名称由来），公元前10世纪由雅典殖民者建立（景点起止年代），是基督教早期最重要的城市之一，是世界上保存最大、最完整的希腊罗马古城遗址，目前已列入联合国教科文组织列管的古迹之一（社会定位）。

序列2：主题信息

以弗所古城是体验和感受罗马时代生活的最好场所。游客可以看到残留的大理石街道、商店、市集广场、市政厅、大会堂（罗马大帝统治时期被用于证券交易和商业营业的场所）和塞尔苏斯图书馆壁龛上代表仁慈、思想、学识、智慧与美德的雕像，柱廊大街，古代世界七大奇迹之一的阿耳忒弥斯神庙及教堂、清真寺、能容纳24000名观众的露天戏院、豪宅、浴场、妓院、公厕等古迹（观赏内容）。

序列3：附加信息

古城景区内提供收费7欧元的英语、汉语语音导游器，可以交100里拉押金或者护照抵押；还销售介绍以弗所的汉语书籍；万人大剧场有免费饮水站（景点的设施和服务）。

土耳其一年一度的骆驼摔跤冠军赛每年冬天在古代以弗所的竞技场举行（游览指南/建议）。

整体保存完好、可以容纳2.4万人的以弗所大剧场历经2000年后直到现在还在使用中，是每年八九月举办"塞尔丘克以弗所文化艺术节"的演出场所。游客在舞台中央高声朗诵和唱歌，可以感受到声音清晰地传遍剧场的每一个角落，传声效果很好（游览指南/建议）。

游客可以朝拜距塞尔丘克7千米的梅雷曼那教堂，据说圣母玛利亚在此度过她生命的最后时光。这座穹顶十字形教堂成为基督教朝圣者的重要膜拜地（游览指南/建议）。

游客也能找到世界卫生组织徽章的来源——权杖与蛇；启发耐克（NIKE）公司老总设计了著名"√"标志的古希腊胜利女神尼克雕像（游览指南/建议）。

游客还可以游览风景秀丽的希林杰小村庄，品尝当地的葡萄酒（游览指南/建议）。

开放时间：10月至次年4月8：00—17：00；5月至9月8：00—19：00。

门票价格：以弗所古城30里拉；露台屋15里拉；除露台屋以外，11岁以下儿童都免费（建议带上护照复印件证明年龄）。

交通：可以乘坐帕姆查克和库沙达瑟的小巴（5里拉，全程5分钟），然后步行20分钟到达后门的售票处；或从塞尔丘克打车前往以弗所古城，车费需15—20里拉。

（二）重构语篇英语书面语介绍

Resort Introduction of Ephesus Relics

Item 1 Background Information

Ephesus Relics is situated in Selcuk Town, 50 kilometres south of Izmir City in Turkey (location). It was named after the old city Ephesus (name origin). The Athens colonists established it in 10th century (time). It is not only one of the most important cities in early christian but also is the most well preserved and well completed relics in Rome, Greek. And now it has been listed into one of the relics by UNESCO (social status).

Item 2 Topic Information

The ancient city of Ephesus is the best place for you to experience and enjoy the life of Roman times. You can see a lot of remains, including streets paved with marbles, shops, market square, council hall, meeting hall (used for stock exchange and commercial business during the reign of Roman empire), the statue on behalf of kindness, thoughts, knowledge, wisdom and virtue in Celsus library, colonnade streets, one of seven ancient world wonders—Temple of Artemis, churches, mosques, openair theater with 24000 spectators, mansions, bathing spots, brothels, public toilets etc. (contents).

Item 3 Additional Information

In the scenic spot, Chinese and English voice guide devices are provided with EUR 7. You can also pay 100 lira or take the passport as deposit. Chinese books about Buddha are sold here and free drinking water stations are provided in the theater holding millions of people (facilities and services).

In every winter, Turkey's annual camel wrestling championship is held in ancient Ephesus arena (guides/advices).

The well preserved Ephesus theater with a capacity of 24000 people, where Selcuk's Cultural Arts Festival is held during the period of every August and September, has gone through more than 2000 years and now is still in use. You can read aloud and sing in the center of the stage, which can be heard clearly, spreading to every corner of the theater with very good sound effect (guides/advices).

You can also worship Meremana church, 7 kilometres to Selcuk, where, it is said that, Virgin Mary spent the last time of her life. This domed cruciform church has now become an important Christian pilgrimage to worship (guides/advices).

You can also find the badge source of WHO—mace and snake, and ancient Greek goddess of victory Nick's statue which inspired Nike company executive designed the famous brand "√" (guides/advices).

You can also tour the beautiful scenery of Sirince Village and taste the local grape wine (guides/advices).

Opening Times: From 8:00 a.m. till 5:00 p.m. from October to next April; from 8:00 a.m. till 7:00 p.m. from May to September.

Ticket Prices: 30 lira to Ephesus; 15 lira to Terrace Houses. Except for Terrace Houses, children under 11 years old are free (we strongly suggest that the replica of passport be taken with them just for proving their ages).

Transportation: Take the minibus which costs 5 lira and 5 minutes to get to Pamucak and Kusadasi, then walk 20 minutes to the ticket office in the back door. Or you can take a taxi from Selcuk to Ephesus with 15-20 lira.

(三) 重构语篇英语口语导游词

Tour Guide Speech of Ephesus Relics

Item 1 Background Information

Hello! Everyone! Today I will take all of you to see around an ancient city—Ephesus Relics. It is located in Selcuk Town, 50 kilometres south of Izmir city in Turkey (location).And it was named after the old city Ephesus (name origin) and was established by the Athens colonists in 10th century (time) . It is not only one of the most important cities in early christian but is the most well preserved and well completed relics in Rome, Greek as well. Now it has been listed into one of the relics by UNESCO (social status).

Item 2 Topic Information

As we all know, the ancient city of Ephesus is the best place for you to experience and enjoy the life of Roman times. Here you can see a lot of remains. There are streets paved with marbles, shops, market square, council hall, meeting hall (used for stock exchange and commercial business during the reign of Roman empire), the statue on behalf of kindness, thoughts, knowledge, wisdom and virtue in Celsus library, colonnade streets, one of seven ancient world wonders—Temple of Artemis, churches, mosques, openair theater with 24000 spectators, mansions, bathing spots, brothels, public toilets etc. (contents).

Item 3 Additional Information

If you want to have a clear introduction of the scenic spot, you just pay

EUR 7 or pay 100 lira or even take the passport as deposit to get Chinese and English voice guide devices. Here Chinese books about Buddha are also sold. You will never imagine that free drinking water stations are provided for millions of people in the theater (facilities and services).

Do you know an interesting game held here? In every winter, Turkey's annual camel wrestling championship is held in ancient Ephesus arena (guides/advices).

You might be amazed that the well preserved Ephesus theater has gone through more than 2000 years and now is still in use. It has a capacity of 24000 people and normally Selcuk's Cultural Arts Festival is held here during the period of every August and September. You can stand in the center of the stage, reading aloud and singing. Because the sound effect is so good in Ephesus theater that people in every corner of the theater can hear the voice clearly (guides/advices).

You can also worship Meremana church which is 7 kilometres to Selcuk. It is said that Virgin Mary spent the last time of her life. This domed cruciform church has now become an important Christian pilgrimage to worship (guides/advices).

You can find the badge source of WHO—mace and snake here. Surprising! The Nick's statue, an ancient Greek goddess of victory, inspired Nike company executive to design the famous brand "√" (guides/advices).

You can also enjoy the beautiful scenery of Sirince Village and taste the local grape wine (guides/advices).

The ancient city opens from 8∶00 a.m. till 5∶00 p.m. from October to next April, and from 8∶00 a.m. till 7∶00 p.m. from May to September. The ticket costs 30 lira to Ephesus; 15 lira to Terrace Houses. Except for Terrace Houses, children under 11 years old are free (we strongly suggest that the replica of passport be taken with them just for proving their ages). You can take the minibus with only 5 lira and 5 minutes' drive to get to Pamucak and Kusadasi, then walk 20 minutes to the back door ticket office. Or you can take a taxi from Selcuk to Ephesus with 15–20 lira.

第四节　基于翻译语境和语篇理论的解释性译文质量评估

天水旅游文化翻译不仅数量少、翻译质量低下而且缺少依据连贯方法论施行的系统翻译活动，更缺少一个译文质量的客观评估体系。在针对译文评估、翻译方法论构建等问题的应用翻译研究领域，尽管有朱莉安·豪斯的功能主义语言学模式[1]，但这些模式关注的仅是译文的语言特征，并未论及影响、制约翻译策略选择的翻译语境问题，同时其操作性也不强。系统功能语言学认为，在构成使用语言的情景语境的各个要素里，只有三个因素对语言的使用产生直接和重要的影响。[2] 即语场、语旨和语式三个语域变量，对于使用语言时如何选择语言形式有着直接的、至关重要的影响。本书运用韩礼德功能语言学的语域理论对天水秦文化及"一带一路"沿线国家人类文明发祥地源文与译文从语场、语旨、语式三方面进行对比分析，客观和具体地评判翻译文本的质量。

一　语场对比分析

语场是关于言语活动的主题或焦点。根据这一情景参数，语用场景一般分为技术场景和日常场景两类，不同场景的语言表现出各自不同的特征。七组语料分别来自天水牧马滩、清水李崖遗址、张家川马家塬战国古墓、甘谷毛家坪遗址、奥林匹亚考古遗址、伊朗波斯波利

---

[1] Juliane House, *Translation Quality Assessment: A Model Revisited*, Tübingen: Gunter Narr Verlag, 1997, pp. 1–23.

[2] 司显柱:《功能语言学与翻译研究——翻译质量评估模式建构》，北京大学出版社2007年版，第6—9页。

斯遗址、土耳其以弗所古城遗址。就语场参数而言，采用哈蒂姆和梅森的语篇分析法① 重构源语语境为背景信息、主题信息和附加信息，与英国旅游网站的语篇结构相比，两者显示出相同的语言特征。重构语篇的主题都相同，都是对景点进行描述和宣传，普遍使用日常用语、标准句法，向潜在的游客提供旅游景点的三类基本信息：包括景点位置、名称由来、起止年代和社会地位等背景信息；观赏内容等主体信息；景点设施与服务、游览指南或建议、气候、当地风土人情、旅游特色项目、开放时间、门票、交通等附加信息。两者均属于呼唤型文本，描述旅游体验，目的都是吸引潜在游客来旅游。

从七组重构语境语料可以看出，天水秦文化及其"一带一路"沿线国家人类文明发祥地的语场特征是相同的。旅游景点的描写都使用日常用语而非技术用语，避免生涩难懂，便于读者阅读，有利于对景点进行宣传介绍。描写多使用标准句法和过程动词。

二 语旨对比分析

语旨是反映言语交际行为的双方，在权势关系、接触密度和亲切程度等方面的情景参数，主要用来区分正式和非正式情景两类。非正式情景中，交际双方一般地位平等，经常见面，关系亲密，语言上常用带有感情色彩的词语、口头用语，使用典型语气；而正式情景里，交际者之间在权势方面是不对等的，接触稀少，关系疏远，语言在形式上，多使用中性词语、正式用语和非常规语气。② 就语旨参数而言，天水秦文化及"一带一路"沿线国家人类文明发祥地在语旨方面的评价潜势都较强，在态度资源的利用上都倾向于"鉴赏资源"，在情感资源方面均以"你指向"情感为主。例句如下。

（1）源语：从公元前8世纪至4世纪末因举办祭祀宙斯主神的体

---

① Basil Hatim and Ian Mason, *Discourse and the Translator*, Shanghai: Shanghai Foreign Language Education Press, 2001, p. 223.

② Suzanne Eggins, *An Introduction to Systemic Functional Linguistics*, London: Pinter, 1994, p. 78.

育盛典而闻名于世。

译语：It... became famous all over the world for holding the sports festival by Lord Jose from 8 Century BC to 4 Century BC.

语料多使用夸张的和具有劝导性的词汇如"闻名于世"（became famous all over the world）并结合鉴赏性词汇"famous""beautiful"等。

（2）源语：在火车站西面的麦积大酒店的入口处乘 34 路到达贾河，在贾河转乘 37 路公交到仙人崖下，再乘坐"天水—利桥"或"天水—党川"的县级班车到达牧马滩。

译语：Take Bus No. 34, which stops at the entrance of Maiji Grand Hotel, west to Tianshui Railway Station, to get to Jiahe, then transfer Bus No. 37 to get to the Immortal Cliff, finally take "Tianshui–Liqiao" or "Tianshui–Dangchuan" county shuttles to get to the Pastureland of Grazing Horses.

多用祈使句来实现呼唤功能。游客直接从祈使句的核心动词成分开始理解，按照不同的句子语境去体会祈使句的功能指向，更能成功完成交际目的。

（3）源语：牧马滩四面环山，有草地和小溪。

译语：The Pastureland of Grazing Horses is surrounded with mountains, vast green grass and clear streams.

汉语为主动语态可译作被动语态。源语中的词类、句型和语态等进行转换使译文更符合目标语的表述方式、方法和习惯。

（4）源语：2006 年在马家塬遗址出土的车辆和车马饰件等 1600 余件实物均收藏在张家川回族自治县博物馆。游客在遗址地面随处可见属于常山、齐家文化类型的横篮纹泥质红陶片和夹砂红陶片，断崖上还有大量的灰坑和房屋遗迹。

译语：Over 1600 objects including vehicles and decorations of carriages and horses, excavated in Majiayuan in 2006, are collected in the Museum of Zhangjiachuan Hui Autonomous County. Mud‑textured red pottery and sand-textured red pottery of Changshan and Qijia Culture category can be seen everywhere in the relics. And a large number of pits and house sites can also be seen on the bluff.

从态度资源上看,七组语料多使用名词、代词、过程动词、数字等来描述景点。分清主从句进行组合,根据需要利用连词、分词、介词、不定式、定语从句、独立结构等把汉语短句连成长句。

(5) 源语:您如果在农历正月十五参观毛家坪遗址,还可以体验著名的"磐安高台"。

译语:If you come to Maojiaping Relics on the 15th day of the first lunar month, you will have the chance to experience the famous "Pan'an Gaotai", a folk culture with strong local features.

"你指向"的大量使用增强了文本的对话性,七组语料多把"您"用作主位,让读者直接参与对话中。描写也更加直白、简单。

三 语式对比分析

语式是描述语言与情景在空间和人际距离方面关系的参数。据埃金斯,这一情景变量主要用来区分口语和书面语的言语特征。口语依赖语境,句子结构松散、动态,使用日常词汇,句子的语法不标准,词汇化密度低。书面语不依赖语境,多使用纲要式结构的句子,使用"声望"词汇,句子语法标准,词汇化密度高。当然,这是对位于语式连续体两极,即典型口语和书面语言辞特征的概括,而实际话语中的多数是介于两极之间,也就是说往往既有口语体又有书面语体特征,差异只是多寡大小而已,即混合语体。① 示例如下。

源语:游客还可参观也位于李崖村的轩辕窑(轩辕指黄帝,古代传说中的中华民族人文始祖之一),相传轩辕母亲曾携轩辕帝居住在此窑。窑内有齐家文化陶片遗存。

---

① Suzanne Eggins, *An Introduction to Systemic Functional Linguistics*, London: Pinter, 1994, p. 78.

书面语介绍：You can also enjoy Xuanyuan Cave (Xuanyuan refers to Huangdi who was one of legend ancestors of Chinese nation in ancient myth). The legend goes that Xuanyuan's mother used to live with him in it. Pottery remains of Qijia Culture were found here.

　　口语导游词：Very exciting thing is that you can also enjoy Xuanyuan Cave (a kind of cave dwelling on the Loess Plateau in northwest China). Who is Xuanyuan? You must be very interested in it. OK, let me tell you. He is said to be the first emperor of China. Chinese people call him Huangdi, and the first legend of our five ancient legends. The legend goes that Xuanyuan's mother used to live with him in it. Pottery remains of Qijia Culture were found here.

　　七组语料均是介于口语和书面语两极之间的混合语体，既包含口语特点又包含书面语特点。汉语重构语境的口语倾向通过英语书面语介绍和口语导游词转换更加清晰。

　　七组语料中除了"寺洼文化""高台""西戎"等少数短语的翻译属于隐性翻译之外，基本上是属于显性翻译的语篇。虽然通过分析发现，语篇中出现了少数的信息不匹配和错误，但是正如豪斯在其翻译评估模式的阐释中指出的，"少数的不匹配与错误的出现是不可避免的"[①]。因此，七组语料的译文中的不匹配现象不会影响语篇的概念功能、人际功能及语篇的质量。

---

① Juliane House, *Translation Quality Assessment：A Model Revisited*, Tübingen：Gunter Narr Verlag, 1997, pp. 1-23.

第五章

天水三国文化描写与解释

第一节 天水三国文化简述

三国文化是近年来学术界约定俗成使用起来的一个概念，泛指与三国（公元220—280年）历史有关的各种文化现象，其内涵和外延仍处在逐步清晰的过程之中。由于特定的时代环境和社会条件，三国历史主要集中在：（1）以黄河中下游的冀鲁豫为主的中原文化圈，是三国前期的袁氏集团以及后来曹魏政权的根据地；（2）长江下游以建业（今南京）及其周围地区为主的吴文化圈，是孙吴集团的主要活动区域；（3）长江中上游以荆州、益州为主的巴蜀文化圈；（4）以关中地区和渭水流域为主的秦陇文化圈，是蜀魏后期激烈角逐的主要地域之一，对三国晚期蜀魏力量对比关系的变化和各自势力的消长产生了重要影响。正是上述四个文化圈的共同作用，塑造了三国历史的独特面貌和该文化的显著地域特色。

三国前期的天水扼陇蜀之咽喉，居关中上游，军事地理位置十分重要。蜀汉《隆中对》北伐战略提出的"西和诸戎"随着形势的变化上升为主导战略，天水也就成为蜀汉北伐的必争之地和北伐战略的轴心。① 三国时期蜀国丞相诸葛亮（公元181—234年）五次北伐、二出祁山，三国时期蜀国大将军姜维（公元202—264年）九次伐魏、七出陇右形成了天水三国文化的主要内容。该文化表现为以三国古遗

---

① 刘雁翔：《天水三国遗迹丛考》，《天水师范学院学报》2004年第4期。

迹为载体，以民间传说、文人墨客凭吊古迹的上乘诗文佳作为主调。徐日辉利用天水在三国时期的重要位置，对三国文化在天水的遗存、影响、传说、习俗等多方面进行了综合研究。①

人们在寻访古战场遗迹的同时，又寻找着一种精神世界。诸葛亮是智慧的化身，有"神奇"的力量。"鞠躬尽瘁，死而后已"的精神激励着天水人的思想境界，"淡泊明志，宁静致远"是修身养德、励精图治的先哲至理。以"三国"为题材的天水文学作品、化装为三国人物的民间马社火、庙会和节日上演的三国故事秦腔、歌颂诸葛亮和感怀的谒拜题诗和楹联、天水三国文化研讨会、民间祭祀诸葛亮活动暨影视三国故事的传播构成地域特色显著的天水三国文化，成为天水人受益不完的文化资源和精神食粮。三国古战场遗址和出土实物形成天水三国文化的主灵魂。馆藏于甘肃省博物馆、天水市博物馆、秦安县博物馆或散藏于民间的古战场遗址出土的实物证明了当年刀光剑影、"鼓角争鸣"三国古战场历史的存在。三国文化旅游区天水雄关、诸葛军垒、街亭古战场、木门古道、姜维墓等三国古遗址已向游客开放。

A Brief Introduction of Tianshui Three Kingdoms Culture

Three Kingdoms Culture is a stereotyped concept formed in the academic circle in recent years. Generally speaking, it refers to all kinds of cultural phenomena concerning Three Kingdoms Time (220 – 280 AD), with its connotation and extension still being in the course of gradual clearness. Because of the specific historical environment and social condition, the Three Kingdoms Time mainly focuses on four aspects. Central Plains Culture Circle, with Ji, Lu and Yu as focus along the middle and lower reaches of the Yellow River, was the base of Yuan Group in early Period of Three Kingdoms and later Cao – Wei regimes Wu Culture Circle, with Jianye

---

① 徐日辉：《三国文化与天水旅游经济发展研究》，《天水师范学院学报》1996年第0期。

(now Nanjing) and its surrounding areas as focus along the lower reaches of the Yangtze River, is main area of Sun-Wu Group. Ba-Shu Culture Circle is Centered around Jingzhou and Yizhou along the upper and middle reaches of the Yangtze River. Qin-Long Culture Circle, focused on Guanzhong areas and the Wei River, is one of the main areas that were violently tussled in late Shu-Wei and has had an important influence on the changes of comparison between Shu-Wei military forces in late Three Kingdoms Time as well as the weakness and strength of their respective forces. It is the joint effects of the four culture circles that shaped the unique appearance of Three Kingdoms Time and its distinctive geographical features.

In early Three Kingdoms Time, Tianshui, located in the upstream of the central Shaanxi plains, was the strategic passage (like a throat in a human's body) between Gansu and Sichuan and had a very important military geographic position. With the situation changing, the military idea of being in amity with various Rong tribes in the west, which was proposed in "Longzhong Plan" as part of Shu-Han's northern expeditionary strategy, rose to a dominate strategy. As a result, Tianshui became a hotly contested spot for Shu-Han's northern expedition and also the axis place for its northern expeditionary strategy.

There were many historic events in Three Kingdoms Period, which formed the main contents of Tianshui Three Kingdoms Culture, including Shu-Han's five times of northern expedition and two times of fight out from Qishan Hill under the leadership of Zhuge Liang (181-234AD, the prime minister of Shu Kingdom in Three Kingdoms Period), and nine times of warfare against the Wei Kingdom, seven times of conquest out from Longyou under the leadership of Jiang Wei (202-264AD, a great general of Shu Kingdom in Three Kingdoms Period). Tianshui Three Kingdoms Culture takes historical remains of Three Kingdoms as its carrier, and also takes folk legends, the excellent poetry and works left by men of letters when paying a visit to these historic sites as its main melody. The important position of Tianshui in Three Kingdoms Period being fully taken advantage of, a comprehensive research has been conducted by Xu Rihui from various aspects such as cultural historical remains, influences, legends and customs etc.

While seeking ancient battlefield remains, people are always looking for a kind of spiritual world. Zhuge Liang is the embodiment of wisdom with a "miraculous" power. His spirits of so called "bending one's back to the task until one's dying day" motivates Tianshui people to improve and perfect their thought realm. His famous saying "One can't show high ideals without simple living; and one can not have lofty aspirations without a peaceful state of mind", is a precious philosophy of life for encouraging people to cultivate their moral character, enlarge their virtue, make vigorous efforts and strive to build a well-off society.

In Tianshui, there are many ways of presenting Tianshui Three Kingdoms Culture-the one with remarkable regional characteristics, including the literary works with topic of Three Kingdoms, folk "Mashehuo" with performers dressing themselves like Three Kingdoms figures and acting on horses, Shaanxi Opera (Qinqiang) with Three Kingdoms stories performed in temple fairs and festivals, Zhuge Liang-praising and inscribed emotionally visiting poems and poetic couplets, Tianshui Three Kingdoms Culture academy seminars, folk Zhuge Liang worship activities, spreading of Three Kingdoms stories through film and TV works, etc. Tianshui Three Kingdoms Culture has become an everlasting beneficial cultural source and spiritual food for Tianshui people. The combination of the ancient Three Kingdoms historic battlefield sites and the unearthed historic relics is the core soul of the culture. The historic relics unearthed from historic battlefield sites, which are preserved in Gansu Museum, Tianshui Museum, Qin'an Museum and even are collected privately, certifies the existence of the Three Kingdoms wars with knives and swords flashing, drums beating and horns sounding. In Three Kingdoms touring area, Three Kingdoms historic sites are available for visitors to see, including Tianshui Pass, Zhuge Rampart, old Jieting Battlefield, Mumen Passageway, Jiang Wei's Tomb, etc.

第二节 天水三国文化语篇语域重构及翻译

一 天水诸葛军垒

（一）汉语语篇重构

天水诸葛军垒

序列1：背景信息

诸葛军垒位于天水市秦州区岷山路南（景点的地理位置）。因传说是蜀军随身携带的预防水土病的盐土堆积而成，且诸葛亮在土墩上布兵点将而得名（景点名称由来），2002年重建于天水市藉河南路（建筑起止年代），是天水境内蜀魏战争留下的大量遗迹之一，是天水人凭吊诸葛亮的胜地（社会定位）。

序列2：主题信息

游客可参观铜铸的诸葛亮雕塑、武侯祠堂、无影墩、八阵图，景仰武侯羽扇纶巾、运筹帷幄的英姿（观赏内容）。

序列3：附加信息

诸葛军垒公园为游客提供了理想的休闲娱乐场所。坐在亭台楼榭上既可驰想三国金戈铁马的烽火景象，又可领略天水山清水秀、鸟语花香的景色（景点的设施与服务）。

游客可在农历六月初六验证"无影墩"的传说。相传这天正午的太阳照在军垒上而四周没有投影（游览指南/建议）。

游客除游览军垒外，还可以参观附近的南郭寺（游览指南/建议）。

开放时间：全天。

门票价格：免费。

交通：乘坐18路内环、23路外环公交车到诸葛军垒站下车。

（二）重构语篇英语书面语介绍

Resort Introduction of Site of the Zhuge Rampart

Item 1 Background Information

The Zhuge Rampart is located on the south of Minshan Road, Qinzhou District, Tianshui City (location). According to the legend, the place was so named because the rampart was formed by the piles of saline soil which the soldiers of Shu army took with them to take precautions against water-soil borne disease and also because Zhuge Liang once called the muster roll of officers and assigned them tasks on the platform (name origin). The rampart, reconstructed in 2002 on Xihe South Road, Tianshui city (time), is one of the numerous historical remains of Shu-Wei war in Three Kingdoms Period in Tianshui city and is also a resort for Tianshui people to pay homage to Zhuge Liang (social status).

Item 2 Topic Information

You can see the bronze sculpture of Zhuge Liang, Wuhou Memorial Temple, the Mound Having No Shadow, Eight Front Strategy, and revere Wuhou Zhuge Liang's heroic posture of waving a feather fan in his hand, wearing a silk kerchief, mapping out army operations in tent and winning victory in battles (contents).

Item 3 Additional Information

Zhuge Rampart park provides you with an ideal leisure and entertainment site. Sitting in its pavilions and towers, you can fall into a reverie of flame scene of war with shining spears and armed horses at the time of Three Kingdoms of China while enjoying the landscape of green hills and beautiful waters, as well as birds' singing and flower's sweetness (facilities and services).

You can examine the reality of the legend "the Mound Having No Shadow" on 6th January of Chinese lunar calendar. According to the legend, at the high noon of that day, in the sun, there is no shadow on the rampart (guides/advices).

Apart from the Zhuge Rampart, you can also visit Nanguo Temple nearby (guides/advices).

Opening Times: The whole day.

Ticket Prices: Free.

Transportation: Take Bus No. 18 (inner ring) or Bus No. 23 (outer ring) to the Zhuge Rampart Stop.

(三) 重构语篇英语口语导游词

Tour Guide Speech of Site of the Zhuge Rampart

Item 1 Background Information

Hello! Dear friends! I feel honored to be your guide. Today I will show everyone around the famous site—Zhuge Rampart. Have you ever heard of Zhuge Liang? Yeah, he is one of the most intelligent persons in China's history and there are a lot of famous stories about him. Zhuge Rampart is just one of them.

The Zhuge Rampart is located on the south of Minshan Road, Qinzhou District, Tianshui City (location). According to the legend, the place was so named because of two reasons. One reason is that the rampart was formed by the piles of saline soil. And the soldiers of Shu army took it with them just to take precautions against water-soil borne disease. The other is because Zhuge Liang once called the muster roll of officers and assigned them tasks on the platform (name origin). The rampart was reconstructed in 2002 on Xihe South Road, Tianshui City (time). It now becomes one of the numerous historical remains of Shu-Wei war in Three Kingdoms Period in Tianshui city and is also a resort for Tianshui people to pay homage to Zhuge Liang (social status).

Item 2 Topic Information

Here you can see some famous sights, such as the bronze sculpture of

Zhuge Liang, Wuhou Memorial Temple, the Mound Having No Shadow, Eight Front Strategy. Here visitor can revere Wuhou Zhuge Liang's heroic posture of waving a feather fan in his hand, wearing a silk kerchief, mapping out army operations in tent and winning victory in battles (contents).

Item 3 Additional information

If you are tired, there is a good place for you to go, Zhuge Rampart Park. It provides you with an ideal leisure and entertainment site. You just sit in its pavilions and towers, falling into a reverie of flame scene of war with shining spears and armed horses at the time of Three Kingdoms of China. At the same time, you can enjoy the landscape of green hills and beautiful waters, as well as birds' singing and flower's sweetness (facilities and services).

You can examine the reality of the legend "Shadowless Pier" on 6th January of Chinese lunar calendar. According to the legend, at the middle time of the day, there is no shadow when sunlight falls across the rampart (guides/advices).

The park opens the whole day. Take Bus No. 18 (inner ring) or Bus No. 23 (outer ring) to the Zhuge Rampart Stop and visit freely.

二 秦安街亭古战场

(一) 汉语语篇重构

秦安街亭古战场

序列1：背景信息

秦安街亭又名街泉亭，简称街亭。街亭古战场地处今天水秦安县城东45千米的陇城镇（景点的地理位置）。相传是因陇城一口年代久远的泉而得名（景点名称由来）。蜀汉建兴六年（公元228年）蜀将马谡（公元190—228年）与魏将张郃（？—公元231年）战于街亭（建筑起止年代），是天水境内蜀魏战争留下的大量遗迹之一，是马谡的败绩处（社会定位）。

序列 2：主题信息

街亭古战场西北 2 千米处薛李川出土的一张铸有"蜀"字的弩机实物现存于甘肃省博物馆。游客可参观六角亭及亭中石碑。石碑正面为习仲勋同志题写的碑名"三国古战场遗址——街亭"，背面为同县的人题写的碑文（观赏内容）。

序列 3：附加信息

总投资 3 亿元的女娲祠至街亭古战场的长 1 千米的步行通道、石凳、凉亭；在街亭古战场入口处的长 100 米的全封闭式通道——时光隧道（外观以木桩、栅栏等材料装饰成军营状，通道内在局部区域建设虚拟现实数码厅）；位于山顶的马谡军营（军营内陈列兵器、古代军服等，绘制街亭之战示意图，并开发参与性项目）；游客服务中心、停车场、旅游厕所、景区标识牌和环卫设施等正在规划实施中（景点的设施与服务）。

除古战场遗址外，游客还可以参观位于陇城镇南门的女娲庙、镇东南约 2 千米的风沟女娲洞和仅 5 千米距离的大地湾遗址（游览指南/建议）。

开放时间：全天。

门票价格：免费。

交通：天水长途汽车站有发往秦安陇城方向的汽车。

（二）重构语篇英语书面语介绍

Resort Introduction of the Site of the Old Battlefield of Jieting

Item 1 Background Information

Jieting is also known as Jiequanting, short for Jieting. Jieting Ancient Battlefield is located in Longcheng Town, 45 kilometres east away from Qin'an County (location). According to the legend, Jieting Ancient Battlefield was named for the reason that there was an ancient spring in Longcheng (name origin). In the sixth year of Jianxing (228 AD), Shu-Han Dynasty of Three Kingdoms, Ma Su, a Shu Kingdom's general, fought against Zhang He, a Wei Kingdom's general, at Jieting (time). The battlefield of

Jieting is one of the many historical relics left by Shu-Wei war, and is also the place where Ma Su was beaten (social status).

Item 2 Topic Information

A crossbow casted in Chinese character "Shu", which was unearthed in Xuelichuan, 2 kilometres northwest away from the ancient battlefield, is preserved in Gansu Provincial Museum. You can see a stone tablet in a hexagonal pavilion. The tablet, in its front face, was engraved with its name—"Ancient Battlefield Site of the Three Kingdoms—Jieting" in Chinese characters, inscribed by Xi Zhongxun, one of the founders of the Shaanxi, Gansu border area and the former secretary of the Northwest Bureau of the Central Committee of the Chinese Communist Party, while in its back face, it was carved with inscription by people from the same county (contents).

Item 3 Additional Information

With investment of 300 million Yuan in total, new construction projects are being under plan, including a pedestrian passageway of 1 kilometre long from Nvwa Temple to Jieting Ancient Battlefield, stone benches, an arbor, a time tunnel, a Ma Su military camp, a tourist service center, a car park, tourist toilets, scenic area signboards and environment-sanitation facilities etc. The time tunnel, starting from the entrance of the battlefield, will be a full closed passageway of 100 metres long, with materials like wood piles and railings decorated on its outside appearance to make it look like a real military camp. In partial area of the tunnel, there will be some virtual reality digital cabinets. Ma Su military camp will be built on the top of the hill, within which will be a schematic diagram of the war of Jieting Fort, weapons and ancient military uniforms displayed, and develop some participation projects. Also, tour service center, parking lot, free toilet, scenic spot signs and the equipment of environment and hygiene are being carried out (facilities and services).

Besides the ancient battlefield, Nvwa Temple (located on the south gate of Longcheng Town), Fenggou Nvwa Cave (2 kilometres southeast away from the town) and Dadiwan Relics (5 kilometres away from this battlefield) are available for you to view (guides/advices).

Openng Times: The whole day.

Ticket Prices: Free.

Transportation: Take any buses heading for Longcheng of Qin'an County from Tianshui Long-distance Bus Station.

(三) 重构语篇英语口语导游词

Tour Guide Speech of the Site of the Old Battlefield of Jieting

Item 1 Background Information

Dear friends! I feel very honored to be your guide. Today I will show everyone of you to see the famous site—the old battlefield of Jieting. Have you ever heard about the place? Yeah, there are some well-known events happening here. I bet all of you must be interested in them. Now, let me give you a detailed and clear explanation of it.

Jieting is also known as Jiequanting, short for Jieting. Jieting Ancient Battlefield is located in Longcheng Town, 45 kilometres east away from Qin'an County (location). Why is it so called? Because it is said that there was an ancient spring in Longcheng (name origin). In the sixth year of Jianxing (228 AD) (time), Shu-Han Dynasty of Three Kingdoms, a Shu Kingdom's general called Ma Su fought against a Wei Kingdom's general called Zhang He at Jieting. It was a very famous battle at that time. Since then, the battlefield of Jieting has been regarded as one of the many historical relics left by Shu-Wei war. Also it is the place where Ma Su was beaten (social status).

Item 2 Topic Information

Very impressively! You can see a crossbow casted in Chinese character "Shu", which was unearthed in Xuelichuan, 2 kilometres northwest away from the ancient battlefield. Now it is preserved in Gansu Provincial Museum. You can also see a stone tablet in a hexagonal pavilion. The front face of the tablet was engraved with its name— "Ancient Battlefield site of the Three Kingdoms—Jieting" in Chinese characters, inscribed by Xi Zhongxun. Do you know who is he? Let me tell you. He is one of the founders of the Shaanxi, Gansu border areas and the former secretary of the Northwest Bureau of the Central Committee of the Chinese Communist Party. Look at the back face, it was carved with inscription by people from the same county (contents).

Item 3 Additional Information

300 million Yuan in total is invested in new construction projects. And now they are being under plan. Among the projects, there is a pedestrian passageway of 1 kilometre long from Nvwa Temple to Jieting Ancient Battlefield, stone benches, an arbor, a time tunnel, a Ma Su military camp, a tourist service center, a car park, tourist toilets, scenic area signboards and environment-sanitation facilities etc. The time tunnel, starting from the entrance of the battlefield, will be a full closed passageway of 100 metres long. Its outside appearance of the tunnel will be made of materials like wood piles and railings to make it look like a real military camp. In partial area of the tunnel, there will be some virtual reality digital cabinets. Ma Su military camp will be built on the top of the hill, within which will be a schematic diagram of the war of Jieting Fort, display weapons and ancient military uniforms, and develop some participation projects. Good news! Travel service center, parking lot, free toilet, scenic spot signs and the equipment of environment and hygiene are being carried out (facilities and services).

Besides the ancient battlefield, there are some other famous sights available for you to view, such as Nvwa Temple (located on the south gate of Longcheng Town), Fenggou Nvwa Cave (2 kilometres southeast away from the town) and Dadiwan Relics (5 kilometres away from this battlefield) (guides/advices).

The ancient battlefield opens the whole day. Take any buses heading for Longcheng of Qin'an County from Tianshui Long-distance Bus Station and visit freely.

三　甘谷姜维墓

（一）汉语语篇重构

甘谷姜维墓

序列1：背景信息

姜维（公元202—264年）墓位于天水市甘谷县六峰镇姜家庄村南将军岭靴子坪上，距县城东5千米（景点的地理位置），相传是姜维衣冠冢而得名（景点名称由来）。传说公元264年姜维兵变被杀后，随从设法偷得衣冠靴子背回故里，家乡人民依南山筑衣冠冢，靴子别葬冢旁。距现在已经1800多年，1988年甘谷县政府在原来的旧址上修复（建筑起止年代），是天水境内蜀魏战争留下的大量遗迹之一，是天水人凭吊姜维的胜地（社会定位）。

序列2：主题信息

游客拜谒时可发现墓葬设计象征着姜维一生。墓前9台石阶代表姜维九伐中原，18台石阶代表姜维距现在已经1800多年。整个墓地与姜维的生平相吻合：墓高3.5米，寓意姜维35岁时就在诸葛亮手下担任重要职务，并屡立战功；墓地直径6.2米，表示姜维享年62岁，举义复蜀，事业未成而含恨九泉；石台高1.2米，寓意姜维12岁时就聪明勇敢，结发从军；姜维塑像高2.7米，寓意姜维27岁时跟随诸葛亮征战疆场。大殿两侧的36幅壁画则描绘了姜维的一生（观赏内容）。

序列3：附加信息

姜维纪念馆由民间自筹资金建于1999年，有杨成武将军题写的"姜维故里"石碑、大殿廊沿明柱上名人题写的匾联、围墙上当代名人题写的诗词名句碑刻、殿内墙壁上的山水人物国画等，还有身高4米的姜维圣像。将军坡上相传是姜维母亲当年居住过的窑洞，曾经是抚养姜维长大成人之处。馆内配备讲解服务等（景点的设施与服务）。

除甘谷姜维墓外，您还可以参观天水关姜维墓。该墓坐落在秦州区天水镇东北的黄家坪山顶，直径约10米，在此远眺可将天水关尽收眼底。姜维62岁兵变被杀后，据传其部下偷偷地割下姜维的头颅，潜回天水关，埋在黄家坪山顶、姜维曾经屯过兵的扎营地里（游览指南/建议）。

每逢姜维诞辰10月18日和清明节，天水人都要举行隆重的祭祀活动来纪念这位"但有远志，不在当归"的大将军（游览指南/建议）。

开放时间：全天。

门票价格：免费。

交通：天水长途汽车站有发往甘谷六峰镇方向的汽车。

（二）重构语篇英语书面语介绍

Resort Introduction of Jiangwei's Tomb

Item 1 Background Information

The Tomb of Jiangwei (202-264 AD) is located on Boots Plateau, General Ridge, south of Jiangjiazhuang Village, Liufeng Town, Gangu County, Tianshui, 5 kilometres east of the county (location). According to the legend, it was named for the reason that there used to bury Jiangwei's clothes and crown (name origin). It was said that after Jiang Wei was killed in 264 AD because of mutiny and his attendant managed to steal his clothes, crown and boots, and then took them to his hometown. His hometown fellows built a tomb against the south mountain and buried his clothes and crown, then buried his boots beside the tomb. Since then, it has been more than 1800 years passed (time). In 1988, Gangu County government rebuilt the tomb on the basis of the old one. The tomb is one of the many historic relics left by Shu-Wei war within the boundary of Tianshui. The tomb is also a resort for Tianshui people to pay homage to Jiangwei (social status).

Item 2 Topic Information

While paying your respect to Jiangwei, you can find that the design of the tomb symbolizes the whole life of Jiangwei. The 9 stone steps before the tomb stand for his 9 times of conquests to the Central Plains. The 18 stone steps refer to that it has been over 1800 years from his time to now. The construction of the whole tomb is identical to the experience of his life. The tomb's 3.5 metres in height implies that he began to take important positions and win many victories at 35 years old under the leadership of Zhuge Liang. The tomb's 6.2 metres in diameter indicates that he died at the age of 62 when rising in revolt for recovering Shu Kingdom, with his cause failing and his life ending with regret. The stone steps' 1.2 metres in height indicates that he was very clever and brave when he was 12 years old, joining army at his early adulthood. And his statue's 2.7 metres in height means that he fought in battlefield following Zhuge Liang from 27 years old. The 36 wall pictures on the two sides of the temple describe Jiangwei's whole life (contents).

Item 3 Additional Information

Jiangwei's Memorial Hall was built in 1999 by civil fund raising. There is a stone tablet in the hall carved with "Jiangwei's Hometown" in Chinese characters inscribed by general Yang Chengwu. On the pillars in the corridor edges, there are horizontal inscribed boards inscribed by famous people. On its enclosing wall, there are poems, famous sentences, inscriptions etc. written by famous people. On its inside walls, there are also some traditional Chinese paintings of mountains, waters and figures. A 4-metre-high Jiangwei icon stands in the hall. According to the legend, there was a cave, on General Hillside, where Jiangwei's mother once lived and brought him up. A full presentation service is available in the hall (facilities and services).

Besides Gangu Jiangwei's Tomb, another Jiangwei's Tomb in Tianshui

Mountain Pass is also available for you to view. The tomb, with about 10 metres in diameter, is on the top of Huangjiaping Hill, northeast of Tianshui Town, Qinzhou District. From there, you can look into the distance and get a wonderful view of Tianshui Pass. According to the hearsay, after Jiang Wei was killed at 62 years old because of mutiny, his attendant secretly cut his head and sneaked back to Tianshui Pass with it, then buried it on the top of Huangjiaping Hill, where was once his campsite to station his troops (guides/advices).

Every year, on his birthday (18th of October) and Tomb-Sweeping Day, Tianshui people would hold grand ceremonial activities to commemorate this great general with ambition of "only great ambition, no consideration of return" (guides/advices).

Openng Times: The whole day.

Ticket Prices: Free.

Transportation: Take any buses heading for Liufeng Town of Gangu County from Tianshui Long-distance Bus Station.

(三) 重构语篇英语口语导游词

Tour Guide Speech of Jiangwei's Tomb

Item 1 Background Information

Hi, everyone! I feel very happy to be your guide today. I will take everyone to visit the famous sight, Jiangwei's Tomb. Jiangwei's tomb, of course the tomb is concerned about the person. Do you know anything about him? OK! You will know about the great general after I explain.

The Tomb of Jiangwei is located on Boots Plateau, General Ridge, south of Jiangjiazhuang Village, Liufeng Town, Gangu County, Tianshui, 5 kilometres east of the county (location). According to the legend, it was so named because Jiang Wei's clothes and crown were buried here. The saying goes that after Jiang Wei was killed in 264 AD because of mutiny, his attendant managed to steal his clothes, crown and boots, then took them to his hometown where people built a tomb against the south mountain and buried his clothes and crown, then buried his boots beside the tomb (name origin). Sounds incredible, isn't it? And now it has been more than 1800 years (time). In 1988, Gangu County government rebuilt the tomb on the basis of the old one. The tomb is one of the many historic relics left by Shu-Wei war within the boundary of Tianshui. The tomb is also a resort for Tianshui people to pay homage to Jiangwei (social status).

Item 2 Topic Information

When you pay your respect to Jiangwei, you will find something interesting, that is the design of the tomb just symbolizes Jiangwei's whole life. Look at these numbers! They all have special meanings. The 9 stone steps before the tomb stand for his 9 times of conquests to the central plain. The 18 stone steps refer to that it has been over 1800 years from his time to now. The construction of the whole tomb is identical to the experience of his life. The tomb's 3.5 metres in height implies that he began to take important position and win many victories at 35 years old under the leadership of Zhuge Liang. The tomb's 6.2 metres in diameter indicates that he died at the age of 62 when he rose in revolt for recovering Shu Kingdom, but unfortunately he failed and died with regret. The stone steps' 1.2 metres in height indicates that he was very clever and brave when he was 12 years old and that he joined army at his early adulthood. And his statue's 2.7 metres in height implies that he fought in battlefield following Zhuge Liang from 27 years old. The 36 wall pictures on the two sides of the temple describe Jiangwei's whole life. Very interesting, right (contents)?

Item 3 Additional Information

Here we are! This is Jiangwei's Memorial Hall. It was built in 1999 by civil fund raising. There is a stone tablet in the hall carved with "Jiangwei's Hometown" in Chinese characters inscribed by general Yang Chengwu. On the pillars in the corridor edges, there are horizontal inscribed boards inscribed by famous people. On its enclosing wall, there are poems, famous sentences, inscriptions etc. written by famous people. On its inside walls, there are some traditional Chinese paintings of mountains, waters and figures. A 4-metre-high Jiangwei icon stands in the hall. The legend goes that there was a cave, on General Hillside, where Jiangwei's mother once lived and brought him up. A full presentation service is available in the hall (facilities and services).

You never imagine that apart from Gangu Jiangwei's Tomb, there is another Jiangwei's Tomb called Tianshui Pass Jiangwei's Tomb. People can go there to visit it. The tomb is on the top of the Huangjiaping Hill, northeast of Tianshui Town, Qinzhou District and it is about 10 metres in diameter. From there, you can look into the distance and get a wonderful view of Tianshui Pass. According to the legend, after Jiang Wei was killed at 62 years old because of mutiny, his attendant secretly cut his head and sneaked back to the Mountain Pass with it, then buried it on the top of the Huangjiaping Hill, where he once stationed his troops (guides/advices).

Every year, on his birthday (18th of October) and the Tomb-Sweeping Day, Tianshui folks would hold grand ceremonial activities to commemorate this great general with "only great ambition, no consideration of return" (guides/advices).

The relics opens the whole day. Take any buses heading for Liufeng Town of Gangu County from Tianshui Long-distance Bus Station and visit freely.

四 天水木门道

（一）汉语语篇重构

天水木门道

序列1：背景信息

木门道古战场遗址地处天水市秦州区牡丹镇木门村（景点的地理位置）。因相传是三国时期蜀国丞相诸葛亮（公元181—234年）设计射死魏国大将张郃（？—公元 231 年）处而得名（景点名称由来）。1996 年秦州区政府将其确定为三国古战场遗址并于同年 8 月立石碑（建筑起止年代），这是天水三国古战场文化遗址建设规模最大、研究价值最高的地方（社会定位）。

序列 2：主题信息

木门道东侧张家坪出土的魏蜀时期的箭头、刀矛等兵器馆藏于天水市博物馆。游客可以参观木门道的武侯纪念祠、当年诸葛亮在山顶上擂鼓指挥作战的擂鼓台石鼓、诸葛亮当年退兵之时垒制的形如巨钟的土钟堆、蜀兵屯兵拴马的拴马湾、蜀兵布伏的伏马湾、诸葛亮与张郃作战时的埋伏地——张郃坪、张郃墓等（观赏内容）。

序列 3：附加信息

为供人们凭吊缅怀诸葛亮，村民于 1996 年开始通过民间集资的渠道兴建了武侯纪念祠。殿内除三国著名人物塑像外还绘有张郃败走木门道的连环壁画；两侧建有卷棚、接待室和陈列室、木门道武侯祠在天水市旅游景点的位置图、木门道及相邻景点示意图、木门道矢镞图（景点的设施与服务）。

游客还可以欣赏著名学者霍松林（1921—2017 年）题写的石碑（游览指南/建议）。

您在每年农历三月十八至二十日庙会期间、农历四月初八可体验有秦腔、羊皮扇鼓舞等各种民间艺术的木门道庙会（游览指南/建议）。

开放时间：全天。

门票价格：免费。

交通：天水长途汽车站有发往牡丹镇木门村的汽车。

（二）重构语篇英语书面语介绍

Resort Introduction of Mumen Passageway

Item 1 Background Information

Mumen Passageway (commonly known as Canyon Door) is located in Mumen Village, Mudan Town, Qinzhou District, Tianshui City (location). According to the legend, it was named for the reason that it was the place where Zhuge Liang (181-234 AD), the prime minister of Shu Kingdom, worked out a plan to kill Zhang He (? -231AD), a Wei Kingdom's general, by shooting arrows (name origin). In 1996, Qinzhou District government determined Mumen Passageway be an ancient battlefield relic of Three Kingdoms and set up a stone tablet there (time). Of all ancient battlefield relics of Three Kingdoms, this attraction is positioned as the biggest in construction size and highest in research value (social status).

Item 2 Topic Information

The weapons of Wei-Shu period such as arrowheads, knives and spears, which were unearthed from Zhangjiaping on the eastern side of the Mumen Passageway, are collected in Tianshui Museum. You can look around the Wuhou Memorial Temple, stone drum with the drum-beating platform, on which Zhuge Liang once beated the drum and commanded battles at the top of hill, the huge bell-like earth mound piled up at the time when Zhuge Liang repulsed the enemy, the Bend of Tying Horses when Shu Kingdom's army stationed their troops, the Ambush Bend where they made ambush, Zhang He Level Ground—the ambushing point where Zhuge Liang fought against Zhang He, Zhang He's Tomb etc. (contents).

Item 3 Additional Information

In order for people to pay homage to and recall Zhuge Liang, villagers built the Wuhou Memorial Temple in 1996 by civil fund raising. Apart from the statues of some famous people during Three Kingdoms in the temple, you can see a series of wall pictures about how Zhang He was defeated at the Mumen Passageway. Also a round ridge roof, a reception room, and a display room built in the two sides. And also some directions of the temple among all Tianshui tourist attractions, site illustration diagrams of Mumen Passageway and other vicinity attractions and the vectogram of Mumen Passageway are available (facilities and services).

Visitors can enjoy the stone tablet inscribed by Huo Songlin (1921 - 2017 AD), a modern famous scholar (guides/advices).

You can enjoy various civil art performances such as Shaanxi Opera and sheep-skin drum dance etc. at Mumen Passageway Temple Fair during the fair periods of 18th to 20th March and 8th April of Chinese lunar calendar every year (guides/advices).

Openng Times: The whole day.

Ticket Prices: Free.

Transportation: Take any buses heading for Mumen Village of Mudan Town from Tianshui Long-distance Bus Station.

(三) 重构语篇英语口语导游词

Tour Guide Speech of Mumen Passageway

Item 1 Background Information

Hello! Everyone! Today I will show you around a small but famous sight—Mumen Passageway. Mumen Passageway (commonly known as Canyon Door) is located in Mumen Village, Mudan Town, Qinzhou District of Tianshui City (location). According to the legend, it was so named because that it was the place where Zhuge Liang (181-234 AD), the prime minister of Shu Kingdom, shot Zhang He (? -231AD), a Wei Kingdom's general, to death (name origin). In 1996, Qinzhou District government recognized Mumen Passageway as an ancient battlefield relic of Three Kingdoms and set up a stone tablet there (time).Of all ancient battlefield relics of Three Kingdoms, this attraction is positioned as the biggest in size and highest in research value (social status).

Item 2 Topic Information

There are many weapons such as arrowheads, knives and spears unearthed from Zhangjiaping on the eastern side of the Mumen Passageway. They are all typical weapons of Wei-Shu Period. And now they are collected in Tianshui Museum. You can enjoy a lot of interesting sights. You can look around the Wuhou Shrine, the stone drum with the drum-beating platform, on which Zhuge Liang once beated the drum and commanded battles at the top of hill, the huge bell-like earth mound piled up at the time when Zhuge Liang repulsed the enemy, the Bend of Tying Horses for tying up horses when Shu Kingdom's army stationed their troops, the Ambush Bend where they made ambush, Zhang He Level Ground—the ambushing point where Zhuge Liang fought against Zhanghe, Zhang He's Tomb etc. (contents).

Item 3 Additional Information

Zhuge Liang's wisdom and military strategies are so unparalleled that people would like to pay homage to and recall Zhuge Liang. So villagers built the Wuhou Memorial Temple in 1996 by civil fund raising. Apart from the statues of some famous people during Three Kingdoms in the temple, you can see a series of wall pictures of how Zhang He was defeated at the Mumen Passageway. Also a round ridge roof a reception room, and a display room built in the two sides. And also some directions of the temple among all Tianshui tourist attractions, site illustration diagrams of Mumen Passageway and other vicinity attractions and the vectogram of Mumen Passageway are available (facilities and services).

You can enjoy the stone tablet inscribed by Huo Songlin (1921-2017 AD), a modern famous scholar (guides/advices).

On 18th to 20th March and 8th April of Chinese lunar calendar every year, Mumen Passageway Temple Fair is held. When going there, you can enjoy various civil art performances such as Shaanxi Opera and sheep-skin drum dance etc. (guides/advices).

The relics opens the whole day. Take any buses heading for Mumen Village of Mudan Town from Tianshui Long-distance Bus Station and visit freely.

第三节 "一带一路"沿线国家军事文化语篇语域重构及翻译

一 斯里兰卡加勒要塞

(一) 汉语语篇重构

斯里兰卡加勒要塞

序列1：背景信息

加勒要塞也叫加勒城堡或者加勒古堡，位于斯里兰卡加勒市的中心地带（景点的地理位置）。因荷兰人建造的牢固坚硬的旧城墙而得名（景点名称由来）。荷兰殖民者于1663年开始建造（建筑起止年代），已经被列入世界文化遗产，也是现存最大的古要塞之一（社会定位）。

序列2：主题信息

游客沿着堡墙顺时针走能看到一系列加勒要塞的碉堡。从主城门到旧门、两侧的库房、最古老的碉堡黑堡，以及乌德勒支碉堡顶上18米高的灯塔等都是要塞的代表性建筑（观赏内容）。

序列3：附加信息

在要塞的正门附近有国家博物馆，陈列着斯里兰卡各时期的文物，还有一些其他博物馆文物的复制品。要塞东部有一处历史博物馆陈列着各种殖民时期的文物，如古董打字机、中国收藏品、瓷器、珠宝、首饰等，这些文物上都有标价。该博物馆免费参观，开放时间为9：00—18：00，有专人介绍。钟楼不远处是由要塞仓库改建的国家海事博物馆，馆内陈列着大量海下发掘的文物，如地图、船只、绳索、陶器、酒杯、烟袋、火炮等，还有一些有关加勒历史、海底生物的介绍。开放时间为周二到周六9：30—16：30，门票为3美元（景点的设施与服务）。

除了堡墙，游客还可以参观灯塔、钟楼、米拉清真寺和老城门

（游览指南/建议）。

城墙西南的海神碉堡是欣赏日落美景的绝妙之处。灯塔不对外开放，游客只能在外围欣赏（游览指南/建议）。

游客付费能在旗石（用来提醒来往船只小心周边危险的水下暗礁）的岩顶上欣赏悬崖跳水表演（游览指南/建议）。

开放时间：全天。

门票价格：免费。

交通：从加勒中心汽车站往南步行五百米即可到达。

（二）重构语篇英语书面语介绍

Resort Introduction of Galle Fort

Item 1 Background Information

Galle Fort, which is located in the heart of Galle of Sri Lanka (location), is also called Galle Castle. It got the name from the old, solid and ironbound city wall made by Dutchmen (name origin). In 1663 AD, the Dutch settlers began building Galle Fort (time), which now has been listed as world cultural heritage and also one of the currently biggest old forts in the world (social status).

Item 2 Topic Information

When walking along the city wall clockwise, tourists can see a series of blockhouse of Galle Fort, such as Main Gate to storehouse in Old Gate, the oldest Zwart Bastion, a 18-metre-long lighthouse on the top of Point Utrecht Bastion etc., which are all the representatives of Galle Fort (contents).

Item 3 Additional Information

There is a National Museum close to the front gate of Galle Fort, where culture relics in Sri Lanka from different periods and other replicas from other museums are displayed. Also there is a Historical Mansion on the way to Leyn Baan, the east side of Galle Fort. In this Historical Mansion, there are culture relics from different colonial days, such as vintage typewriter,

Chinese collections, china and jewelry with price tags on them. Historical Mansion is free for every one, and it opens from 9:00 a.m. till 6:00 p.m. with a guide available. National Maritime Museum, located close to the Bell Tower, is remodeled from a fort storehouse. A large amount of culture relics were excavated in the sea, for example, maps, ships, ropes, china, wineglasses, tobacco pouches, cannons and introduction about the time of Galle and sea creatures. National Maritime Museum opens at 9:30 a.m. and closes at 4:30 p.m., from Tuesday to Saturday. The ticket is 3 dollars for each (facilities and services).

Besides city walls, tourists can also visit Light Tower, Bell Tower, Jumeirah Mosque and the old city gate (guides/advices).

Triton Bastion, located at the southwest of city wall, is the perfect place to view the fascinating sunset. Lighthouse is not open to visitors so they can only enjoy it from outside (guides/advices).

If you buy tickets, you can enjoy the cliff diving from Flag Rock, which is for warning passing ships from reef dangers (guides/advices).

Opening Times: The whole day.

Ticket Price: Free.

Transportation: Walk 500 metres to the south from Galle bus stop and you will arrive at the destination.

(三) 重构语篇英语口语导游词

Tour Guide Speech of Galle Fort

Item 1 Background Information

Hello! Dear friends! Today I will show all of you around Galle Fort. Galle Fort is located in the heart of Galle of Sri Lanka. It is also called Galle Castle (location). Do you know where is this name from? It is from the old, solid and ironbound city wall made by Dutchmen (name origin). The Dutch settlers built Galle Fort in 1663 AD (time). And now it has been listed as world heritage and also is one of the biggest old forts in the world (social status).

Item 2 Topic Information

When you walk along the city wall clockwise, you can see a series of blockhouse of Galle Fort, such as Main Gate to storehouse in Old Gate, the oldest Zwart Bastion and a 18-metre-long lighthouse on the top of Point Utrecht Bastion. These are all the representatives of Galle Fort (contents).

Item 3 Additional Information

You can visit National Museum if you are interested in. It is close to the front gate of Galle Fort. There are culture relics in Sri Lanka from different periods and other replicas from other museums. And the Historical Mansion is on your way to Leyn Baan, the east side of Galle Fort. In it you can see tons of culture relics from different colonial days, such as vintage typewriter, Chinese collections, china and jewelry with price tags. By the way, Historical Mansion is free for every one. It usually opens from 9 : 00 a. m. to 6 : 00 p. m. and a special guide is offered. Besides, there is another museum called National Maritime Museum, which is close to the Bell Tower. It is remodeled from a fort storehouse. You can see a great number of culture relics in the sea, for example, maps, ships, ropes, china, wineglasses, tobacco pouches, cannons and introduction about the time of Galle and sea creatures. Remember Nation Maritime Museum opens at 9 : 30 a. m. and closes at 4 : 30 p. m., from Tuesday to Saturday. The ticket is 3 dollars for each (facilities and services).

Apart from city walls, you can also visit Light Tower, Bell Tower, Jumeirah Mosque and the old city gate (guides/advices).

I highly recommend you a perfect spot for viewing fascinating sunset. It is Triton Bastion, which is located at the southwest of city wall. But lighthouse is not open to people so you can only enjoy it from outside (guides/advices).

If you buy a ticket, you can enjoy the cliff diving from Flag Rock, which is for warning passing ships from reef dangers (guides/advices).

Good news! It is open all day and it is free. Walk 500 metres to the south from Galle bus stop and you will arrive at the destination.

二　阿曼巴赫莱要塞

(一) 汉语语篇重构

阿曼巴赫莱要塞

序列1：背景信息

巴赫莱要塞坐落在阿曼首都马斯喀特西南部约200千米处（景点的地理位置）。因要塞所在地巴赫莱村庄而得名（景点名称由来）。建造于13—14世纪，当时正是巴赫莱绿洲一代在巴努·内布罕部落统治下繁荣昌盛的历史时期（建筑起止年代），1987年被列入联合国教科文组织世界遗产名录，是阿曼全国最早的世界遗产（社会定位）。

序列2：主题信息

这个庞大的堡垒的废墟，有土制的城墙和碉堡以及用石头打的地基，是这个类型的防御工事中突出的例子。围绕要塞的城墙总长12千米，是用晒干了的砖头修建而成的。该要塞采用砖石结构，底层由数米高的大型石块作为基石，上层用砖垒砌而成。城墙直通巡逻小路，城墙上建有许多监视塔，至今还残留着几座方形或圆形的监视塔（观赏内容）。

序列3：附加信息

经过20年的恢复工作，现在要塞在限制时间内向公众部分开放。里面有许多陈列物品，但很少有标签或描述；要塞没有关于城堡的介绍，需要网上搜寻资料；现存的要塞只是整个巴赫莱城防御系统的一部分，地基下面是阿曼著名的地下水道系统（景点的设施与服务）。

马斯喀特港是古代中国和阿拉伯国家贸易的重要港口，是"21世纪海上丝绸之路"途经阿拉伯半岛的唯一港口城市。阿曼是北京奥运会火炬传递途经的唯一阿拉伯国家（游览指南/建议）。

游客还可以感受10千米外建于17世纪的贾布林城堡的军事和防

御功能（游览指南/建议）。

开放时间：周六至周四 9：00—16：00，周五 8：00—11：00。

门票价格：不详。

交通：在迪拜机场巴吉租车公司租车到巴赫莱 21 号公路下即可到达。

（二）重构语篇英语书面语介绍

Resort Introduction of Bahla Fort in Oman

Item 1 Background Information

Bahla Fort is located about 200 kilometres southwest of Oman capital Muscat (location). It got the name for Bahla Village (name origin). It was built in the 13th-14th century, when the oasis of Bahla was prosperous under the control of the Banu Nebhan tribe (time). The fort became a UNESCO World Heritage Site in 1987 and is also the earliest World Heritage Site in Oman nationwide (social status).

Item 2 Topic Information

The ruins of the immense fort, with its walls and towers of unbaked brick and its stone foundations, is a remarkable example of this type of fortification. The walls surrounding the fort is 12 kilometres in all and they are built of the bricks dried in the sun. The fort takes the structure of stones and bricks, the bottom of the fort being a huge stone of several metres high as the cornerstone, and the upper being laid with bricks. The walls of city lead directly to the patrol lane. Many surveillance towers are built on the walls and there are still a few square and circular surveillance towers (contents).

Item 3 Additional Information

After a twenty-year restoration effort, the fort is now partially open to the public for limited hours. There are a number of displays inside, but few labels or descriptions. There is no introduction of the fort. So you need to surf the Internet to get some information. The existing fort is only a part of the defensive systems of Bahla. Under the foundation is Oman's famous underground system (Falaj) (facilities and services).

Muscat harbour is an important port of ancient China and Arabic countries' trade, which is the only port city of "Maritime Silk Route" on the sea passing Arabian Peninsula. Oman is also the only Arabian country that the Beijing Olympic torch relay passes (guides/advices).

You can also enjoy the military and defensive functions of Jabrin Fort, which was built 10 kilometres away in 17th century (guides/advices).

Opening Times: From 9:00 a.m. till 4:00 p.m. from Saturday to Thursday; from 8:00 a.m. till 11:00 p.m. on Friday.

Ticket Prices: Unknown.

Transportation: You can hire a car to get to No. 21 highway of Bahla from Dubai airport.

(三) 重构语篇英语口语导游词

Tour Guide Speech of Bahla Fortin Oman

Item 1 Background Information

Dear friends! Today I will be your guide and take everyone of you to visit Bahla Fort. Bahla Fort is located about 200 kilometres southwest of Oman capital Muscat (location). It was named after Bahla Village (name origin). It was built in the 13th–14th century, when the oasis of Bahla was prosperous under the control of the Banu Nebhan tribe (time). The fort became a UNESCO World Heritage Site in 1987 and is also the earliest World Heritage Site in Oman nationwide (social status).

Item 2 Topic Information

The ruins of the immense fort includes walls made of earth, towers of unbaked brick and stone foundations. It is a remarkable example of this type of fortification. Firstly, the walls surrounding the fort is 12 kilometres in all and they are built of the dried bricks. Secondly, the fort takes the structure of stones and bricks. The bottom of the fort is a huge stone of several metres high as the cornerstone, and the upper is laid with bricks. Thirdly, the walls of city lead directly to the patrol lane. Many surveillance towers are built on the walls and there are still a few square and circular surveillance towers (contents).

Item 3 Additional Information

After a twenty-year restoration effort, the fort is now partially open to the public for limited hours. There are a number of displays inside, but few labels or descriptions are on them. One strange thing is that there is no introduction of the fort. So you need to surf the Internet to get some information. The existing fort is only a part of the defensive systems of Bahla. Under the foundation is Oman's famous underground system (Falaj) (facilities and services).

Muscat harbour is an important port of ancient China and Arabic countries' trade. It is the only port city of "Maritime Silk Route" on the sea passing Arabian Peninsula. Oman is also the only Arabian country that the Beijing Olympic torch relay passes (guides/advices).

You can also enjoy the military and defensive functions of Jabrin Fort. You will be amazed by the technology and wisdom of people at that time, because Jabrin Fort was built in 17th century. Long long time ago, isn't it (guides/advices)?

The fort opens from Saturday to Thursday from 9：00 a.m. till 4：00 p.m., and opens from 8：00 a.m. till 11：00 p.m. on Friday. Ticket prices information is not available. You can hire a car to get to No. 21 highway of Bahla from Dubai airport.

三 特洛伊考古遗址

（一）汉语语篇重构

特洛伊考古遗址

序列1：背景信息

特洛伊考古遗址位于土耳其达达尼尔海峡主要港口恰纳卡莱以南

40 千米处的希沙立克（景点的地理位置）。因 1871 年挖掘于土耳其古城特洛伊而得名（景点名称由来）。其跨越公元前 3000 年至公元 400 年时期（景点起止年代），考古成就证实《荷马史诗》是有史为据的。1998 年联合国教科文组织将特洛伊考古遗址作为文化遗产列入《世界遗产名录》（社会定位）。

序列 2：主题信息

游客除可在景区门口欣赏到仿建的巨大木马模型外，还可以身临其境地观赏分属 9 个时期、从公元前 3000 年至公元 400 年的特洛伊古城在历史上不同时期的景象。有公元前 400 年罗马帝国时期的雅典娜神庙、会议厅、市场和剧场的废墟，还有大量公元前 2600 年至公元前 2300 年城堡中的铜制兵器、金银饰品、马车道、雕刻精美的石饰、保留完好的供水系统等（观赏内容）。

序列 3：附加信息

游客可以在景区内聘请当地导游，费用约 115 里拉，时长一个半小时左右，具体情况可到售票亭咨询。由于古城面积较大，没有语音讲解器可供租借，可以聘请导游或者在入口处的纪念品商店购买游览地图，费用 5 里拉。同时还可购买特罗伊木马模型纪念品（景点的设施和服务）。

除古城遗址外，游客还可以体验毗邻恰纳卡莱城的亚洲与欧洲两大陆的分界线达达尼尔海峡、拥有奥斯曼帝国清真寺和雅典娜神庙的阿索斯、海港边地标性的建筑钟楼等自然、建筑景观（游览指南/建议）。

特洛伊考古遗址是当地学校周末组织旅游的热门地点，因此最好不要在周末游玩。建议游览前查询天气状况，天气好的时候游览更佳。秋天是游览特洛伊古城的最佳时间。在木马的平台上，可以眺望五颜六色的特洛伊平原（游览指南/建议）。

景区还有《特洛伊》电影的道具木马，游客可以钻入马肚体验希腊人木马屠城时藏身马肚的感受。旁边还有可以扮演战士的服装配饰，并且还有武士可以一起合影。木马的楼梯有点陡峭，建议老年人或体力不好的游客不要攀爬（游览指南/建议）。

开放时间：5月1日至9月15日8：30—19：00，9月16日至次年4月30日8：30—17：00。

门票价格：成人20里拉。儿童免费。注意：景区关闭前一小时停止售票。

交通：乘坐土耳其航班到达伊斯坦布尔，再转恰纳卡莱方向旅游中巴，搭载大轮渡横渡达达尼亚海峡最后到达特洛伊考古遗址。

（二）重构语篇英语书面语介绍

Resort Introduction of Archaeological Site of Troy

Item 1 Background Information

Archaeological Site of Troy is located on the mound of Hisarlik, which overlooks the plain along the Turkish Aegean coast, 40 kilometres from the southern entrance to the Dardanelles (location). It was named after Troy, an old town unearthed in Turkey (name origin). It covers a long period from 3000 BC to 400 AD (time). The achievements in archaeology testify that *the Homer Epic* leaves no doubt in time. It was inscribed on the world heritage list by UNESCO in 1998 (social status).

Item 2 Topic Information

Apart from the copy wooden horse models, you can also enjoy the spectacular sights of old Troy Town in different times, ranging nine periods from 3000 BC to 400 AD, which surprisingly makes you personally experience it. Among the sights there are famous Temple of Athena built around 400 BC at the time of the Roman Emperor Augustus, meeting hall, and the ruins of markets and theaters. In addition, here you can see copper arms, jewelry, horse lanes, well-engraved stone decorations and well-preserved water supply systems (contents).

Item 3 Additional Information

If you pay around TRY 115, a local guide will be hired to give you a clear and detailed explanation of sights, which takes about one and a half hour to finish the toured guide. If you want to acquire further information, you can hire a guide or go directly to the ticket office. Because the old town covers a large area and does not offer or rent you any voice intercoms, you can purchase a map of travel in souvenir shops at the entrance of scenic spot for clear instructions of tour. And this would only cost TRY 5. Also you can purchase the souvenirs of Troy wooden horse models (facilities and services).

Besides the ruins of old town of Troy, you can enjoy many natural and architectural sceneries such as Dardanelles, Temple of Athena and Mosques of Roman Emperor Augustus in Assos, and the landmark towers at the seaport (guides/advices).

Archaeological Site of Troy is one of the most popular scenic spots that local schools would organize the students to visit during the weekends, so you are strongly advised not to go there during that two days. Moreover, checking the weather broadcast before leaving is strongly suggested as fine days help enjoy the sights. In fact, autumn is the best time to visit the Archaeological Site of Troy. You can enjoy a panoramic view of colorful plains of Troy (guides/advices).

There is also a prop wooden horse of the film *Troy* here, you are allowed to climb into the abdomen of the horse to experience the feeling of hiding in it when the Greeks invaded and slaughtered the old town. There are also some clothes for acting as soldiers and you are lucky enough to take a photo with warriors. The steps of wooden horse are a bit steep, so the senior citizens or the weak are not suggested climbing (guides/advices).

Opening Times: Visiting the ruins of Troy is possible during the opening hours: from 8:30 a.m. till 7:00 p.m. from 1st May to 15th September; from 8:30 a.m. till 5:00 p.m. from 16th September to next 30th April.

Ticket Prices: A ticket costs TRY 20. Small children enter for free. Note: the ticket office closes one hour earlier.

Transportation: You have three choices to get to the ruins of Troy.

By public transport—There are regular minibuses connecting Troy with Çanakkale. Minibuses depart from Çanakkale every hour between 9:30 a.m. and 4:30 p.m. (in summer till 7:00 p.m.). The ride costs around TRY 5, and takes 40 minutes. Please note the last return minibus from Troy to Çanakkale departs at 3:00 p.m. (5:00 p.m. in summer), which means that you might need to stay in Troy if you decide to visit this site in the afternoon as there are no other public transport options in the evenings.

By taxi—It is possible to organize a taxi tour from Çanakkale to Troy and back, and the price depends on the result of negotiations with a driver.

By car—Take D550 route from Çanakkale, and turn to the west after 26 kilometres. The turnoff is clearly signposted, and the total distance from Çanakkale is 30 kilometres.

(三) 重构语篇英语口语导游词

Tour Guide Speech of Archaeological Site of Troy

Item1 Background Information

Dear friends! Today I will take everyone to look around a famous scenic spot—Archaeological Site of Troy. It is located in Hisarlik, 40 kilometres away from southward Canakkale, the main harbor of the Dardanelles, Turkey (location). It was named after Troy, an old town unearthed in Turkey (name origin). It covers a long period from 3000 BC to 400 AD (time). The achievements in archaeology testify that *the Homer Epic* leaves no doubt in time (social status).

Item 2 Topic Information

In addition to the huge copy Trojan models, you can also enjoy the spectacular sights of old Troy Town in different times. During the times there are nine periods from 3000 BC to 400 AD. When you watch the scenes, you will undoubtedly have the feeling of experience them on the scene. Now I will list some of famous scenes. First, the well-known Temple of Athena which was built around 400 BC at the time of the Roman Emperor Augustus. Next is the meeting hall and the ruins of markets and theaters. Also, here you can see copper arms, jewelry, horses lanes, well-engraved stone decorations and well-preserved water supply systems (contents).

Item 3 Additional Information

If you want to have a clear and detailed explanation of scenic spot, you just need to pay around TRY 115 to hire a local guide for one and a half hour toured guide. If you want to get further information, you can go directly to the ticket office to inquire. Because the old town covers a large area and does not offer or rent you any voice intercoms, you can hire a guide or purchase a map of travel in souvenir shops at the entrance of scenic spot for clear instructions of tour. And this would only cost TRY 5. Also you can purchase the souvenirs of Trojan horse models if you are interested (facilities and services).

Besides the ruins of old town of Troy, you can enjoy many natural landscapes such as Dardanelles Strait, Temple of Athena and Mosques of Roman Emperor Augustus in Assos, and the landmark towers at the seaport (guides/advices).

You know Archaeological Site of Troy is one of the most popular scenic spots, so local schools would organize the students to visit it during the weekends and you are strongly advised not to go there during the two days. Moreover, you would better check the weather broadcast before going there as fine days would be preferable. In fact, autumn is the best time to visit the Archaeological Site of Troy. Standing on the platform of Trojan horse, you can enjoy a panoramic view of colorful plains of Troy (guides/advices).

Excitedly, there is also a prop wooden horse of the film *Troy*, you are allowed to climb into the abdomen of horse to experience the moment the

Greeks invaded and slaughtered the old town. There are also some clothes for acting as soldiers. If you like, you can take photos with warriors. By the way, one thing I have to warn everyone, the steps of wooden horse is a bit steep, so the senor citizens or the weak are not suggested climbing (guides/advices).

Visiting the ruins of Troy is possible during the opening hours: from 8:30 a.m. till 7:00 p.m. from 1st May to 15th september; from 8:30 a.m. till 5:00 p.m. from 16th September to next 30th April. A ticket costs TRY 20. Free for Small children. Note, the ticket office closes one hour earlier. You'll have three choices to get there.

By public transport—There are regular minibuses connecting Troy with Çanakkale. Minibuses depart from Çanakkale every hour between 9:30 a.m. and 4:30 p.m. (in summer till 7:00 p.m.). The ride costs around TRY 5, and takes 40 minutes. Please note the last return minibus from Troy to Çanakkale departs at 3:00 p.m. (5:00 p.m. in summer), which means that you might need to stay in Troy if you decide to visit this site in the afternoon as there are no other public transport options in the evenings.

By taxi—It is possible to organize a taxi tour from Çanakkale to Troy and back, and the price depends on the result of negotiations with a driver.

By car—Take D550 route from Çanakkale, and turn to the west after 26 kilometres. The turnoff is clearly signposted, and the total distance from Çanakkale is 30 kilometres.

第四节 基于翻译语境和语篇理论的解释性译文质量评估

天水旅游文化翻译不仅数量少、翻译质量低下而且缺少依据连贯方法论施行的系统翻译活动，更缺少一个译文质量的客观评估体系。

在针对译文评估、翻译方法论构建等问题的应用翻译研究领域,尽管有朱莉安·豪斯的功能主义语言学模式[1],但这些模式关注的仅是译文的语言特征,并未论及影响、制约翻译策略选择的翻译语境问题,同时其操作性也不强。系统功能语言学认为,在构成使用语言的情景语境的各个要素里,只有三个因素对语言的使用产生直接和重要的影响。[2] 即语场、语旨和语式三个语域变量,对于使用语言时如何选择语言形式有着直接的、至关重要的影响。本书运用韩礼德功能语言学的语域理论对天水大三国文化及"一带一路"沿线国家军事文化源文与译文从语场、语旨、语式三方面进行对比分析,客观和具体地评判翻译文本的质量。

一 语场对比分析

语场是关于言语活动的主题或焦点。根据这一情景参数,语用场景一般分为技术场景和日常场景两类,不同场景的语言表现出各自不同的特征。七组语料分别来自天水诸葛军垒、秦安街亭古战场、甘谷姜维墓、天水木门道、斯里兰卡加勒要塞、阿曼巴赫莱要塞、特洛伊考古遗址。就语场参数而言,采用哈蒂姆和梅森的语篇分析法[3] 重构源语语境为背景信息、主题信息和附加信息,与英国旅游网站的语篇结构相比,两者显示出相同的语言特征。重构语篇的主题都相同,都是对景点进行描述和宣传,普遍使用日常用语、标准句法,向潜在的游客提供旅游景点的三类基本信息:包括景点位置、名称由来、起止年代和社会地位等背景信息;观赏内容等主体信息;景点设施与服务、游览指南或建议、气候、当地风土人情、旅游特色项目、开放时

---

[1] Juliane House, *Translation Quality Assessment*: *A Model Revisited*, Tübingen: Gunter Narr Verlag, 1997, pp. 1–23.

[2] 司显柱:《功能语言学与翻译研究——翻译质量评估模式建构》,北京大学出版社2007年版,第6—9页。

[3] Basil Hatim and Ian Mason, *Discourse and the Translator*, Shanghai: Shanghai Foreign Language Education Press, 2001, p. 223.

间、门票、交通等附加信息。两者均属于呼唤型文本，描述旅游体验，目的都是吸引潜在游客来旅游。

从七组重构语境语料可以看出，天水三国文化及"一带一路"沿线国家军事文化的语场特征是相同的。旅游景点的描写都使用日常用语而非技术用语，避免生涩难懂，便于读者阅读，有利于对景点进行宣传介绍。描写多使用标准句法和过程动词。

二 语旨对比分析

语旨是反映言语交际行为的双方，在权势关系、接触密度和亲切程度等方面的情景参数，主要用来区分正式和非正式情景两类。非正式情景中，交际双方一般地位平等，经常见面，关系亲密，语言上常用带有感情色彩的词语、口头用语，使用典型语气；而正式情景里，交际者之间在权势方面是不对等的，接触稀少，关系疏远，语言在形式上，多使用中性词语、正式用语和非常规语气。[①] 就语旨参数而言，天水三国文化及"一带一路"沿线国家军事文化在语旨方面的评价潜势都较强，在态度资源的利用上都倾向于"鉴赏资源"，在情感资源方面均以"你指向"情感为主。例句如下。

（1）源语：这是天水三国古战场文化遗址建设规模最大、研究价值最高的地方。

译语：This attraction is positioned as the biggest in construction size and highest in research value.

语料多使用夸张的和具有劝导性的词汇如"规模最大"（the biggest in construction size）"研究价值最高"（highest in research value）并结合鉴赏性词汇"famous""beautiful"等。

（2）源语：在天水长途汽车站乘坐发往甘谷六峰方向的汽车。

译语：Take any buses heading for Liufeng Town of Gangu County from

---

① Suzanne Eggins, *An Introduction to Systemic Functional Linguistics*, London: Pinter, 1994, p. 78.

Tianshui Long-distance Bus Station.

多用祈使句来实现呼唤功能。游客直接从祈使句的核心动词成分开始理解，按照不同的句子语境去体会祈使句的功能指向，更能成功完成交际目的。

（3）源语：相传是因陇城一口年代久远的泉而得名。

译语：According to the legend, Jieting Ancient Battlefield was named for the reason that there was an ancient spring in Longcheng。

汉语为主动语态可译作被动语态。源语中的词类、句型和语态等进行转换使译文更符合目标语的表述方式、方法和习惯。

（4）源语：游客拜谒时可发现墓葬设计象征着姜维一生。墓前9台石阶代表姜维九伐中原，18台石阶代表姜维距现在已经1800多年。整个墓地与姜维的生平相吻合：墓高3.5米，寓意姜维35岁时就在诸葛亮手下担任重要职务，并屡立战功；墓地直径6.2米，表示姜维享年62岁，举义复蜀，事业未成而含恨九泉；石台高1.2米，寓意姜维12岁时就聪明勇敢，结发从军；姜维塑像高2.7米，寓意姜维27岁时跟随诸葛亮征战疆场。大殿两侧的36幅壁画则描绘了姜维的一生。

译语：While paying your respect to Jiangwei, you can find that the design of the tomb symbolizes the whole life of Jiangwei. The 9 stone steps before the tomb stand for his 9 times of conquests to the Central Plains. The 18 stone steps refer to that it has been over 1800 years from his time to now. The construction of the whole tomb is identical to the experience of his life. The tomb's 3.5 metres in height implies that he began to take important position and win many victories at 35 years old under the leadership of Zhuge Liang. The tomb's 6.2 metres in diameter indicates that he died at the age of 62 when rising in revolt for recovering Shu Kingdom, with his cause failing and his life ending with regret. The stone steps' 1.2 metres in height indicates that he was very clever and brave when he was 12 years old, joining army at his early adulthood. And his statue's 2.7 metres in height means that he fought in battlefield following Zhuge Liang from 27 years old. The 36 wall pictures on the two sides of the temple describe Jiangwei's whole life.

从态度资源上看，七组语料多使用名词、代词、过程动词、数字等来描述景点。分清主从句进行组合，根据需要利用连词、分词、介词、不定式、定语从句、独立结构等把汉语短句连成长句。

（5）源语：您在每年农历三月十八日至二十日庙会期间、农历四月初八可体验有秦腔、羊皮扇鼓舞等各种民间艺术的木门道庙会。

译语：You can enjoy various civil art performances such as Shaanxi Opera and sheep-skin drum dance etc. at Mumen Passageway Temple Fair during the fair periods of 18th to 20th March and 8th April of Chinese lunar calendar every year.

"你指向"的大量使用增强了文本的对话性，七组语料多把"您"用作主位，让读者直接参与对话中。描写也更加直白、简单。

三 语式对比分析

语式是描述语言与情景在空间和人际距离方面关系的参数。据埃金斯，这一情景变量主要用来区分口语和书面语的言语特征。口语依赖语境，句子结构松散、动态，使用日常词汇，句子的语法不标准，词汇化密度低。书面语不依赖语境，多使用纲要式结构的句子，使用"声望"词汇，句子语法标准，词汇化密度高。当然，这是对位于语式连续体两极，即典型口语和书面语言辞特征的概括，而实际话语中的多数是介于两极之间，也就是说往往既有口语体又有书面语体特征，差异只是多寡大小而已，即混合语体。[①] 示例如下。

源语：除甘谷姜维墓外，您还可以参观天水关姜维墓。该墓坐

[①] Suzanne Eggins, *An Introduction to Systemic Functional Linguistics*, London: Pinter, 1994, p. 78.

落在秦州区天水镇东北的黄家坪山顶，直径约 10 米，在此远眺可将天水关尽收眼底。姜维 62 岁兵变被杀后，据传其部下偷偷地割下姜维的头颅，潜回天水关，埋在黄家坪山顶上姜维曾经屯过兵的扎营地里。

书面语介绍：Besides Gangu Jiangwei's Tomb, another Jiangwei's Tomb in Tianshui Mountain Pass is also available for you to view. The tomb, with about 10 metres in diameter, is on the top of Huangjiaping Hill, northeast of Tianshui Town, Qinzhou District. From there, you can look into the distance and get a wonderful view of Tianshui Mountain Pass. According to the hearsay, after Jiang Wei was killed at 62 years old because of mutiny, his attendant secretly cut his head and sneaked back to the Mountain Pass with it, then buried it on the top of Huangjiaping Hill, where was once his campsite to station his troops.

口语导游词：You never imagine that apart from Gangu Jiangwei's Tomb, there is another Jiangwei's Tomb called Tianshui Pass Jiangwei's Tomb. People can go there to visit it. The tomb is on the top of the Huangjiaping Hill, northeast of Tianshui Town, Qinzhou District and it is about 10 metres in diameter. From there, you can look into the distance and get a wonderful view of Tianshui Pass. According to the legend, after Jiang Wei was killed at 62 years old because of mutiny, his attendant secretly cut his head and sneaked back to the Mountain Pass with it, then buried it on the top of the Huangjiaping Hill, where he once stationed his troops.

七组语料均是介于口语和书面语两极之间的混合语体，既包含口语特点又包含书面语特点。汉语重构语境的口语倾向通过英语书面语介绍和口语导游词转换更加清晰。

七组语料中除了"鞠躬尽瘁，死而后已""淡泊明志，宁静致远""但有远志，不在当归"等少数短语的翻译属于隐性翻译之外，基本上是属于显性翻译的语篇。虽然通过分析发现，语篇中出现了少数的信息不匹配和错误，但是正如豪斯在其翻译评估模式的阐释中指出的,"少数的不匹配与错误的出现是不可避免的"。① 因此,七组语料的译文中的不匹配现象不会影响语篇的概念功能、人际功能及语篇的质量。

---

① Juliane House, *Translation Quality Assessment: A Model Revisited*, Tübingen: Gunter Narr Verlag, 1997, pp. 1–23.

第六章

天水石窟文化描写与解释

第一节 天水石窟文化简述

石窟是一种人工雕凿在山体上的特殊建筑形式,是古代佛教遗迹。佛教石窟首先在印度开始营造,造窟之风循丝绸古道波及中国新疆并通过河西走廊逐渐发展到山西及中原地区。传统的石窟文化主要指石窟佛文化,是指随着佛教文化传入中国而产生的融建筑、雕塑、绘画于一体的艺术文化。在众多的石窟艺术文化中,最具代表性的要数甘肃敦煌莫高窟、山西大同云冈石窟、河南洛阳龙门石窟和甘肃天水麦积山石窟。

随着古印度的佛教从丝绸之路传入,并以讲读佛经的方式传播,之后又逐渐传入印度的凿窟造像技术,以艺术文化的形式由西向东弘扬。石窟艺术文化同佛教的文化思想传播情况一样,融进了诸种民族文化的影响,约形成于公元前100年至公元300年,所谓的犍陀罗艺术就是印度佛教与希腊艺术的结合体。这种专为佛界神灵开窟造像的佛教艺术传入中国,即刻便同中国秦汉以来已达到很高水平的雕刻艺术相融合,最后形成了以北魏时期雕像为代表的完全中国化的佛教雕刻艺术。这种艺术以石窟为载体逐渐脱离了早期外来艺术的范围,形成独特的民族化、中原化造像风格并反哺今甘肃所在区域。[①]

---

① 萧易:《甘肃石窟——佛从西来相自东传》,2015年10月,国家地理中文网(http://www.national geographic.com.cn/science/archaeology/4328.html)。

甘肃是西域通向中原的走廊地带,随着佛教传入河西以至在甘肃全省兴起和发展起来,石窟在甘肃得到迅速发展,从而使甘肃成为全国石窟最多的省份,被誉为"石窟之乡"。① 按照地域特色可划分为河西、陇中、陇南和陇东四个石窟群,石窟走廊主要包括敦煌莫高窟、安西榆林窟、玉门昌马石窟、肃南裕固族自治县文殊山石窟和马蹄寺石窟、永靖县炳灵寺石窟、武山县水帘洞石窟、甘谷县大像山石窟、天水麦积山石窟、泾川县王母宫石窟、庆阳市北石窟寺等。形成了始凿时间早、规模大,反映出佛教思想在我国的快速传播;开凿时间跨度长,不同时期开凿的洞窟反映不同时期的社会文化经济特征及审美观等具有浓郁地方特色的石窟文化。

天水地处古丝绸之路的要冲地带,丝绸古道的兴盛使天水成为石窟兴盛发展的沃土,以麦积山石窟为代表的石窟寺与仙人崖、甘谷大像山、甘谷华盖寺、武山水帘洞、武山木梯寺等众多石窟组成了丝绸之路东段的"石窟走廊"。

这些石窟沿交通要道分布,沿着通过古秦州丝绸之路的主干道自东向西分布,如仙人崖、麦积山、大像山、华盖寺、水帘洞、木梯寺等石窟。这样,北上进入河西走廊,沿途洞窟崖阁相连不断、佛陀菩萨形影相伴。特别是在甘谷县,几乎是五里有佛窟、十里见崖阁;僧侣参拜的身影和梵乐鼓鸣之声相继不绝。这些石窟或高居于绝壁,或息隐于丛林;或近于乡村之旁供善男信女参拜,或处于深山峡谷供僧侣禅思苦修。这就在天水境内形成了一道纵横数百里、奇特而神秘的佛教石窟走廊景观,也就构成了天水一种独特的文化现象。这些分布于天水各地的石窟,由于各种原因,如所处的地理位置、艺术形式的传承、发展的时间段等,都突出地表现出各自不同的文化面貌。

这条石窟走廊,从时限上讲,上起4世纪末的十六国时期(公元301—460年),下至清朝(公元1644—1912年),涵盖了1600余年

---

① 王宗光:《甘肃石窟文化综述》,《西北民族学院学报》(哲学社会科学版)2002年第4期。

的历史；从地域上看，贯通了古代天水的大部分地区。各石窟之间内容相互补充、完善了以麦积山石窟为代表的天水石窟文化。石窟走廊似一条宽阔而美丽的文化纽带，不但将本地区的区域文化结为一体，更重要的是它将天水和其他地区紧密地联系起来，使天水源源不断地从丝绸之路上接受新的文化形式和思想源泉，从而补充和完善了区域文化的内容。

这些石窟主要以佛教题材为表现形式，承担了大量的历史文化信息。身处石窟走廊如同穿越时空而置身于历史长河中，可以清晰地触摸和感受天水历史和文化，如美术（雕塑、绘画）、建筑（宫殿、民居、宗教建筑）、民俗（服饰、仪礼、葬俗）、宗教思想、民间崇拜、道路交通等。因而，这些石窟可以说是为一部无字的史书，它们以独特的形式传达出深刻的文化内涵。①

A Brief Introduction of Grotto Cultures in Tianshui

Rock cave, the remains of ancient Buddhist, is a special type of buildings carved manually in mountains. Originally, rock caves were constructed in India, then the winds of cave-building "blew" to Xinjiang, China along the Ancient Silk Route, and finally spread gradually to Shanxi and Central Plains through Hexi Corridor. Traditional rock cave culture mainly refers to Buddhist rock cave culture, representing an artistic culture which integrates into whole three kinds of arts: architecture, sculpture and painting arts created by the introduction of Buddhist culture into China. Among the numerous grotto artistic cultures, the most representative ones are Dunhuang Mogao Grottoes in Gansu Province, Yungang Grottoes in Datong, Shanxi Province, Longmen Grottoes in Luoyang, Henan Province and Maiji Mountain Grottoes in Tianshui, Gansu Province.

At the beginning, ancient India Buddhism was introduced to China through the Ancient Silk Route by the way of teaching and reading Buddhist

---

① 董广强等：《石窟走廊》，《文化天水》2006年12月18日。

scriptures, then India cave-building and sculpture-carving techniques were gradually introduced to China, and finally it was developed and expanded from west to east in the way of artistic culture. The transmission of rock cave artistic culture, in the same way as that of Buddhist culture and ideology, was integrated with influence of various national cultures. The rock cave artistic culture was formed from around 100 BC to 300 AD, with the sign of so called Gandhara Buddhist art—a combination of India Buddhist art and Greco-Buddhist art. As soon as the Buddhist arts of cave-building and sculpture-carving, which were specially created for Buddha field Gods, were introduced to China, they were integrated into China's sculptural art which had reached very high level by that time since China's Qin-Han Dynasties, and finally formed fully sinicized Buddhist sculptural arts, with the statue art in the Northern Wei Dynasty as their representative. The sinicized arts, taking rock caves as their carrier, gradually separated themselves from the early exotic art territory and became the ones with unique nationalized and central-plainized sculpture-carving style, and further reflected the area around Gansu currently.

Gansu is a corridor area leading to central-plains from Western Regions. With the upsurge and development of Buddism in Hexi and even in the full range of Gansu Province, rock caves were developed rapidly in this province, making Gansu Province have the biggest number of rock caves in China and therefore be honored as "Hometown of Grottoes". Based on their regional characteristics, the rock caves are divided into the following four cave groups: Hexi, Longzhong, Longnan and Longdong. The Grottoes Corridor mainly contains: Mogao Grottoes in Dunhuang, Yulin Grottoes in Anxi County, Changma Grottoes in Yumen, Wenshu Mountain Grottoes and Matisi Grottoes in Sunan Yugu Autonomous County, Grottoes of Binglingsi in Yongjing County, the Water Curtain Cave Grottoes in Wushan County, the Grottoes of Giant Buddha in Gangu County, the Maiji

Mountain Grottoes in Tianshui, the Palace Grotto in Jingchuan County, North Cave Temple in Qingyang. The fact that rock caves were built in early time and in big scale reflects that Buddhist ideology in China was once spread rapidly. With their building time span being very long, the rock caves constructed in a certain period will reflect the cave culture of that period with strong local characteristics from all aspects like social culture, economical feature and aesthetic idea and so on.

Tianshui is located at the communications centre of the Ancient Silk Route. The thriving of the Silk Route made the city become a fertile land for the development and the prosperity of rock caves. With the Grottoes of Maiji Mountain as their representative, the numerous rock caves, such as the Immortal Cliff Grottoes, the Grottoes of Giant Buddha in Gangu, the Canopy Temple Grottoes in Gangu, the Water Curtain Cave Grottoes in Wushan, the Wood Ladder Temple Grottoes etc., formed a "Grottoes Corridor" in the eastern section of the Silk Route.

These rock caves were distributed along the main arteries of traffic. Some of them, such as the Immortal Cliff Grottoes, the Grottoes of Maiji Mountain, the Grottoes of Giant Buddha, the Canopy Temple Grottoes, the Water Curtain Cave Grottoes, and the Wood Ladder Temple Grottoes etc., were distributed from the east to the west along the backbone road of the Ancient Qinzhou Silk Route. In this way, if going up north to enter Hexi Corridor, you could see rock caves, cliffs and temples linked one by one, and you might feel Buddha and Bodhisattva following you like your shadow. Especially, if you go to Gangu County, as there is almost a Buddha cave every 2.5 kilometres and a cliff palace every 5 kilometres, the figures of monks and priests' worshiping, accompanied by the sound of Buddhist music and drum beating, would continuously come to your eyes or ears. Some of these rock caves are built high in cliffs, some are built in hidden forests, some are close to villages so as for Buddhist pilgrims to worship, and some are in remote mountains and canyons so as for monks to practice meditation thoughts and mortification of the flesh. All of the above described elements form a striking and mysterious landscape of the Buddhist rock cave corridor which covers several kilometres, and also constitute a unique cultural phenomenon in Tianshui. These rock caves, which spread everywhere in Tianshui, outstandingly show different cultural characteristics because of various factors—different geographical location, inheritance of artist form and phases of development.

In terms of the time span, this rock cave corridor covered over 1600 years of time, dating back from the end of 4th century, in the period of the Sixteen States (301-460 AD), down to the Qing Dynasty (1644-1912 AD). As far as the geographic location is concerned, the corridor links up most areas of ancient Tianshui.

The caves were complementary in content with each other, improved and perfected the Tianshui rock cave culture with the Grottoes of Maiji Mountain as its representative. The corridor, looking like a wide and beautiful cultural link, not only combines regional cultures in the area into one, but also, or the most important, closely communicates Tianshui with other districts, providing Tianshui with more opportunities of accepting new cultural forms and idea sources continuously from the Silk Route so as to supplement and improve the content of regional culture.

These caves, mainly taking Buddhist themes as their expressing form, carry great amount of historical and cultural information. Physically loitering in the corridor, you will have the feeling of passing the veil of time. As you place yourself in the long river of time, you can clearly touch and feel time and culture of Tianshui, such as works of art (sculptures and paintings), buildings (palaces, folk houses and religious buildings), folk customs (dress, personal adornment, etiquette and burial custom), religious philosophy, folk worship, road transport and so on. Therefore, the rock caves, you can say, are a serial of wordless historical records, which express profound cultural connotations in a unique way.

第二节　天水石窟文化语篇语域重构及翻译

一　天水麦积山石窟

（一）汉语语篇重构

天水麦积山石窟

序列1：背景信息

麦积山石窟坐落在甘肃省天水市东南方向50千米的麦积区麦积乡南侧（景点的地理位置）。因开凿在形似农家麦垛的峭壁上而得名（景点名称由来）。开凿于十六国晚期（公元383—417年）（建筑起止年代），是中国四大石窟之一，2014年被联合国教科文组织列入《世界遗产名录》（社会定位）。

序列2：主题信息

麦积山石窟现存194个洞窟，7200余尊造像。分泥塑、石雕和石刻造像碑三类，以泥塑为主。具有深厚的民族传统、鲜明的世俗化气息和浓郁的生活情趣。游客可以欣赏到位于山东侧的"西方三圣"雕塑。中间的阿弥陀佛高13米，威严壮观，神形兼备，琉璃珠做的眼睛炯炯有神，衣服上的褶皱细致入微，因为在和泥时加入了发丝等材料，使得佛像看起来光滑细嫩像真的一样。被称为"东方微笑"的小沙弥两眼微闭，嘴巴上翘，头微微低下，显出东方人特有的可爱与含蓄（观赏内容）。

序列3：附加信息

距景区8千米的游客服务中心正在建造中；2.5千米处设有停车场；提供景区观光车交通服务，往返票价15元，单程8元；英语/汉语导游讲解售团体票（5人起团），每人10元；景点门口免费提供电子导游设备；景区免费寄存行李和饮用水（景点的设施与服务）。

石窟完全被雕凿在悬崖绝壁上,游客必须攀爬悬空栈道才能参观,可以带手电筒看壁画(游览指南/建议)。

"麦积烟雨"是麦积山石窟的一景。麦积山海拔 1617 米,在下雨天您能见到麦积山"头顶戴帽子"的美景(游览指南/建议)。

游客还可以游览景区以东 2 千米处的麦积山植物园、景区外 14 千米处的仙人崖石窟(游览指南/建议)。

开放时间:夏季为 8:30—17:30;冬季为 9:30—16:00。

门票价格:从 2015 年 10 月起执行淡旺季门票价格。旺季时间为每年 5 月 1 日至 10 月 31 日,淡季时间为每年 11 月 1 日至次年 4 月 30 日。旺季为 110 元/人;淡季为 70 元/人。进入景区,但不参观石窟为 25 元。60 岁以上老人及学生半价。

交通:在天水麦积区火车站前搭乘 34 路麦积山旅游专线车,车程约 1 小时,每 7 分钟即有一趟。可以在大门口购买门票时再买 10 元的观光车费用(单程)送到离石窟很近的地方,也可以徒步 30 分钟缓坡到达。

(二)重构语篇英语书面语介绍

Resort Introduction of the Grottoes of Maiji Mountain

Item 1 Background Information

The Grottoes of Maiji Mountain is located in the south of Maiji Town, Maiji District, 50 kilometres southeast of Tianshui, Gansu Province (location).It was named for the reason that it was built in a cliff with the similar shape of farmers' wheat-stalk (name origin). The Grotto, one of the four biggest caves in China, was constructed in Late Sixteen States (383-417 AD) (time). In 2014, it was listed into the World Heritage List by UNESCO (social status).

Item 2 Topic Information

In the Grottoes, currently there are 194 caves and over 7200 sculptures, including clay sculptures, stone sculptures and stone carving joss statues, with the first one as main type. Maiji Mountain Cave Culture has profound national tradition, distinctive secularization and strong sense of life delights. You can enjoy viewing the statues of "Three Western Saints" on the eastern side of the mountain. The statue for Amitabha, the one in the middle place, is 13 metres long, with his image being dignified and magnificent from both form and spirit, his glass ball-made eyes being bright and piercing, and his clothes being with fine and subtle detailed wrinkles on them. Since some materials like hairline were mixed to the clay used for making the statues, the statues look so smooth and delicate that they seemed to be real people. In his statue, a little monk, known as "Oriental Smile", with an image of his eyes slightly closed, his mouth curled up and his head lowered a little, shows the oriental's unique loveliness and implication (contents).

Item 3 Additional Information

A tourist service center, 8 kilometres away from the scenic spot, is under construction. There is a car park available, 2 kilometres away from the scenic spot. Sightseeing bus services are available at the spot, with return tickets of RMB 15 per person, and single ones of RMB 8 per person. English/Chinese tourist guiding services are available for groups of 5 or more people, with RMB 10 per person. There is a free baggage depository and free water drinking point at the spot (facilities and services).

As the rock caves were completely carved in a cliff, you have to climb the suspended plank road for your visiting. You are allowed to take electric torches with you to view frescoes (guides/advices).

"The Misty Rain of Maiji Mountain" is a scene of the Maiji Mountain Grottoes. The mountain is 1617 metres above sea level, so, on a rainy day, you can enjoy the extremely beautiful scenery of the mountain like wearing a hat on its top (guides/advices).

Near the Grottoes, you can also look around Maiji Mountain Botanical Garden (2 kilometres east of the spot), or the Grottoes of Immortal Cliff

(12 kilometres away from the spot) (guides/advices).

Opening Times: From 8:30 a.m. till 5:30 p.m. on summer; from 9:30 a.m. till 4:00 p.m. on winter.

Ticket Prices: Peak season (from 1st May to 31st October) RMB 110 per person, Off-peak season (from 1st November to 30th April of the next year) RMB 70 per person. Admission fee for the spot area is only (no visiting the caves) RMB 25 per person. All tickets are half price for seniors of over 60 years old and students.

Transportation: Take Maiji Mountain's special tourist bus No. 34 at Tianshui Maiji rail station, with 1 hour drive, buses going every 7 minutes. You can pay RMB 10 extraly to buy a single ticket for sight-seeing bus when you buy your admission tickets. By the sight-seeing bus, you can be taken to the place very close to the caves. It takes 30 minutes' walk to there through a gently sloping road.

(三) 重构语篇英语口语导游词

Tour Guide Speech of the Grottoes of Maiji Mountain

Item 1 Background Information

Dear friends! Today I will show you around a very famous grotto—the Grottoes of Maiji Mountain. It is regarded as one of the four most well known grottoes in China. The Maiji Mountain Mountain Grottoes is located in the south of Maiji Town, Maiji District, 50 kilometres southeast of Tianshui, Gansu Province (location). It got such a name because it was built in a cliff with the similar shape of farmers' wheat stalk (name origin). Do you know that? The Grottoes here is one of the four biggest caves in China and it was constructed in Late Sixteen States (383-417AD) (time). In 2014, it was listed into the World Heritage List by UNESCO (social status).

Item 2 Topic Information

There are 194 caves and over 7200 sculptures in the Grottoes. So many, isn't it? The sculptures can be divided into three types: clay sculptures, stone sculptures and stone carving joss statues. The clay sculptures is the main type. Maiji Mountain Cave Culture has profound national tradition, distinctive secularization and strong sense of life delights. There are two typical statues that you will never miss seeing. First is the statues of "Three Western Saints" on the eastern side of the mountain. The statue of Amitabha in the middle is 13 metres long. Look at it carefully! His image is dignified and magnificent from both form and spirit. His glass ball–made eyes are bright and piercing and his clothes are subtle with fine and detailed wrinkles. When making the statues, some materials like hairline were mixed to the clay, and the statues look so smooth and delicate that they seemed to be real people. The second is a little monk, known as "Oriental Smie". Look at it closely! His eyes are slightly closed. His mouth is curled up and his head is lowered a little. All of these characters show the oriental's unique loveliness and implication (contents).

Item 3 Additional Information

Some tourist services are available. There is a car park available, 2 kilometres away from the scenic spot. And a tourist service center which is 8 kilometres away from the scenic spot is under construction. The spot also provides you with sightseeing bus services. Return tickets is RMB 15 for one person and single tickets is RMB 8 for one person. English/Chinese tourist guiding services are available for groups of five or more people and the ticket price is RMB 10 for one person. Good news! There is a free baggage depository and free water drinking point at the spot (facilities and services).

Look at the rock caves. They were completely carved in a cliff. It looks so dangerous for you to climb. Right? Don't worry! If you want to go close to the caves and have a good look, you have to climb the suspended plank road to enjoy. In order to view the frescoes carefully, you are allowed to take electric torches with you (guides/advices).

Near the Maiji Mountain Grottoes, there are some other scenic spots. You can look around Maiji Mountain Botanical Garden（only 2 kilometres east of the spot）, or the Grottoes of Immortal Cliff（only 12 kilometres away from the spot）（guides/advices）.

The Grottoes open in Summer from 8：30 a. m. till 5：30 p. m., in winter from 9：30 a. m. till 4：00 p. m. Price in peak season（from 1st May to 31st October）is RMB 110 per person, in off-peak season（from 1st November to 30th April of the next year）is RMB 70 per person. Admission fee for the spot area is only（no visiting the caves）RMB 25 per person. All tickets are half price for seniors of over 60 years old and students. Take Maiji Mountain's special tourist bus No. 34 at Tianshui Maiji rail station, with 1 hour drive, buses going every 7 minutes. You can pay RMB 10 extraly to buy a single ticket for sight-seeing bus when you buy your admission tickets. By the sight-seeing bus, you can be taken to the place very close to the caves. It takes 30 minutes' walk to there through a gently sloping road.

二 天水仙人崖石窟

（一）汉语语篇重构

天水仙人崖石窟

序列1：背景信息

仙人崖石窟位于甘肃省天水麦积山风景名胜区东南65千米朱家后川（景点的地理位置）。因有仙人点灯指路的传说，被认为是仙人集聚之地而得名。宋朝（公元960—1279年）称"华严寺"，明朝永乐皇帝在任时（公元1403—1424年）赐名"灵应寺"，从此灵应寺成为仙人崖的通称（景点名称由来）。始建于南北朝时期（公元420—589年），距今近1600年（建筑起止年代），现为佛、道合一的石窟寺庙（社会定位）。

序列2：主题信息

仙人崖石窟由三崖、五峰、六寺组成，保存有明清时期（公元1368—1912年）殿宇27座、房屋54间，以及南北朝（公元420—589

年)、宋朝(公元960—1279年)、明朝(公元1368—1644年)、清朝(公元1644—1912年)各类塑像197尊、壁画83平方米。其中,永乐年间(公元1403—1424年)的珍贵铜佛像5尊。仙人崖三崖中,以西崖面积和佛殿数量为最,14座殿宇内有唐朝(公元618—907年)、宋朝(公元960—1279年)、明朝(公元1368—1644年)、清朝(公元1644—1912年)佛像100多尊,艺术价值极高(观赏内容)。

序列3:附加信息

入口旁设有仙人崖景区导览图和游客服务中心;山下1.5千米处设停车场;景区提供观光车交通服务,往返票价10元/人;英语/汉语导游讲解售团体票(5人起团),每人10元(景点的设施与服务)。

在景区内可以品尝到当地居民自家制作的浆水面、凉粉、手工面条等当地的特色小吃。景区有供游客住宿的旅店,也有很有特色的草地帐篷供游客住宿(景点的设施与服务)。

游客可以乘坐快艇游览仙人湖,湖北岸建有水榭和观鱼台等;夏日里可以直接到甘露泉和仙人泉饮水(景点的设施与服务)。

仙人崖石窟内容除佛教题材之外,还大量融入道、儒题材。如明清时期三教祠(佛教、道教、儒家)内塑三教圣人塑像。正壁塑释迦牟尼佛,左侧塑道教创始人老子像,右侧塑儒家创始人孔子像。殿堂内左壁绘剃度图、孔子问礼图、佛教题材画各一幅,右壁绘孔子讲经图、释迦牟尼涅槃图、道教题材画各一幅(游览指南/建议)。

仙人崖有许多关于仙人的传说,游客游览时可以在天然景观中寻觅。相传南崖燃灯阁有天然仙灯,每当夏秋深夜,天然磷光与阁中的油灯和烛光浮动辉映,人传是神仙携灯往来,故有"仙人送灯"之说(游览指南/建议)。

裸露的崖壁也是游客经常觅奇的景点之一。最宏伟壮观的是由"五峰"和罗汉沟群峰共同构成的"十八罗汉朝玉帝"的景象。其景象的具体构成为:东、西峰和玉皇峰三峰参列,玉皇峰处于正中;宝盖峰和献珠峰与三峰比列,宛若仙童侍立;另有罗汉沟的群峰似具若揖若拜之势,故有"十八罗汉朝玉帝"之美称(游览指南/建议)。

除了部分已然残缺的泥塑菩萨石窟之外，仙人崖山体本身能展现出典型的丹霞地貌（游览指南/建议）。

仙人崖地势较高，有山有水，树木成林。温度一般比别处要低4—5度，夏季是仙人崖旅游的最佳季节（游览指南/建议）。

游客还可以游览另一个位于朱家后川的天水最有名的佛教净土宗寺院（游览指南/建议）。

开放时间：8：00—17：00。

门票价格：40元/人。距仙人崖3.5千米的净土寺为20元/人。

交通：在天水火车站或麦积区都有通往仙人崖景区的37路专线旅游车。

（二）重构语篇英语书面语介绍

Resort Introduction of the Immortal Cliff Grottoes

Item 1 Background Information

The Immortal Cliff Grottoes is situated in Zhujia Houchuan, about 65 kilometres southeast of the Maiji Mountain scenic zone of Tianshui (location). It was named according to the legend— "an immortal shows the way with lamps" and was thought of as a gathering place for immortals. It was called "Huayan Temple" in the Song Dynasty (960 - 1279AD) while it was granted by Emperor Yongle (1403 - 1424AD) of the Ming Dynasty a new name— "Lingying Temple", which has become a general name of the Grottoes (name origin). It was built from the Northern and Southern Dynasties (420-589AD), and it has been about 1600 years so far (time). Now it is a Buddhism and Daoism two-in-one grotto temple (social status).

Item 2 Topic Information

The Immortal Cliff Grottoes consists of three cliffs, five peaks and six temples. In the Grottoes, there are 27 palaces and 54 houses of the Ming and Qing Dynasties (1368-1912AD), 197 statues of various types in different dynasties, including the Northern and Southern Dynasties (420-589AD), the Song Dynasty (960-1279AD), the Ming Dynasty (1368-1644AD) and the Qing Dynasty (1644-1912AD), 83 square metres of frescoes and 5 precious Buddhist bronze statues from the period of Emperor Yongle's reign. Of the three cliffs, the west cliff has the largest area and the biggest number of Buddha temples. In the 14 palaces, the Grottoes contains more than 100 statues of Buddha from different periods, covering the Tang Dynasty (618-907AD), the Song Dynasty (960-1279AD), the Ming Dynasty (1368-1644AD) and the Qing Dynasty (1644-1912AD), all of which being of precious artistic value (contents).

Item 3 Additional Information

At the entrance of the scenic spot, there is a guide map of Immortal Cliff scenic spot and a tourist service center. There is also a car park 1.5 kilometres away from the spot. A sight-seeing bus service in the spot is available, with return ticket of RMB 10 per person. English/Chinese tourist guiding services are available for groups of 5 or more people, with RMB 10 per person (facilities and services).

At the scenic spot, you can taste Semifluid Noodles, grass jelly and hand-made noodles made by local residents and other local snacks. Hotels and featured lawn tents are available at the spot for you to live in (facilities and services).

You can take speedboats to go sight-seeing on the Immortal Lake. On its north bank, there is a waterside pavilion, a fish-observation platform and so on. Around the lake, there are two springs named Ganlu Spring and Immortal Spring, from which people can drink its water directly in summer time (facilities and services).

In the Immortal Cliff Grottoes, apart from Buddhism theme, there are also ones integrating Taoism and Buddhism themes. For example, in the Three Religions (Buddhism, Taoism and Confucianism) Shrine built in the Ming-Qing Dynasties, there are statues for the three sages—the middle one for Sakyamuni, the founder of Buddhism, the left one for Lao Zi, the founder of Taoism and the right one for Confucius, the founder of Confucianism. On the left internal wall of the shrine, there is a tonsure ceremony picture, a Confucius propriety preaching picture and a Buddhist picture. While on its right internal wall, there is a Confucius Confucianism-texts expounding picture, a Sakyamuni Parinirvana picture and a Taoism - related picture (guides/advices).

There are many immortal related legends as to the Immortal Cliff Grottoes, which you can search from the natural landscapes. It was said that there were some natural immortal lanterns in a burning pavilion of the South Cliff, where natural phosphorescence, the oil burning lanterns and candle light in the pavilion would shine floatingly with addition to each other's splendor, which referred to the immortals "coming and going" each with a lantern in a hand based on the legend, which is so called "Immortals have brought lanterns" (guides/advices).

The exposed cliffs are also one of the scenic sites where tourists often seek marvelous spectacles. The most magnificent and spectacular one is the sight called "Eighteen Arhats worship the Jade Emperor", which was presented by five peaks and a group of peaks in Arhat Ravine as follows. The three peaks (the East, the West and the Jade Emperor) participate in the parade with the last one being in the right center, accompanied by Baogai Peak and Xianzhu Peak as their side parade, seemingly like fair-children standing and waiting for the Emperor. While other peaks in the Arhat Ravine facing the Jade Emperor Peak are in bowing-like posture and worshiping-like posture, which therefore was enioyed this laudatory reputation— "Eighteen Arhats worship the Jade Emperor" (guides/advices).

Apart from the caves with incomplete clay sculptures of Buddha, the immortal cliffs can also show its landform to you with typical Danxia Landform (guides/advices).

As the immortal cliffs has relative high altitude, with mountains, water and forests around it, with a temperature of 4 - 5 degree lower than other places, summer is the best season to visit the cliffs (guides/advices).

You can also have a view of a Pure Land Buddhism Temple in Rear Zhujia Plains, which is the most famous temple in Tianshui (guides/advices).

Opening Times: From 8 : 00 a. m. till 5 : 00 p. m.

Ticket Prices: RMB 40 per person per time. And RMB 20 per person per time for visiting Buddhist Jingtuzong Temple, 3.5 kilometres away from the Immortal Cliff Grottoes.

Transportation: A special tourist bus No. 37 is available from Tianshui railway station or Maiji District to the Immortal Cliff Grottoes.

(三) 重构语篇英语口语导游词

Tour Guide Speech of the Immortal Cliff Grottoes

Item 1 Background Information

Hello, everyone! I feel honored to be your guide. Today I will take everyone to look around a famous scenic spot—the Immortal Cliff Grottoes. From the given name, we can guess it is a beautiful place full of interesting stories. Yes! It is located in Zhujia Houchuan which is about 65 kilometres southeast of the Maiji Mountain scenic zone of Tianshui (location). It was so named because of a legend "an immortal shows the way with lamps" and it was also thought of as a gathering place for immortals (name origin). In the Song Dynasty (960 - 1279AD) it was called "Huayan Temple" while it was granted a new name— "Lingying Temple" by Emperor Yongle (1403-1424AD) of the Ming Dynasty. Now it has become a general name of the Grottoes (name origin). Do you know the time of it? It has been about 1600 years since it was built from the Northern and Southern Dynasties (420-589AD) (time). Now it is a Buddhism and Daoism two-in-one grotto temple (social status).

Item 2 Topic Information

The Immortal Cliff Grottoes includes three cliffs, five peaks and six temples. In the Grottoes, there are 27 palaces and 54 houses of the Ming and Qing Dynasties (1368-1912AD), 197 statues of various kinds from different periods, including the Northern and Southern Dynasties (420-589AD), the Song Dynasty (960-1279AD), the Ming Dynasty (1368-1644AD) and the Qing Dynasty (1644-1912AD), 83 square metres of frescoes and 5 precious Buddhist bronze statues from the period of Emperor Yongle's reign. Of the three cliffs, the largest area and the biggest number of Buddha temples are in the west cliff. In the 14 palaces, the Grottoes contains more than 100 statues of Buddha from different periods, including the Tang Dynasty (618-907AD), the Song Dynasty (960-1279AD), the Ming Dynasty (1368-1644AD) and the Qing Dynasty (1644-1912AD). All of these status are of precious artistic value (contents).

Item 3 Additional Information

There are some useful information you need to know. At the entrance of the scenic spot, there is a guide map of Immortal Cliff scenic spot and a tourist service center. Also there is a car park 1.5 kilometres away from the spot. A sight-seeing bus service in the spot is also available. The fare is RMB 10 per person for return tickets. English/Chinese tourist guiding services are available as well. For groups of five or more people, the service will cost each person RMB 10 (facilities and services).

Dear friends! If you come to Tianshui, I strongly suggest all of you tasting the local delicious food. Semifluid Noodles, grass jelly and hand-made noodles made by local residents are very popular at the scenic spot. Don't miss the chance to taste them. Delicious! And other convenient facilities are hotels and featured lawn tents. You will have free choice to live in (facilities and services).

There are some beautiful sights for you to go. For example, you can take speedboats to go sight-seeing on the Immortal Lake. On its north bank, there is a waterside pavilion, a fish-observation platform and so on. Around the lake, there are two springs named Ganlu Spring and Immortal Spring, from which people can drink its water directly in summer time (facilities and services).

Apart from Buddhism theme, there are also themes which integrate Taoism and Buddhism themes in the Immortal Cliff Grottoes. For example, in the Three Religions (Buddhism, Taoism and Confucianism) Shrine built in the Ming-Qing Dynasties, there are statues for the three sages. The middle one is for Sakyamuni who is the founder of Buddhism, the left one is for Lao Zi who is the founder of Taoism and the right one is for Confucius who is the founder of Confucianism. On the left internal wall of the shrine, there is a tonsure ceremony picture, a Confucius propriety preaching picture and a Buddhist picture. On its right internal wall, there is a Confucius Confucianism-texts expounding picture, a Sakyamuni Parinirvana picture and a Taoism-related picture (guides/advices).

There are many legends related to the immortals. So you can find them in the natural landscapes. The saying goes that there were some natural immortal lanterns in a burning pavilion of the south cliff, where natural phosphorescence, the oil burning lanterns and candle light in the pavilion would shine closely. Based on the legend, people say that it is the immortals "coming and going" each with a lantern in a hand. So it enjoys the fame "Immortals have brought lanterns" (guides/advices).

The most marvelous spectacle that you often seek is the exposed cliffs. And the most magnificent and spectacular one is the sight called "Eighteen Arhats worship the Jade Emperor". Five peaks and a group of peaks in Arhat Ravine present it as follows. The three peaks (the East, the West and the Jade Emperor) participate in the parade. The last one is in the right center, accompanied by Baogai Peak and Xianzhu Peak as their side parade, just like fair-children standing and waiting for the Emperor. Other peaks in the Arhat Ravine are in bowing-like posture and worshiping-like posture facing the Jade Emperor Peak. So it was given this laudatory reputation— "Eighteen Arhats worship the Jade Emperor" (guides/advices).

Apart from partial caves with incomplete clay sculptures of Buddha, the immortal cliff can also impress you with its typical Danxia Landform (guides/advices).

The immortal cliff has relatively high altitude, and mountains, water and forests are around it, so the temperature here is 4-5 degree lower than other places. When is the best time to visit the cliff? Of course summer! So pleasant and comfortable! Summer is the best season to visit the cliff (guides/advices).

Near the Immortal Cliff Grottoes there is a Pure Land Buddhism Temple in Rear Zhujia Plains. It is very famous in Tiansui. You can go there to have a good time (guides/advices).

The grottoes open from 8∶00 a.m. till 5∶00 p.m. The price is RMB 40 per person per time. And the price for visiting Buddhist Jingtuzong Temple, 3.5 kilometres away from the Immortal Cliff Grottoes, is RMB 20 per person per time. A special tourist bus No. 37 is available from Tianshui railway stop or Maiji District to the Immortal Cliff Grottoes.

三 甘谷大像山石窟

(一) 汉语语篇重构

甘谷大像山石窟

序列1：背景信息

大像山石窟，又名大象山石窟，坐落在甘肃省天水市甘谷县大像山镇五里铺村（景点的地理位置）。因山巅修凿有一躯身高23.3米的石胎泥塑释迦牟尼大佛像而得名（景点名称由来）。成型于北魏（公元386—534年），完善于盛唐（公元8世纪上半叶）（建筑起止年代），是中国相对地面高度最高的大佛，是古丝绸之路上甘肃东南部融石窟和古建为一体的重要文化遗存之一（社会定位）。

序列 2：主题信息

游客可以看到以大像窟为中心的 23 处石窟群、15 处姿态各异的明清木结构古建筑群、东汉隗嚣歇凉台、阅兵台（均在无量殿）等遗址，"羲皇故里"碑、"圣门石子故里"碑、"重修汉平襄侯祠记"碑等文物。其中大佛的形象和衣饰可视为西方装饰性雕塑和中国写意性雕塑的完美结合。大佛石胎泥塑，身高 23.3 米，腰阔 10.4 米。右手作拔济众生印，左手平放于膝，蓄有笈多王朝时期（约公元 320—500 年）佛教造像的蓝色螺型头发和两撇蝌蚪状短须，双足各踩莲花座，袒胸赤足，上着双领下垂袈裟，衣褶为阳纹（观赏内容）。

序列 3：附加信息

景区入口旁设有大像山景区导览图和游客服务中心；停车场免费停车；大像山文化主题公园内有青海云杉、垂柳、银杏、红叶石楠等树种和祭坛、人工湖、姜维祠、音乐喷泉等景观（景点的设施与服务）。

游客将会惊讶于大佛在中国极为罕见的蝌蚪状胡须（游览指南/建议）。

雕凿者通过对视觉误差的准确计算塑造出比例和谐的大佛像。游客不论从佛窟内还是山脚下甚至渭河北岸更远的地方观看大佛的比例总是那么匀称，眼神总是那么安详（游览指南/建议）。

游客可以体验农历四月初八的大像山庙会，观看各种文艺活动并且游山祭拜大佛（游览指南/建议）。

游客还可以游览附近另一个景点姜维墓（游览指南/建议）。

开放时间：8：00—17：00。

门票价格：30 元/人，半票 15 元/人。1.2 米以下儿童、老年人持甘肃省颁发的老年证、现役军人持军官证、残疾人持残疾证免费。

交通：大像山距离天水火车站 87 千米，在车站有直达甘谷的汽车，也可乘火车直接在甘谷车站下车。

（二）重构语篇英语书面语介绍

Resort Introduction of the Grottoes of Giant Buddha

Item 1 Background Information

The Grottoes of Giant Buddha, also known as Daxiangshan Mountain Grottoes, is located in Wulipu Village, Daxiang Mountain Town, Gangu County, Tianshui City, Gansu Province (location). It was named for the reason that there is a giant stone casing, clay sculpture statue of Sakyamuni Buddha of 23.3 metres high in the mountain, which was built on the mountaintop (name origin). This Giant Buddha was completed in the Northern Wei Dynasty (386 – 534AD) and perfected in Flourish, Tang Dynasty (the first half of the 8th century) (time). The Grottoes of Giant Buddha is the highest one in relative height in China and also is one of the important cultural relics of combining rock cave culture and ancient building techniques together in southeastern area of Gansu Province on the Ancient Silk Route (social status).

Item 2 Topic Information

Visitors, taking the Buddha statue as the area center, can wateh a number of ruins, including 23 cave complex, 15 various styles of ancient wood structural building complex in the Ming – Qing Dynasties, the Rest Palace of Wei Xiao and the Military Parade Platform of Wei Xiao (Wei Xiao (? –33 AD), a general of the Eastern Han Dynasty (25-220 AD) and governor of Tianshui area), these are all in Zhenwu Emperor Hall (Zhenwu Emperor, the third Emperor of Heaven after the Jade Emperor). You can also see some cultural relics of stone tablets carved in Chinese characters respectively, such as Tablet of "Hometown of Fuxi" (according to the legend that Fuxi was born in Gufeng Plateau of Southern Gangu County), Tablet of "Hometown of Shi Zuoshu" [Shi Zuoshu (519-479 BC), one of seventy-two sages of confucius' student] and Tablet of "Record of Rebuilding Jiang Wei's Shrine" [Jiang Wei (202-264 AD), a great general of Shu Kingdom of Period of Three Kingdoms (220 - 280 AD)]. The image of Buddha, together with his clothing and ornaments, can be regarded as the art works created by the perfect combination of western ornamental sculptural art and Chinese sculptural art of freehand brushwork. The Giant Buddha, a stone casing clay sculpture, is 23.3 metres high and 10.4 metres wide at its waist, with blue heliciform hair used for Buddhist sculpture in the Gupta period on his head, the tadpole-shaped beards on his mouth and a dual collared dipping cassock with male threaded pleats on his body. He rests in a lotus place, with his right hand making varada mudra, his left hand putting flatly on his left knee, his feet bared and his chests keeping bared (contents).

Item 3 Additional Information

Beside the entrance of the scenic area, there is a guide map of the Grottoes of Giant Buddha and a tourist service center. Also there is a free car parking lot. In the Cultural Theme Garden of the Giant Buddha, there are many rare trees like Qinghai dragon spruce, weeping willow, ginkgo tree, photinia fraseri etc. and some landscapes like the man-made lake, the Jiang Wei's Shrine and musical springs etc. (facilities and services).

Visitors will surprisingly find that the Giant Buddha has the tadpole-shaped beards, which is extremely rare in China (guides/advices).

The sculptors of the Giant Buddha sculptured the statue with harmonious proportion based on their accurate visual error calculation. Whether from inside of the cave or from the foot of the mountain, or even from far distance on the north bank of the Wei River, visitors can see Giant Buddha with its proportions being always harmonious and his eyes being always so serene (guides/advices).

Visitors can stroll around the fairground of the Fair of the Giant Buddha held on the 8th of April of Chinese lunar calendar, watch various performances, go sightseeing among the hills and worship the Giant Buddha (guides/advices).

Another nearby attraction, Jiang Wei's Tomb, is also available for visitors to view (guides/advices).

Opening Times: From 8:00 a.m. till 5:00 p.m.

Ticket Prices: RMB 30 per person, RMB 15 per person as half price applicable. Free for children of less than 1.2 metres tall, elderly people who hold senior people certificate issued, servicemen with officer certificate and disable people with disable certificate.

Transportation: Rail service is available from the Grottoes to Tianshui railway station, with 87 kilometres journey, also both direct bus and rail services are available from the Grottoes to Gangu Town.

(三) 重构语篇英语口语导游词

Tour Guide Speech of the Grottoes of Giant Buddha

Item 1 Background Information

OK! Here we are! Look at the giant Buddha. This is the well known Grottoes of Giant Buddha, also called Daxiang Mountain Grottoes. It is located in Wulipu Village, Daxiang Mountain Town, Gangu County, Tianshui City, Gansu Province (location). Why is it called so? You can see clearly that a giant stone casing, clay sculpture statue of Sakyamuni Buddha of 23.3 metres high was built on the mountaintop (name origin). This Giant Buddha was completed in the Northern Wei Dynasty (386 – 534AD) and perfected in Flourish Tang Dynasty (the first half of the 8th century) (time). The Grottoes of Giant Buddha is the highest one in China and also is one of the important cultural relics of combining rock cave culture and ancient building techniques together in southeastern area of Gansu on the Ancient Silk Route (social status).

Item 2 Topic Information

Visitors can see a number of ruins. Of course the Buddha statue is the center. Among the ruins, there are 23 cave groups, 15 various styles of ancient wood structural building complex in the Ming-Qing Dynasties, the Rest Palace of Wei Xiao and the Millitary Parade Platform of Wei Xiao. Wei Xiao was a general of the Eastern Han Dynasty (25-220AD) and governor of Tianshui area (all in the Wuliang Palace). Also visitors can find some cultural relics, including the three stone tablets carved in Chinese characters respectively. They are Tablet of "Hometown of Fuxi", according to the legend that Fuxi was born in Gufeng Plateau of southern Gangu County, Tablet of "Hometown of Shi Zuoshu", who was one of seven-two sages of Confucius' student, and Tablet of "Record of Rebuilding Jiang Wei's Shrine", who was a great general of Shu Kingdom of Three Kindoms Period. The clothing and ornaments of Buddha can be regarded as the art works created by the perfect combination of western ornamental sculptural art and Chinese sculptural art of freehand brushwork. The Giant Buddha, a stone casing clay sculpture, is 23.3 metres high and 10.4 metres wide at its waist. Look at the image of Buddhist sculpture carefully. His blue heliciform hair in the Gupta period on his head, the tadpole-shaped beards on his mouth and a dual collared dipping cassock with male threaded pleats on his body. He rests in a lotus place. He was bare chested with bare feet. His right hand is making varada mudra and his left hand is putting flatly on his left knee. The Buddha looks so benevolent and divine (contents).

Item 3 Additional Information

At the entrance of the scenic area, there is a guide map of the Grottoes of Giant Buddha and a tourist service center. Also there is a free car parking lot. In the Cultural Theme Garden of the Giant Buddha, there are many rare trees, for example, Qinghai dragon spruce, weeping willow, Ginkgo tree, photinia fraseri etc. And visitors can also enjoy some landscapes here like a man-made lake, the Jiang Wei's Shrine and musical springs etc. (facilities and services).

Are all of you amazed at the tadpole-shaped beards that the Giant Buddha has? The shape of them is extremely rare in China (guides/advices).

The sculptors of the Giant Buddha sculptured the statue with harmonious proportion by their accurate visual error calculation. So whether seen from inside of the cave or from the foot of the mountain, or even from far distance on the north bank of the Wei River, Giant Buddha's proportions are always harmonious and his eyes are always so serene (guides/advices).

Visitors can experience the Fair of the Giant Buddha. It is normally held on the 8th of April of Chinese lunar calendar. On that day, thousands of people would throng here, to watch various performances, go sightseeing among the hills and worship the Giant Buddha (guides/advices).

By the way, Jiang Wei's Tomb is just near Giant Buddha. Visitors can go there if they like (guides/advices).

The temple opens from 8:00 a.m. till 5:00 p.m. Tickets are RMB 30 for each person, and RMB 15 for per person as half price applicable. Free for children of less than 1.2 metres tall, elderly people who hold senior people certificate issued, servicemen with officer certificate and disable people with disable certificate. Rail service is available from the Grottoes to Tianshui railway station. The journey covers only 87 kilometres. Also both direct buses and rail services are available from the Grottoes to Gangu Town.

四 甘谷华盖寺石窟

（一）汉语语篇重构

甘谷华盖寺石窟

序列1：背景信息

华盖寺石窟位于甘肃省天水市甘谷县城西二十里铺村（景点的地理位置）。因山崖红体绿顶，远看恰似一顶喇嘛帽而得名（景点名称由来）。开凿于元朝泰定年间（公元1323—1328年）（建筑起止年代），是甘谷县保存最完好的石窟，是天水百里石窟走廊的重要组成部分（社会定位）。

序列 2：主题信息

华盖寺现存洞窟 18 个、塑像 53 尊、壁画 204 幅，内容涉及道教（太上老君洞等 10 个）、佛教（释迦洞等 4 个）、儒家（孔子洞）及祖先崇拜（伏羲洞和鲁班洞）。游客可以看到寺内最珍贵的《唐僧取经图》和《唐僧取经归来图》两幅元代壁画。该壁画早于《西游记》成书，是《西游记》来源的重要证据（观赏内容）。

序列 3：附加信息

本寺所有洞窟农历初一、十五全部开放；寺内常住僧众 20 多人（景点的设施与服务）。

除了石窟和壁画之外，游客可以观察华盖寺岩体半圆柱形丹霞地貌地质结构（游览指南/建议）。

华盖寺为宗教活动场所，每年农历四月初八、七月十五都会举行盛大的佛事活动。游客如遇佛事活动可以选择静立默视或安静离开（游览指南/建议）。

游客还可以欣赏距华盖寺 7 千米的大像山石窟（游览指南/建议）。

开放时间：8：00—18：00。

门票价格：免费。

交通：在甘谷县城大十字乘坐到西二十里铺的公交车，不到 20 分钟就可到华盖寺。

（二）重构语篇英语书面语介绍

Resort Introduction of the Canopy Temple Grottoes

Item 1 Background Information

The Canopy Temple Grottoes is situated in Ershilipu Village, west of Gangu Town, Tianshui City, Gansu Province (location). It was named for the reason that the cliff there has red body with green top, looked from a long distance like a Lama cap (name origin). The Grottoes, built in the yesrs of Taiding (1323-1328AD) in the Yuan Dynasty (time), is the best reserved cave in Gangu County, and is also an important part of the

"Tianshui Baili" Grottoes Corridor (social status).

Item 2 Topic Information

In the Canopy Temple Grottoes, there are 18 caves, 53 statues and 204 frescoes, among them there are 10 ones related to Taoism (such as the Cave of Lord Lao Zi), 4 ones related to Buddhism (such as Sakyamuni Cave), one related to Confucianism (Confucius Cave) and two related to ancestor worship (Fuxi Cave and Lu Ban Cave). Visitors can also see the most precious frescoes of the Yuan Dynasty in the Temple—*The Paintings of the Tang Priest's Pilgrimage to Ancient Indian for Buddhist Scriptures* and *The Paintings of the Tang Priest's Back from Pilgrimage to Ancient Indian for Buddhist Scriptures*.

The two frescoes were completed earlier than the completion of the book *Journey to the West*, and show important value for being the creation source of the book (contents).

Item 3 Additional Information

All grottoes in the temple are open on the 1st and 15th of January of Chinese lunar calendar. There are over 20 inhabitant monks living in the temple (facilities and services).

Besides looking around the grottoes and frescoes, visitors can observe the temple's semi cylindrical geologic structure of Danxia Landform (guides/advices).

The Canopy Temple is a place for holding religious activities, with grand Buddhist events held every 8th April and 15th July of Chinese lunar calendar. If meeting Buddhist events, visitors can choose either to stand silently or leave quietly (guides/advices).

Visitors can see another tourist attraction—The Grottoes of Giant Buddha, just 7 kilometres away from the Canopy Temple (guides/advices).

Opening Times: From 8:00 a.m. till 6:00 p.m.

Ticket Prices: Free.

Transportation: Public bus service is available from the Big Crossing in Gangu Town to the West Ershilipu Village stop, with less than 20 minutes journey.

(三) 重构语篇英语口语导游词

Tour Guide Speech of the Canopy Temple Grottoes

Item 1 Background Information

Hello! Everyone! Today I will take you to see another small grottoes—the Canopy Temple Grottoes. It is in Ershilipu Village, west of Gangu Town in Tianshui City, Gansu Province (location). The reason why it got the name is because the cliff there has red body with green top. So it looks like a Lama cap from a long distance (name origin). The Grottoes were built in the years of Taiding (1323 – 1328AD) in the Yuan Dynasty (time). It is the best reserved cave in Gangu County. Now it is an important part of the "Tianshui Baili" Grottoes Corridor (social status).

Item 2 Topic Information

In the Canopy Temple Grottoes, you can see 18 caves, 53 statues and 204 frescoes. Among them, 10 ones are related to Taoism (such as the Cave of Lord Lao Zi), 4 ones are related to Buddhism (such as Sakyamuni Cave), one is related to Confucianism (Confucius Cave) and 2 ones are related to ancestor worship (Fuxi Cave and Lu Ban Cave). Visitors can also see the most precious frescoes of the Yuan Dynasty in the Temple—*The Paintings of the Tang Priest's Pilgrimage to Ancient Indian for Buddhist Scriptures* and *The Paintings of the Tang Priest's Back from Pilgrimage to Ancient Indian for Buddhist Scriptures*. Have you ever heard of the Tang Priest? He was the most famous monk in Chinese history. The two frescoes were completed earlier than the completion of the book *Journey to the West*. So we can say that the creation source of the book derived from this (contents).

Item 3 Additional Information

All grottoes in the temple are open on the 1st and 15th of January Chinese lunar calendar. More than 20 inhabitant monks are now living in the temple (facilities and services).

Apart from visiting the grottoes and frescoes, visitors can also enjoy the temple's semi cylindrical geologic structure of Danxia Landform (guides/advices).

The Canopy Temple is a place for holding religious activities. Normally grand Buddhist events are held every 8th April and 15th July of Chinese lunar calendar. If visitors happen to meet Buddhist events, they can choose either to stand silently or leave quietly (guides/advices).

There is another tourist attraction—The Grottoes of Giant Buddha nearby, just 7 kilometres away from the Canopy Temple. If visitors like, they can go there and see it (guides/advices).

The temple opens from 8∶00 a.m. till 6∶00 p.m. Tickets are free. Public bus service is available. You can take a bus from the Big Crossing in Gangu Town to the West Ershilipu Village stop. The journey is less than 20 minutes.

五 武山水帘洞石窟

(一) 汉语语篇重构

武山水帘洞石窟

序列1：背景信息

武山水帘洞石窟坐落在甘肃省天水市武山县东北约25千米的鲁班峡谷中（景点的地理位置）。因每当雨季，洞檐下流水如注恰似珠帘掩门而得名（景点名称由来）。始建于北周武成元年（公元559年）（建筑起止年代），是拱形自然洞穴（社会定位）。

序列2：主题信息

游客可以观赏北魏（公元386—534年）、隋朝（公元581—618

年)、唐朝（公元618—907年)、元朝（公元1271—1368年）的佛教巨幅壁画，涉及飞天、朝圣人、佛、菩萨以及表现世俗生活的牛拉大篷车等；千年筥刷树；不溢不竭的"摸子泉"；清朝康熙帝于公元1710年立的《水帘洞功德碑记》等（观赏内容）。

序列3：附加信息

景区售票处免费存放行李；景区中心建有停车场；随处可见水帘洞景区导游图（景点的设施与服务）。

游客可以参与每年6月23日本寺举办的"中国·武山水帘洞拉梢寺世界第一摩崖大佛祈福文化旅游节"（游览指南/建议）。

本寺在5月19日中国旅游日对前来参观游览的游客实行免门票优惠活动（游览指南/建议）。

水帘洞附近的丹霞地貌近年已被确立为省级地质公园，一线天、试斧山、莲花山、象鼻山、笔尖峰、单乳峰、圣贤壁等丹霞地貌风光为佛教石窟添加了独特壮丽的自然景观（游览指南/建议）。

游客还可以欣赏景区内拉梢寺、千佛洞、显圣池石窟群。其中拉梢寺拥有世界最大的摩崖浮雕景观和北宋（公元960—1127年）"东方维纳斯"菩萨头像（游览指南/建议）。

开放时间：8：00—18：00。

门票价格：30元/人，观光车往返票价10元/人。

交通：在天水市秦州区南湖汽车站乘坐开往武山的班车，每半小时一班，到洛阳门汽车站下车，然后打车约30元可到；也可从武山县城或武山县洛门镇乘坐前往钟楼山、党口等地的中巴车前往，票价5—10元左右。

(二) 重构语篇英语书面语介绍

Resort Introduction of Water Curtain Cave Grottoes

Item 1 Background Information

The Water Curtain Cave Grottoes is situated in Luban Valley, about 25 kilometres northeast of Wushan Town, Tianshui City, Gansu Province (location). When in rainy seasons, the spring in the peak and walls of the cave pour out together. The spring water runs from the eaves of the cave, just like the bead curtains shutting the door of the cave, which is the reason why it was given the name "Water Curtain Grottoes" (name origin). The grottoes, built from the first year of Wu Cheng (559 AD), the Northern Zhou Dynasty (time), is a natural arched cave (social status).

Item 2 Topic Information

Visitors can enjoy the sight of huge Buddhist murals of the Northern Wei Dynasty (368-534AD), the Sui Dynasty (581-618AD), the Tang Dynasty (618-907AD) and the Yuan Dynasty (1271-1368AD), which are in relation to flying to the sky, Buddhist pilgrims, the Buddha, the Bodhisattvas and ox-drawn caravans of showing secular life etc. Visitors can also see the broom-brush trees of thousand years old, the so-called Bodhisattva Spring, where people touch stone to divine the gender of birthing child, with no overflowing or no drying out, and the *Record of Merit Monument of Water Curtain Grottoes* set up in 1710 AD by Emperor Kangxi of the Qing Dynasty (contents).

Item 3 Additional Information

At the ticket office of the scenic spot, there is a baggage deposit office for free depositing. Also there is a car park in the center of the spot. Tourist guiding maps are available everywhere at the spot (facilities and services).

Visitors can participate in "The World's Biggest Ciff Buddha Praying Cultural Tourism Festival of Lashao Temple in Wushan Water Curtain Grottoes" every 23rd June (guides/advices).

The temple offers free visiting activities to tourists on 19th of May—the China's Tourist Day every year (guides/advices).

The surrounding district of the Grottoes, with its beautiful Danxia Landform, has been established as a provincial-level geological park. The natural sceneries of Danxia Landform, such as Thin Strip of Sky, Axe-hewed Hill, Lotus Hill, Elephant Trunk Peak, Penpoint Peak, Single

Breast Peak and Saints Cliff etc., provides the Grottoes with extra unique and magnificent natural landscapes (guides/advices).

Visitors can enjoy the view of the Lashao Temple, the Thousand-Buddha Cave and the Saints Visitation Pool. Among them, the Lashao Temple owns the world's largest relief sculpture and "Oriental Venus" Buddha head in the Northern Song Dynasty (960-1127AD) (guides/advices).

Opening Times: From 8:00 a.m. till 6:00 p.m.

Ticket Prices: RMB 30 per person, and the sight-seeing bus service is RMB 10 per person for the return ticket.

Transportation: A public bus service is available. Visitors can take a bus from Nanhu Bus Stop in Qinzhou District, Tianshui, to the direction of Wushan Town, with an interval of half an hour, then drop out at Luoyangmen stop, last take a taxi to the Grottoes with RMB 30. They can also take mini-bus heading for Zhongloushan, Dangkou etc. from Wushan Town or Luomen Town, Wushan County to the Grottoes. The fare is about RMB 5 to RMB 10.

(三) 重构语篇英语口语导游词

Tour Guide Speech of Water Curtain Cave Grottoes

Item 1 Background Information

Hi, dear friends! I am happy to be your guide. Today I will show everyone around a famous kind of grottoes—the Water Curtain Cave Grottoes. It is in Luban Valley, about 25 kilometres northeast of Wushan Town in Tianshui, Gansu Province (location). The name sounds interesting, isn't it? Do you know why it is so called? OK, let me tell you. When in rainy seasons, the spring in the peak and walls of the cave pour out together. The spring water runs from the eaves of the cave, just like the bead curtains shutting the door of the cave. So people gave it a beautiful name "Water Curtain Cave Grottoes" (name origin). The grottoes was built from the first year of Wu Cheng (559 AD) (time), the Northern Zhou Dynasty. It is a natural arched cave (social status).

Item 2 Topic Information

When going into the grottoes, visitors will be amazed at the sight of huge Buddhist murals of the Northern Wei Dynasty (368–534AD), the Sui Dynasty (581–618AD), the Tang Dynasty (618–907AD) and the Yuan Dynasty (1271–1368AD). They are in relation to flying to the sky, Buddhist pilgrims, the Buddha, the Bodhisattvas and ox-drawn caravans of showing secular life etc. Visitors can also see some peculiar sights. First, broom-brush trees of thousand years old. Next, a so-called Bodhisattva Spring, also named as spring where people touch stone to divine the gender of birthing child, with no overflowing or no drying out. Last is the most precious the Record of Merit Monument of Water Curtain Grottoes. Do you know why? Because it was set up in 1710 AD by Emperor Kangxi of the Qing Dynasty (contents).

Item 3 Additional Information

At the ticket office, a baggage deposit office is offered. It's free. Also there is a car park the center of the spot. You will notice that tourist guiding maps are available everywhere at the spot (facilities and services).

Good news! If visitors happen to come on 23rd June, they will have the chance to participate in "The World's Biggest Ciff Buddha Praying Cultural Tourism Festival of Lashao Temple in Wushan Water Curtain Grottoes of china" every 23rd June (guides/advices).

Also the temple offers free visiting activities to tourists on the day 19th of May—the China's Tourist Day every year (guides/advices).

The government has set the beautiful Danxia Landform in the surrounding district of the Grottoes as a provincial-level geological park. The natural sceneries of Danxia Landform, such as Thin Strip of Sky, Axe-hewed Hill, Lotus Hill, Elephant Trunk Peak, Penpoint Peak, Single Breast Peak, Saints Cliff etc., undoubtedly adds extra unique and magnificent natural landscapes to the Grottoes (guides/advices).

Visitors can enjoy the view of the Lashao Temple, the Thousand-Buddha Cave and the Saints Visitation Pool. Among them, the Lashao Temple has the world's largest relief sculpture and "Oriental Venus" Buddha head in the Northern Song Dynasty (960-1127AD) (guides/advices).

The temple opens from 8:00 a.m. till 6:00 p.m., and cost RMB 30 per person. The sight-seeing bus service costs RMB 10 per person for the return ticket. A public bus service is available. Visitors can take a bus from Nanhu bus stop in Qinzhou District, Tianshui, to Wushan Town, then get off at Luoyangmen stop. It usually takes half an hour to drive. Then they have to take a taxi to the Grottoes for RMB 30. They can also take mini-bus heading for Zhongloushan, Dangkou ect. from Wushan Town or Luomen Town, Wushan County to the Grottoes. The fare is about RMB 5 to RMB 10.

六　武山木梯寺石窟

（一）汉语语篇重构

武山木梯寺石窟

序列1：背景信息

木梯寺石窟位于甘肃省天水市武山县马力乡杨家坪（景点的地理位置）。因于绝壁处置木梯供人们攀登入寺而得名（景点名称由来）。始建于北魏（公元386—534年）（建筑起止年代），其现存的宋朝（公元960—1279年）塑像填补了天水佛教洞窟的空白（社会定位）。

序列2：主题信息

木梯寺内现存窟龛18个，殿堂4座，造像80余尊，壁画234幅共2100平方米。游客可以观赏大佛阁14米高的唐朝（公元618—907年）彩塑大佛（天水排名第三）、宋朝（公元960—1279年）跷腿菩萨和采用白象装饰的斗拱等特色建筑（观赏内容）。

序列3：附加信息

景区售票处免费存放行李；景区中心建有停车场；随处可见木梯

寺景区导游图（景点的设施与服务）。

游客可以体验农历五月初五端午节木梯寺庙会，观看旋鼓、杂耍、摆武等文艺活动并且游山祭拜大佛（游览指南/建议）。

白皮松也是木梯寺一景。树干上鱼鳞似的树皮就像蛇蜕皮一样，每年进行一次。据说脱落的树皮有治疗皮肤病的奇效，游客可以采摘、捡拾这些"鳞片"（游览指南/建议）。

木梯寺山势陡峭有一定危险性，游客要量力而行（游览指南/建议）。

开放时间：8：00—17：00。

门票价格：25元/人，持学生证半价。

交通：在武山县火车站乘坐马力或漳县新寺的班车即可到达木梯寺石窟，单程约35千米，车费约8元。

（二）重构语篇英语书面语介绍

Resort Introduction of Wood Ladder Temple Grottoes

Item 1 Background Information

Wood Ladder Temple Grottoes is situated in Yangjiaping, Mali Village of Tianshui City in Gansu Province (location). The name comes from the time that originally a tall wood ladder was installed on the precipice, through which you can climb up into the grottoes (name origin). The Wood Ladder Temple was built in the Northern Wei Dynasty (386-584AD) (time). The statue in the Song Dynasty (960-1279AD) has filled in gaps of Buddhist cave in Tianshui (social status).

Item 2 Topic Information

There are 18 shrine-caves, 4 palaces, more than 80 statues and 234 frescoes, which occupy 2100 square metres in the Wood Ladder Temple. You can visit 14-metre-high sculptures of Buddha of the Tang Dynasty (618-907AD) (rank the third in Tianshui), Feet-up Bodhisattva of the Song Dynasty (960-1279AD) and brackets furnished with white elephants in Buddha Pavilion etc. (contents).

Item 3 Additional Information

Luggage storage is free at the spot of ticket office and there is a parking lot in scenic center. And scenic guide maps are available everywhere (facilities and services).

You can enjoy the Wood Ladder Temple Fair on the Dragon Boat Festival where there are rotary drum, juggle and folk dance. Besides, you can worship Buddha in the mountain (guides/advices).

Pinus bungeana is also worthy to be visited. The barks that look like scales on the trunk molt every year like a snake. It is said that the molted barks can cure the skin disease. And you can pick up these molted barks (guide/advices).

The mountains in Wood Ladder Temple are very steep, so you should tour according to your abilities (guides/advices).

Open Times: From 8:00 a.m. till 5:00 p.m.

Ticket Prices: RMB 25 for adults and half price for students.

Transportation: Take the bus heading for Mali Village or Zhang Village Xinsi at the Wushan railway station to get to Wood Ladder Temple Grottoes. The one-way trip will be 35 kilometres and the ticket is RMB 8.

(三) 重构语篇英语口语导游词

Tour Guide Speech of Wood Ladder Temple Grottoes

Item 1 Background Information

Hello! Dear friends! I am your guide and I will take you to see around the Wood Ladder Temple Grottoes. It is located in Yangjiaping, Mali Village of Tianshui City in Gansu Province (location). People used to use this ladder to go into the temple when the ladder was a disposed ladder on cliffs. So that's how the name comes from (name origin). Do you know when the Wood ladder Temple was built? It was in the Northern Wei Dynasty (time) and the statue in the Song Dynasty has filled in gaps of Buddhist cave in Tianshui (social status).

Item 2 Topic Information

There are 18 shrine-caves, 4 halls, more than 80 statues and 234 murals which occupy 2100 square metres in the Wood Ladder Temple. You can visit 14-metre-high sculptures of Buddha of the Tang Dynasty, Feet-up Bodhisattva of the Song Dynasty and brackets furnished with white elephants in Buddha Pavilion (contents).

Item 3 Additional Information

There is a free luggage repository at the ticket office and a parking lot in scenic center. You can see scenic guide maps everywhere (facilities and services).

You can enjoy the Wood Ladder Temple Fair on the Dragon Boat Festival where there are rotary drum, juggle and folk dance. Besides, you can worship Buddha in the mountain if you are interested (guides/advices).

Pinus bungeana is also worthy to be visited. The barks that look like scales on the trunk molt every year like a snake. It is said that the molted barks can cure the skin disease. And you can pick up these molted barks if you want (guides/advices).

The mountains in Wood Ladder Temple are very steep, so you should tour according to your abilities (guides/advices).

The temple opens from 8:00 a.m. till 5:00 p.m. Tickets are RMB 25 for adults and half price for students. Just take the bus to Mali Village or Zhang Village Xinsi at Wushan railway station. The single way trip will be 35 kilometres and the ticket is RMB 8.

第三节 "一带一路"沿线国家石窟文化语篇语域重构及翻译

一 柬埔寨吴哥石窟

(一) 汉语语篇重构

柬埔寨吴哥石窟

序列1：背景信息

吴哥石窟雄踞在柬埔寨西北方的暹粒市以北约6千米处（景点的地理位置）。因建于吴哥古王朝遗址而得名，是整个古遗迹群吴哥寺（小吴哥）、吴哥王城（大吴哥）等的总称（景点名称由来）。始建于公元802年，完成于公元1201年（景点起止年代），是世界上最大的宗教建筑。1992年，联合国教科文组织世界遗产委员会把整个吴哥古迹列为世界文化遗产（社会定位）。

序列2：主题信息

古遗迹群因全部用石头建构及精美浮雕而著称。表情、面貌、衣着完全不同的天女浮雕墙、反衬寺庙倒影的护城河、情人梯、四面佛雕像、宏伟的斗象场、十二生肖塔均让游客流连忘返（观赏内容）。

序列3：附加信息

景区提供自行车租借；包车司机可兼做导游；专业汉语导游20—25美元/天；可购买中英文吴哥石窟古迹的旅游指南和以吴哥窟为主题发展出来的艺术品。大吴哥由于整个景点规模较大，有出租机动和非机动车辆。两轮摩托5—8美元/天，三轮摩托10—16美元/天，小型轿车20美元/天，面包车25美元/天（景点的设施和服务）。

除寺内建筑群外，游客还可以从附近唯一的制高点巴肯山顶一边观日落一边俯瞰吴哥窟（游览指南/建议）。

寺前莲花池畔既是观赏日出的最佳地点之一，也是捕捉吴哥窟及其倒影的最佳之处（游览指南/建议）。

如果您碰巧在吴哥举办国际马拉松比赛时参观古建筑群，就可以和亿万观众一起为世界各地的运动健儿加油喝彩，观赏他们从世界奇迹吴哥窟前跑过的壮观景象（游览指南/建议）。

开放时间：5：00—17：30。吴哥寺第三层的开放时间是7：40—17：00，限制人数，游客必须排队攀登进入。

门票价格：1日票20美元；3日票40美元，可以选择连续3天或1周内任意3天参观；7日票60美元，可以选择连续7天或1个月内任意7天。买票时当场拍照，照片会印在自己的门票上。吴哥窟售票时间为5：00—17：30，所以看日出的旅行者不用担心购票问题。另外每天下午17：00开始卖第二天的门票，买好门票后即可进入景区，门票期限从第二天开始计算。

交通：从暹粒机场至吴哥窟景区约5千米车程，乘出租车约8美元。

（二）重构语篇英语书面语介绍

Resort Introduction of Angkor Wat Relics in Cambodia

Item 1 Background Information

Angkor Wat is located in about 6 kilometres north of Siem Reap, northwest of Cambodia (location). It is named after the remains of ancient Angkor Wat and called by the combination of Temple of Angkor Wat and Angkor City (name origin). It was first built in 802 AD and completed in 1201AD (time). Now it is well-acknowledged as the biggest religion construction in the world. It was inscribed on the World Heritage List by UNESCO in1992 (social status).

Item 2 Topic Information

Angkor Wat is well known for its construction made of stones and beautiful relief sculptures. And visitors are bound to be attracted by the beautiful sights—the walls of relief sculptures with Apsaras which are different in facial expression, features and clothes, the moat which reflects the Temple of Angkor Wat, lover ladder, the statue of four-sided Buddha, the magnificent arena for fighting elephants and towers of 12 zodiac signs so that they would be unable to tear themselves away (contents).

Item 3 Additional Information

Bikes can be rented here and a charted driver can also acts as a guide. If you want to hire a professional Chinese guide, you just pay 20 to 25 dollars for one-day toured guide. Besides, you can purchase handbooks in both English and Chinese of the relics of Angkor Wat and works of art promoted on the basis of the theme of Angkor Wat. Finally, you can get there by renting motorized vehicles or non-motorized vehicles as Angkor has a large area. Visitors can just pay 5 dollars to 8 dollars a day to rent a two-wheeled motors or 10 dollars to 16 dollars for a three-wheeled motor. Also they can pay 20 dollars a day to rent a car or 25 dollars for a minibus (facilities and services).

Besides group of buildings in Temple, you will be able to enjoy the sunset standing on the summit of Bakeng which is the only highest place nearby while you can overlook Angkor Wat at the same time (guides/advices).

The Lotus Pool in front of the Temple serves not only one of the best locations to enjoy the sunset, but the best vantage ground to capture Angkor Wat and its reflection as well (guides/advices).

If you happen to be visiting the ancient group of buildings at the time when the International Marathon is held in Angkor, you will be able to cheer for the players all over the world with billions of people and watch the spectacular scenes when they are running past Angkor Wat, the world wonder (guides/advices).

Opening Times: Angkor Wat usually opens from 5:00 a.m. till 5:30 p.m. The opening time of the third layer of the Temple of Angkor Wat is 7:40 a.m. till 5:00 p.m. For the sake of the protecting Angkor Wat from being damaged, the number of visitors is restricted. Therefore, all of visitors have to queue in line and enter by climbing.

Ticket Prices: There is a variety of alternatives for tickets, ranging from 20 dollars for one-day ticket, 40 dollars for three-day ticket (you can choose three-day visit in succession or random three days' visit within one week) and 60 dollars for seven-day ticket (similarly, you can choose seven-day visit in succession or random seven days' visit within one month). Interestingly, you will be taken a photo when buying tickets and the photo will also be printed on the ticket. In addition, the time of selling tickets is from 5∶00 a.m. till 5∶30 p.m., so you do not have to worry about the tickets. And tickets are usually sold from 5∶00 p.m. in the afternoon every day for the next day's visit. Once you have bought the ticket, you can enter the scenic spot directly. To your delight, the time limit of ticket starts from next day, which obviously will make you enjoy yourselves to the full.

Transportation: There are roughly 5 kilometres away from Siem Reap airport to the relics of Angkor Wat. If you choose to take a taxi, you just need to pay 8 dollars to get there.

(三) 重构语篇英语口语导游词

Tour Guide Speech of Angkor Wat Relics in Cambodia

Item 1 Background Information

Hello! Everyone! I am honored to be your guide. Today I will take all of you to visit the famous scenic spot—Angkor Wat Relics in Cambodia. Angkor Wat Relics is located in the north, about 6 kilometres away from Siem Reap, northwest of Cambodia (location). It is named after the remains of ancient Angkor Wat. Interestingly, the Temple of Angkor Wat and Angkor City constitute the remains of ancient Angkor Wat (name origin). It was first built in 802 AD and completed in 1201 (time). Now it is regarded as the biggest religion construction in the world. In 1992, WHC (World Heritage Centre) in UNESCO (United Nations Educational, Scientific, and Cultural Organization) ranked the relics of Angkor Wat as world cultural heritage (social status).

Item 2 Topic Information

Angkor Wat is famous for its stones construction and beautiful relief sculptures. There are many so beautiful and amazing scenic spots here that you will be astonished by them. There are walls of relief sculptures with Apsaras who are varied in facial expression, features and clothes. There is the moat which reflects the Temple of Angkor Wat. And there is a lover ladder, a statue of four-sided Buddha, a magnificent arena for fighting elephants and towers of 12 zodiac signs. No wonder all of these amazing sights would make you wander around and forget to go home (contents).

Item 3 Additional Information

If you want to have an all-around and quick tour, you can rent bikes here. Also you can hire a charted driver as a guide if you like. If you want to hire a professional Chinese guide, you just pay 20 to 25 dollars for one-day toured guide. Besides, you can buy handbooks of the relics of Angkor Wat both in English and Chinese and works of art developed on the basis of the theme of Angkor Wat. I bet you must be concerned with how to get there. OK, let me tell you. There are several convenient ways to go there. One way is that you can rent motorized vehicles or non-motorized vehicles to reach there because Angkor occupies a large area. What you need to do is to pay just 5 dollars to 8 dollars a day to rent a two-wheeled motor or 10 dollars to 16 dollars a three-wheeled motor. Another way to get there is that you can pay 20 dollars a day to rent a car or 25 dollars for a minibus (facilities and services).

In addition to group of buildings in Temple, there is another pleasant place to visit. If you stand on the summit of Bakeng, the only highest place nearby, you will be able to enjoy the wonderful sunset while overlooking Angkor Wat (guides/advices).

The Lotus Pool in front of the Temple is another place worth a visit. Because it serves not only one of the best locations to enjoy the sunset, but the best vantage ground to capture Angkor Wat and its reflection as well (guides/advices).

Another lucky thing! If you happen to be visiting the ancient group of buildings at the time when the International Marathon is held in Angkor, you, together with billions of people, will have the chance to cheer for athletes all over the world. You will be lucky to watch the spectacular scenes when the players are running past Angkor Wat, the world wonder (guides/advices).

Angkor Wat is usually open from 5 : 00 a.m. till 5 : 30 p.m. The opening time of the third layer of the Temple of Angkor Wat is from 7 : 40 a.m. till 5 : 00 p.m. In order to protect Angkor Wat from being damaged, the number of visitors is restricted. Therefore, all of you have to queue in line and climb into it. There is a variety of options for tickets, ranging from 20 dollars for one-day ticket, 40 dollars for three-day ticket (you can choose three-day visit in succession or random three days' visit within one week) and 60 dollars for seven-day ticket (similarly, you can choose seven-day visit in succession or random seven days' visit within one month). Dear friends, when you buy tickets, you have to be careful with three things. First, when buying tickets, your photo will be taken on the spot and the photo will also be printed on the ticket. In addition, the time of selling tickets is from 5 : 00 a.m. till 5 : 30 p.m., so you do not have to worry whether the tickets have been sold out. And tickets are usually sold from 5 : 00 p.m. in the afternoon every day for the next day's visit. As soon as you buy the ticket, you can enter the scenic spot directly. Last, to make it more humane, the time limit of ticket starts from the next day, which will obviously make you enjoy yourselves to the full. There are roughly 5 kilometres away from Siem Reap airport to the relics of Angkor Wat. If you choose to take a taxi, you just need to pay 8 dollars to get there.

二 印度尼西亚婆罗浮屠石窟

（一）汉语语篇重构

印度尼西亚婆罗浮屠石窟

序列1：背景信息

婆罗浮屠石窟坐落于印度尼西亚日惹西北40千米处的高地，爪哇岛中部马吉冷婆罗浮屠村（景点的地理位置）。这座宏伟的寺庙因其所在地而得名（景点名称由来），大约公元750—850年由当时统治爪哇岛的夏连特拉王朝统治者兴建（景点起止年代），是世界上规模最大、最具有佛教哲理与艺术的古迹，与中国的长城、埃及的金字塔和柬埔寨的吴哥窟并称为古代东方四大奇迹（社会定位）。

序列2：主题信息

"救人一命，胜造七级浮屠（指七层宝塔）"，自古以来就是中国人乐善好施的通俗用语。游客在世界上最大的佛教遗迹中能看到鲜活的例子。整个建筑完全用附近河流中的安山岩和玄武岩砌成的没有门窗与梁柱的实心佛塔；长达3000多米的浮雕描绘了佛陀从降生到涅槃的全部过程；用火山灰制作的人物和各种图案都非常逼真（观赏内容）。

序列3：附加信息

景区入口处提供免费饮料，游客可以在水、茶、咖啡中选其一；景区内英语讲解员讲解婆罗浮屠从发掘、修复到保存背后的故事；为便于第二天一早欣赏日出，游客可选择紧邻景区的旅馆。玛塔哈利旅馆位于景区内，可以不受开放时间的限制（景点的设施和服务）。

除山顶的佛塔外还可以参观出口附近的博物馆，日出和云海景观也值得一看（游览指南/建议）。

游客不允许穿背心和短裤游览。如果您的下装比较短，服务中心会提供一块富有当地特色的布帮您围起来，参观完后请归还（游览指南/建议）。

开放时间：6：00—17：00。

门票价格：成人 20 美元，儿童 10 美元。

交通：日惹市区的吉旺安和占宝巴士总站都有前往婆罗浮屠的客车，票价 5000 印尼盾，车程分别约 1.5 小时和 40 分钟。

（二）重构语篇英语书面语介绍

Resort Introduction of Borobudur Indonesia

Item 1 Background Information

Borobudur Indonesia is located in an elevated area, approximately 40 kilometres northwest of Jogia, central Java Magelang, Village of Borobudur (location). This magnificent temple is named after its location (name origin). Evidence suggests that it was built during the reign of Sailendra Dynasty when governing Java from 750 AD to 850 AD (time). It is regarded as the world's largest Buddhist temple and one of the greatest Buddhist monuments full of philosophy and art in the world. Now it has been known as one of the four wonders of the ancient eastern countries, together with China's Great Wall, Egypt's Pyramid and Angkor Wat in Cambodia (social status).

Item 2 Topic Information

"Saving a life is better than build a seven-storied pagoda (refers to seven pagodas)" is a Chinese colloquial expression, which means that Chinese people have been kind and charitable since ancient time. Such vivid cases can be seen in the world's biggest Buddhist relics. The whole building made of andesite and basalt bricks in the river nearby is a solid Buddhist temple without windows and pillars. The reliefs with the length of 3000 metres depict the life process of Buddha from birth to nirvana. The characters made of volcano ash and various patterns are very realistic (contents).

Item 3 Additional Information

Free drinks are offered at the entrance of scenic spots and you can choose one of the three—water, tea and coffee. The English instructors in the scenic area explain the time of Borobudur from its excavation, repair to preservation. In order to enjoy the sunset in the early morning, you can choose the hotels adjacent to scenic spot. Among the hotels, Matahari Hotel lies inside the scenic area, so you do not have to worry about the opening time of Borobudur (facilities and services).

Apart from Buddhist temples on the mountain, you can also visit the museum, sunrise and the sea of clouds near the exit. The landscape is really worth seeing (guides/advices).

You are not allowed to wear vests and shorts when visiting. If your pants or skirts are too short, the service center will offer you a cloth full of local characteristics and ask you to wrap you with it. Then after finish visiting, you need to return the cloth (guides/advices).

Opening Times: From 6:00 a. m. till 5:00 p. m.

Ticket Prices: 20 dollars for adults, 10 dollars for children.

Transportation: At Terminal Giwangan and Terminal Jombor of Jogia, there are coaches heading for Borobudur. The fare is 5000 rupiah. The drives are approximately 1.5 hours and 40 minutes.

(三) 重构语篇英语口语导游词

Tour Guide Speech of Borobudur Indonesia

Item 1 Background Information

Hello, Dear friends! Today I will take all of you to see around a famous temple. Yeah, it is Borobudur Indonesia. Very famous! Borobudur Indonesia is located in an elevated area, approximately 40 kilometres northwest of Jogia, central Java Magelang, Village of Borobudur (location).This magnificent temple got its name because of its location (name origin).It was built during the reign of Sailendra Dynasty when governing Java from 750 AD to 850 AD (time).To the world's surprise, it is regarded as the world's largest Buddhist temple and one of the greatest Buddhist monuments full of philosophy and art in the world. You may not know that it has now been known as one of the four wonders of the ancient eastern countries. What are the other three wonders in eastern countries? OK. Let me tell you. They are China's Great Wall, Egypt's

Pyramid and Angkor Wat in Cambodia (social status).

Item 2 Topic Information

There is a colloquial saying in China— "Saving a life is better than build a seven-storied pagoda (refers to seven pagodas)". What's the meaning of it? That is just a popular expression to show that Chinese people are kind and charitable from ancient times to the present. And you can see such vivid cases in the world's biggest Buddhist relics. The whole building is made of andesite and basalt bricks near the river. Even though there are no windows and pillars, it is still a solid Buddhist temple. The 3000 metres long reliefs depict the life process of Buddha from birth to nirvana. The characters made of volcano ash and various patterns are very lifelike (contents).

Item 3 Additional Information

OK, you must be tired and thirsty after you take a long tour to the temple. Don't worry. At the entrance of scenic spots free drinks are offered and you can choose one of the three—water, tea and coffee. It is so considerate, isn't it? Want to know the time of Borobudur? An English instructor in the scenic area would explain the time of Borobudur from its excavation, repair to preservation. Also, if you want to enjoy the sunset in the early morning, you can choose the hotels near the scenic spot. Matahari Hotel is one of them. The advantage of it is that it lies inside the scenic area, so you do not have to worry about the opening time of Borobudur (facilities and services).

In addition to Buddhist temples on the mountain, you can also visit the museum, sunrise and the sea of clouds near the exit. The landscape is really worth seeing (guides/advices).

Next, I have to warn everyone of one thing. You are not allowed to wear vests and shorts. If your pants or skirts are too short, the service center will offer you a cloth full of local characteristics and ask you to wrap you with it. After finish sightseeing, you need to return the cloth (guides/advices).

The temple opens from 6:00 a.m. till 5:00 p.m. Tickets are 20 dollars for adults, 10 dollars for kids. At Terminal Giwangan and Terminal Jombor of Jogia, there are coaches heading for Borobudur. The fare is 5000 rupiah. The drives are about 1.5 hours and 40 minutes.

三　斯里兰卡丹布勒石窟寺

(一) 汉语语篇重构

斯里兰卡丹布勒石窟寺

序列1：背景信息

丹布勒石窟寺坐落在斯里兰卡岛的中部，距离科伦坡城东北149千米，位于古都康提北60千米处（景点的地理位置）。因相传国王在外敌侵略躲到丹布勒被佛教徒所救，为了表达感激，在此地修建了洞窟寺庙而得名（景点名称由来）。建于公元前1世纪（建筑起止年代），是斯里兰卡最大、保存最完好的洞穴寺庙建筑群，也是人们朝圣的圣地。1991年联合国教科文组织将其列入《世界遗产名录》（社会定位）。

序列2：主题信息

游客可以看到黑色山岩中欧式风格的白色寺庙和由整块岩石雕刻的形态各异的雕像。洞穴的石壁及顶部都布满了树汁绘制的壁画，2100平方米的壁画与157尊雕像描述着佛陀的修炼与讲道等场景，并且为了纪念祖先抵抗印度人攻击时脚底沾满红土的艰辛，佛像的脚底都涂成了红色（观赏内容）。

序列3：附加信息

五个石窟虽然并排开凿但彼此之间并没有相通，需要从各自的入口进去参观；在石窟内可以拍照，但不能用闪光灯；每天上午10：30，寺庙会关闭专供信徒们祈祷（景点的设施与服务）。

游客可以带手电筒看壁画；进寺庙参观需着长袖长裤，并且脱鞋进入；不要故意惹逗山上猴子（游览指南/建议）。

游客还可以欣赏附近另一个世界遗产——锡吉里耶狮子岩，是在斯里兰卡历史上唯一流传下来的非宗教题材壁画（游览指南/建议）。

开放时间：上午8：00—11：00，下午2：00—7：00。

门票价格：免费。

交通：在康提前往锡吉里耶的必经之路上的长途车站乘坐大巴即可到达，从波隆纳鲁沃乘大巴也可以到达，两个路程都需大约2小时。

（二）重构语篇英语书面语介绍

Resort Introduction of Dambulla Rock Temple

Item 1 Background Information

Dambulla Rock Temple is located in the central section of Sri Lanka Island and it is 149 kilometres away from north east of Colombo City and 60 kilometres from north side of old Kandy (location). It got the name for the reason that the king was saved by Buddhists when he hid from foreign enemy in Dambulla (name origin) and in order to express his gratitude, Dambulla Rock Temple was built here in the first century BC (time). Now it has been the biggest and the most well-preserved temple building and also a sacred place where people make a pilgrimage. In 1991, it was listed on the World Heritage List by UNESCO (social status).

Item 2 Topic Information

You can see the white temples of European style on black rocks and different statues carved from a piece of rock. Murals with sap are full of cliff and top. There are 2100-square meter frescoes and 157 statues. On stone walls and top of the cave are dotted with frescoes painted with sap, which vividly describe the scenes of practice and sermon of Buddha. In honor of their ancestors' hardships as their soles of feet were covered with red mud when resisting the attack of Indians, the soles of Buddha statue are also painted red (contents).

Item 3 Additional Information

Although five grottoes were built side by side, they are not connected with one another. You have to walk into each entrance to visit. Photos without flashlight are allowed in grottoes. And temple closes at 10∶30 a.m.

for believers to pray (facilities and services).

You can view the frescoes with an electric torch. Besides, you have to wear long sleeves and pants and take off your shoes before going into the temple. Teasing monkeys in the mountains on purpose is not allowed (tour guides/advices)

Moreover, you can visit another world heritage—Sigiriya Lion Rock, the only non-religious theme fresco in Sri Lanka's history that has still existed so far (tour guides/advices).

Opening Times: From 8:00 a.m. till 11:00 a.m. and from 2:00 p.m. till 7:00 p.m.

Ticket Prices: Free.

Transportation: Take a coach at the coach station on the way from Kandy to Sigiriya. Or you can take a bus from Polonnaruwa. Both routes take approximately two hours.

(三) 重构语篇英语口语导游词

Tour Guide Speech of Dambulla Rock Temple

Item 1 Background Information

Dear friends! Let's go and visit Dambulla Rock Temple today. As you can see, Dambulla Rock Temple is located in the centre of Sri Lanka Island and it is 149 kilometres away from northeast of Colombo City and 60 kilometres from north side of old Kandy (location). The reason why it got such a name is that the king was saved by Buddhists when he hid from foreign enemy in Dambulla and in order to express his gratitude, he built Rock Temple in Dambulla in the first century BC. And it now becomes the biggest and the most well-preserved temple building where people make a pilgrimage. Also, UNESCO added it to the World Heritage List in 1991.

Item 2 Topic Information

Look at the white temples! Do you notice anything special? Yeah, the white temples of European style are on the black rocks and statues in different shapes are all carved from a piece of rock. The most amazing part is that some frescoes on stone walls and top of the cave are painted with sap. There are also 2100-square meter frescoes and 157 statues. All of them depict the practice and sermon of Buddha and hardships of ancestors when fighting against Indians.

Item 3 Additional Information

There are five grottoes in all. They are built side by side but they are not connected with one another. So if you want to visit them, you have to enter each entrance. You can take photos inside but remember, do not use flashlight. By the way, temple closes at 10：30 a.m., because the believers will pray at that time (facilities and services).

You can view the frescoes with an electric torch. Besides, before going into the temple, you need to wear long sleeves and pants and take off your shoes too. And you are not allowed to play with monkeys in the mountains (tour guides/advices).

Moreover, you can visit another world heritage called Sigiriya Lion Rock. It is very famous. I suggest that you should not miss visiting because it is the only non-religious theme fresco handed down in Sri Lanka's history (tour guides/advices).

It is open from 8：00 a.m. till 11：00 a.m. and from 2：00 p.m. till 7：00 p.m. Good thing is that it is free for everyone! You can take a coach from coach station on the way from Kandy to Sigiriya. Or you can take a bus from Polonnaruwa. Both routes will take about two hours.

四 斯里兰卡锡吉里耶狮子岩

(一) 汉语语篇重构

斯里兰卡锡吉里耶狮子岩

序列1：背景信息

锡吉里耶狮子岩坐落在斯里兰卡锡吉里亚连接丹布勒与哈伯勒内

之间的主干道以东约10千米处（景点的地理位置）。因修建于貌似狮子的橘红色巨岩上而得名，如今只剩下狮身，狮头早已风化掉落（景点名称由来）。建于公元5世纪达都舍那王朝时期（建筑起止年代），以其在斯里兰卡历史上唯一流传下来的非宗教题材壁画而著名，1982年联合国教科文组织将其列入《世界遗产名录》（社会定位）。

序列2：主题信息

游客可以通过螺旋形楼梯欣赏仅存的21帧"天使般的少女"壁画。图中仕女上裸半身，戴宝冠头饰，垂着美丽璎珞，佩戴夸张耳环，金钏环臂，手托花盘或轻拈莲花，丰姿绰约。以红黄绿黑为主色，不同肤色的绘图传说是国王来自世界各国的嫔妃和侍女画像。步下螺旋梯可观察被抛光得明如镜面的金黄色镜墙，欣赏涂写在墙面的赞叹诗句。经过走道就可到达狮爪平台。两尊巨大的狮爪是当时统治者依照迷信雕刻而成，为的就是包围自己的领地。只有穿过这对狮爪城门才能一睹空中宫殿的真容（观赏内容）。

序列3：附加信息

如果额外付费，游客可以得到汉语或英语的讲解及爬山搀扶服务；有螺旋形铁楼梯设施辅助游客攀爬；为了避免对残留壁画的再度伤害，岩洞里有专人守护（景点的设施与服务）。

如果游客碰巧遇到好天气，在日出或者日落时登顶会看到很壮观的景色（游览指南/建议）。

游客不可以在洞内使用闪光灯照相；不可以触摸镜墙；不要故意惹逗园区猴子，避免在吃东西时被抓伤（游览指南/建议）。

在狮子岩以北1.5千米的皮杜兰加拉岩石寺不仅能远眺狮子岩全景甚至能清楚看到狮子岩上攀爬移动的游客。但需花500卢比购买寺庙门票方可攀登（游览指南/建议）。

开放时间：8：30—17：30（17：00停止售票）。

门票价格：成人30美元，6—12岁儿童15美元（包括大门票、壁画和博物馆，要查验三次，注意不要把票丢掉）。

交通：丹布勒有往返狮子岩的长途汽车，一般从7：00开始，每

30 分钟一班，车程约 45 分钟。最后一班回丹布勒的汽车在 19∶00 左右发车。前往狮子岩还可搭乘包车，车程约 30 分钟，费用约 600 卢比，请事先谈好价钱。

(二) 重构语篇英语书面语介绍

Resort Introduction of Sigiriya Lion Rock

Item 1 Background Information

Sigiriya Lion Rock is located in Sigiriya, Sri Lanka, about 10 kilometres east to the backbone road between Dambulla and Habarana (location). It got the name because it was built on the orangered colored huge rock with the similar appearance to a lion. Currently, there is only "lion's body" left, while the "lion's head" has been weathered away and dropped out (name origin). Sigiriya Lion Rock was built in the 5th century AD, in Dhatusena Dynasty period (time). It is well known all over the world in that it is the only non-religious fresco handed down in Sri Lanka history. Sigiriya Lion Rock today is a UNESCO listed World Heritage Site (social status).

Item 2 Topic Information

Mounting a spiral stairway, you can enjoy the only existed 21 frescoes of "angelic young maidens", the portraits of ladies in plump and fit postures. They are all with their naked upper bodies, wearing treasured crown and the lop beautiful necklaces, and also wearing exaggerate encircling earrings and gold bracelets. They were all in different manners, with one supporting flower plate on her hands, while another one gently picking up lotus flowers and so on. According to the legend, painted with red, yellow, green and black as their main skin colors, the portraits indicated that the King's concubines and maidservants appeared in the paintings were from all over the world. Walking down the spiral stairway, you can see the golden Mirror Wall, which was polished bright like mirror, and also you can enjoy reading beautiful praised verses written on the wall. Through an aisle way, you can reach Lion's Paws Platform, where there are two huge stone-made lion's paws which were engraved by the ruler of that time based on superstitions, with aims to protect his dominions. It is only through the city gate formed by the two lion's paws that you can have a view of the real scape of the temple in the sky (contents).

Item 3 Additional Information

By paying extra money, you can get Chinese or English tourist guide service, or hill climbing assistance service by hand supporting. There are steel spiral stairway facilities for assisting your climbing. There are special staff on duty in every cave to prevent the remaining frescoes from being further damaged (facilities and services).

If you happen to come on a fine day, you will enjoy a magnificent sight of sunrise or sunset when reaching the top of the hill (guides/advices).

You are not allowed to take photos with flashing lights, not allowed to touch mirror walls, and also not allowed to purposely tantalize monkeys in the temple. You should not eat so as to avoid being scratched by monkeys as well (guides/advices).

From Pidurangala Rock Temple, 1.5 kilometres north of Sigiriya Lion Rock, you can not only enjoy a panoramic view of the Lion Rock, but also see other visitors climbing and moving on the Lion Rock. However, you need to buy temple admission fee of 500 rupees for this climbing (guides/advices).

Opening Times: From 8:30 a.m. till 5:30 p.m. (ticket sale until 5:00 p.m.).

Ticket Prices: 30 dollars for each adult, 15 dollars for each child of 6-12 years old (including admissions to the main entrance, frescoes and museum). The ticket will be checked three times. Please note do not discard your ticket.

Transportation: Long distance of returning bus service is available from Dambulla to Lion Rock, normally starting from 7:00 a.m., leaving every

30 minutes, with 45 minutes of drive. The last bus to Dambulla departs at about 7∶00 p. m.. Charter bus services to the Lion Rock are available with about 30 minutes' drive, for about 600 rupees. As to the charter bus service, you should agree upon a price in advance.

(三) 重构语篇英语口语导游词

Tour Guide Speech of Sigiriya Lion Rock

Item 1 Background Information

Hello! Dear friends! I feel honored to be your guide. Today I will show you around the famous place of interest—Sigiriya Lion Rock. It is located in Sigiriya, Sri Lanka, about 10 kilometres east to the backbone road connecting Dambulla and Habarana (location). Do you know why is it so called? Because it was built on the orangered colored huge rock with the similar appearance to a lion (name origin). But Sigiriya Lion Rock was built in the 5th century AD, in Dhatusena Dynasty period, very long time ago. You see, there is only "lion's body" left, and the "lion's head" has been weathered away and dropped out (time). Now it is famous all over the world because it is the only non-religious fresco handed down in Sri Lanka history. Today the Sigiriya Lion Rock is a UNESCO listed World Heritage Site (social status).

Item 2 Topic Information

There are some very famous sights you should never miss. One is the fresco. When you climb a spiral stairway, you can enjoy the only existed 21 frescoes of "angelic young maidens", the portraits of ladies in plump and fit postures. They are all upper bodies naked, wearing treasured crown and the drooping beautiful necklaces, and also wearing exaggerate encircling earrings and gold bracelets. They were all in different manners, with one supporting flower plate on her hands, while another one gently picking uplotus flowers and so on. According to the legend, painted with red, yellow, green and black as their main skin colors, the portraits indicated that the

King's concubines and maidservants appeared in the paintings were from all over the world. Another one is the Mirror Wall. When you walk down the spiral stairway, you can see the golden Mirror Wall, which was polished bright like mirror, and also can enjoy reading beautiful praised verses written on the wall. Last is the famous Lion's Paws Platform. Through an aisle way, you can reach Lion's Paws Platform, where there are two huge stone-made lion's paws which were engraved by the ruler of that time based on superstitions. His purpose is obviously to protect his dominions. It is only through the city gate formed by the two lion's paws that you can have a view of the real scape of the temple in the sky (contents).

If you pay extra money, you can get Chinese or English tourist guide service, or hill climbing assistance service by hand supporting. There are steel spiral stairway facilities for assisting your climbing. There are special staff on duty in every cave to prevent the remaining frescoes from being further damaged (facilities and services).

If you happen to come on fine a fine day, you will enjoy a magnificent sight of sunrise or sunset when reaching the top of the hill (guides/advices).

I have to remind every visitor of something. You are not allowed to take photos with flashing lights, not allowed to touch mirror walls, and also not allowed to purposely tantalize monkeys in the temple. You should not eat so as not to be scratched as well (guides/advices).

From Pidurangala Rock Temple, 1.5 kilometres north of Sigiriya Lion Rock, you can not only enjoy a full sight of the Lion Rock, but also see other visitors climbing and moving on the Lion Rock. However, you need to buy temple admission fee of 500 rupees for this climbing (guides/advices).

The temple opens from 8 : 30 a. m. till 5 : 30 p. m. (ticket sale until 5 : 00 p. m.). Tickets are 30 dollars for each adult, 15 dollars for each child of 6 - 12 years old (including admissions to the main entrance,

第六章 天水石窟文化描写与解释

frescoes and museum). The ticket is usually checked three times. Please note do not discard your ticket.

Long distance of returning bus service is available from Dambulla to Lion Rock, normally starting from 7:00 a. m., leaving every 30 minutes, with 45 minutes of drive. The latest bus to Dambulla departs at about 7:00 p. m. Charter bus services to the Lion Rock are available with about 30 minutes' drive, for about 600 rupees. As to the charter bus service, you should agree upon a price in advance.

五 印度阿旃陀石窟

(一) 汉语语篇重构

印度阿旃陀石窟

序列1：背景信息

阿旃陀石窟坐落在印度孟买奥兰加巴德市东北104千米的瓦格拉河断崖中（景点的地理位置）。因源于附近的小村阿旃陀，梵语"阿谨提那"，意为"无想"而得名（景点名称由来）。最初的佛教石窟始建于公元前2世纪至公元前1世纪，再修于公元5世纪至公元6世纪的笈多时期及之后（建筑起止年代），是印度古代最优秀的绘画、雕塑和壁画，对当时的中国和东南亚佛教石窟有很大影响。1983年联合国教科文组织将其列入《世界遗产名录》（社会定位）。

序列2：主题信息

阿旃陀石窟是印度古代建筑、雕刻和绘画三种艺术结合的范例。游客可欣赏描绘的释迦牟尼佛生平故事和当时印度社会生活和宫廷生活等情景，包括山林、田舍、战争、乐舞以及劳动人民狩猎、畜牧、生产等场面（观赏内容）。

序列3：附加信息

从景区入口到石窟陡峭山路，老年游客可以花费600卢比选择四人抬轿子；景区入口处有水晶销售摊位；售票点旁边有餐厅提供印餐和印式中餐；8—10人有英文导游付费服务；景区存包处设在购物广场;景区门口有观光车服务,15—20卢比(景点的设施与服务)。

阿旃陀石窟的开凿依发展阶段可划分成三个时期,早期佛教石窟、笈多王朝石窟及之后的石窟。年代久远的石窟位于峡谷的正中央,依序往两边扩展,并非以年代顺序排列;每一个石窟前均有一个号显示,这与开凿的年代无关,是从入口开始顺序排列的;共有29窟,9、10、19、26号窟为支提洞(佛殿),其余均为毗可罗洞(僧房)(游览指南/建议)。

游客还可以到石窟对面观景台俯瞰石窟全貌(游览指南/建议)。

游客可以随意拍照,不可以在洞穴内使用闪光灯。所有石窟都必须脱鞋才能进入(游览指南/建议)。

除了带上强光手电外,游览之前可以准备好食品和饮用水(游览指南/建议)。

唐僧玄奘(公元602—664年)在《大唐西域记》(卷十一)中曾概括生动地把阿旃陀石窟的位置、建筑、雕刻、民间传说等记述下来。这些记述现在已成为记载印度阿旃陀石窟最宝贵的古代文献,其壁画是东南亚、中国、日本古代佛教绘画的源流。它存在时期相当于中国魏晋南北朝,但对中国佛教艺术的影响集中反映在唐朝佛教艺术之中(游览指南/建议)。

开放时间:9:00—17:30,星期一休息。

门票价格:500卢比。

交通:从奥兰加巴德到阿旃陀,可以在中心巴士站乘豪华沃尔沃巴士(往返623卢比),大约3小时车程到景区路口。再花15—20卢比乘景区观光车到达石窟。

(二) 重构语篇英语书面语介绍

Resort Introduction of Ajanta Caves in India

Item 1 Background Information

Ajanta Caves is located in the cliff of Wagle River, 104 kilometres northeast of Aurangabad District, Maharashtra State, India (location). It was named for the reason that it started from a small village—Ajanta, whose meaning, in Sanskrit language is "no thinking" (name origin).Early Buddhist caves were constructed from the 2nd century BC to 1st century BC, reconstructed in its second and third phase from the 5th century AD to 6th century AD during and after Gupta period (time). Ajanta Caves had the most outstanding drawing, sculpture and frescoing arts in ancient India, which had a significant influence on the Buddhist caves in China and Southeast Asian countries. Ajanta Caves was listed on the World Heritage Site by UNESCO in 1983 (social status).

Item 2 Topic Information

Ajanta Caves in India is an outstanding example of combining India's ancient buildings, sculptures and painting arts together. You can enjoy the scenes which described the life story of Sakyamuni—the founder of Buddhism, India's social life and court life at that period, including the ones such as mountain forests, farmhouses, wars, music and dance, as well as working people's hunting, raising livestock and producing etc (contents).

Item 3 Additional Information

From the scenic area entrance to the steep hill road, elderly visitors can spend 600 rupees to hire a sedan chair with 4 carrying people. At the scenic area entrance, there are some booths for selling crystals. Next to the ticket office, there is a restaurant of selling India food and Chinese food of India style . Payable English tourist guide service is available for a group of 8-10 people. Baggage Depository is located in Shopping Plaza near the scenic area entrance. At the scenic area entrance, sightseeing coach service is available for 15-20 rupees each (facilities and services).

Ajanta Caves was constructed in three different phases, namely the early Buddhist caves, caves constructed in Gupta period, the caves constructed after Gupta period. The older caves are in the center of the canyon, then the following ones were extended sequentially from the two sides. So their listing sequence was not arranged based on their construction dates. Every cave was given a digital code, but the code is not relevant to the cave's construction date. The order was arranged starting from the entrance. There are 29 caves in all, of which the 9th, 10th, 19th and 26th caves are chaitya (Buddha Halls), and the rest are vihara (Buddhist monks' rooms) (guides/advices).

You can go to the viewing platform opposite to the caves to overlook the whole caves (guides/advices).

You can take photos as you like, but you are not allowed to use flashing light in the caves. You have to take off your shoes before entering the caves (guides/advices).

Apart from taking glare flashlights, you are reminded to get food and drinking water ready before viewing (guides/advices).

Tang Priest Xuanzang (602 - 664AD) once put the caves down in writing. The frescoes in the Ajanta Caves were the original sources of the ancient Buddhist paintings of Southeast Asian counties, China and Japan. The Caves' existent period was equivalent to the period of the Wei and Jin Dynasties, and the Southern and Northern Dynasties in China. However, the influence of Ajanta Caves on Buddhist art in China was mainly reflected in China's Tang Dynasty (guides/advices).

Opening Times: From 9:00 a.m. till 5:30 p.m., with Monday off.

Ticket Prices: 500 rupees.

Transportation: From Aurangabad to Ajanta Caves, luxury Volvo buses are available, departing from the central bus station, with return ticket for 623 rupees. It takes 3 hours to get to the scenic area entrance. At scenic area entrance, you can pay 15 - 20 rupees to take sighting buses to the Caves.

(二) 重构语篇英语口语导游词

Tour Guide Speech of Ajanta Caves in India

Item 1 Background Information

Now, dear friends! Today I will show you around a famous cave-Ajanta Caves. It is located in the cliff of Wagle River, 104 kilometres northeast of Aurangabad District, Maharashtra state, India (location). It got named because it started from a small village—Ajanta. Sounds strange? In Sanskrit language it means "no thinking" (name origin). Early Buddhist caves were constructed from the 2nd and 1st centuries BC, during the Gupta period, to the 5th and 6th centuries AD (time). Ajanta Caves had the most outstanding drawing, sculpture and frescoing arts in ancient India and they had a significant influence on the Buddhist caves in China and Southeast Asian countries. In 1983, Ajanta Caves was listed on the World Heritage Site by UNESCO (social status).

Item 2 Topic Information

Ajanta Caves in India is an outstanding example of combining India's ancient buildings, sculptures and painting arts. You can enjoy many vivid scenes, for example, the life story of Sakyamuni who was the founder of Buddhism, India's social life and court life at that period. Among the scenes, mountain forests, farmhouses, wars, music and dance, as well as working people's hunting, raising livestock and producing etc. are depicted (contents).

Item 3 Additional Information

As the road to the caves is slightly steep, some aid service is available. So from the scenic area entrance to the steep hill road, elderly visitors can just spend 600 rupees to hire a sedan chair with 4 carrying people. At the scenic area entrance, there are some booths for selling crystals. Next to the ticket office, there is a restaurant of selling India food and India style of Chinese food. If you pay, English tourist guide service is available for a group of 8-10 people. So it is convenient for you to have a clear understanding of the sight. Baggage Depository is located in Shopping Plaza near the scenic area entrance. At the scenic area entrance, sightseeing coach service is available for 15-20 rupees each (facilities and services).

According to the stage of its development, the excavation of Ajanta Caves can be divided into three different phases, namely the early Buddhist caves, caves constructed in Gupta period, the caves constructed after Gupta period. Usually the older caves are in the center of the canyon, then the following ones were extended sequentially from the two sides. So their listing sequence was not arranged according to the dates. Every cave is given a digital code, but the code is not relevant to the cave's construction date. The order was arranged starting from the entrance. There are 29 caves in all. The 9th, 10th, 19th and 26th caves are chaityas (Buddha Halls), and the rest are viharas (Buddhist monks' rooms) (guides/advices).

You can go to the viewing platform across from the caves to overlook the whole caves (guides/advices).

Also you can take photos as you like, but you are not allowed to use flashing light in the caves. I have to remind everyone again. All of you have to take off your shoes before entering the caves (guides/advices).

Apart form taking glare flashlights with you, I have to remind you that you should get food and drinking water ready before viewing (guides/advices).

Chinese famous Tang Priest Xuanzang (602-664AD) once put the caves on record. So the frescoes in the Ajanta Caves were the original sources of the ancient Buddhist paintings of southeast Asian counties, China and Japan. The Caves' existent period was equivalent to the period of the Wei and Jin Dynasties, and the Southern and Northern Dynasties in China. However, the influence of Ajanta Caves on Buddhist art in China was mainly reflected in China's Tang Dynasty (guides/advices).

The grottoes open from 9∶00 a. m. till 5∶30 p. m. during the whole week except Monday. Tickets are 500 rupees. From Aurangabad to Ajanta Caves, luxury Volvo buses are available, departing from the central bus station, with return ticket for 623 rupees. It takes 3 hours to get to the scenic area entrance. At scenic area entrance, you can pay 15-20 rupees to take sighting buses to the Caves.

第四节　基于翻译语境和语篇理论的解释性译文质量评估

天水旅游文化翻译不仅数量少、翻译质量低下而且缺少依据连贯方法论施行的系统翻译活动，更缺少一个译文质量的客观评估体系。在针对译文评估、翻译方法论构建等问题的应用翻译研究领域，尽管有朱莉安·豪斯的功能主义语言学模式[1]，但这些模式关注的仅是译文的语言特征，并未论及影响、制约翻译策略选择的翻译语境问题，同时其操作性也不强。系统功能语言学认为，在构成使用语言的情景语境的各个要素里，只有三个因素对语言的使用产生直接和重要的影响。[2] 即语场、语旨和语式三个语域变量，对于使用语言时如何选择语言形式有着直接的、至关重要的影响。本书运用韩礼德功能语言学的语域理论对天水石窟文化及"一带一路"沿线国家石窟文化源文与译文从语场、语旨、语式三方面进行对比分析，客观和具体地评判翻译文本的质量。

一　语场对比分析

语场是关于言语活动的主题或焦点。根据这一情景参数，语用

---

[1] Juliane House, *Translation Quality Assessment: A Model Revisited*, Tübingen: Gunter Narr Verlag, 1997, pp.1-23.

[2] 司显柱：《功能语言学与翻译研究——翻译质量评估模式建构》，北京大学出版社2007年版，第6—9页。

场景一般分为技术场景和日常场景两类，不同场景的语言表现出各自不同的特征。十一组语料分别来自天水麦积山石窟、天水仙人崖石窟、甘谷大像山石窟、甘谷华盖寺石窟、武山水帘洞石窟、武山木梯寺石窟、柬埔寨吴哥石窟、印度尼西亚婆罗浮屠石、斯里兰卡丹布勒石窟寺、斯里兰卡锡吉里耶狮子岩、印度阿旃陀石窟。就语场参数而言，采用哈蒂姆和梅森的语篇分析法①重构源语语境为背景信息、主题信息和附加信息，与英国旅游网站的语篇结构相比，两者显示出相同的语言特征。重构语篇的主题都相同，都是对景点进行描述和宣传，普遍使用日常用语、标准句法，向潜在的游客提供旅游景点的三类基本信息：包括景点位置、名称由来、起止年代和社会地位等背景信息；观赏内容等主体信息；景点设施与服务、游览指南或建议、气候、当地风土人情、旅游特色项目、开放时间、门票、交通等附加信息。两者均属于呼唤型文本，描述旅游体验，目的都是吸引潜在游客来旅游。

从十一组重构语境语料可以看出，天水石窟文化及"一带一路"沿线国家石窟文化语场特征是相同的。旅游景点的描写都使用日常用语而非技术用语，避免生涩难懂，便于读者阅读，有利于对景点进行宣传介绍。描写多使用标准句法和过程动词。

二 语旨对比分析

语旨是反映言语交际行为的双方，在权势关系、接触密度和亲切程度等方面的情景参数，主要用来区分正式和非正式情景两类。非正式情景中，交际双方一般地位平等，经常见面，关系亲密，语言上常用带有感情色彩的词语、口头用语，使用典型语气；而正式情景里，交际者之间在权势方面是不对等的，接触稀少，关系疏远，语言在形

---

① Basil Hatim and Ian Mason, *Discourse and the Translator*, Shanghai: Shanghai Foreign Language Education Press, 2001, p. 223.

式上，多使用中性词语、正式用语和非常规语气。① 就语旨参数而言，天水石窟文化及"一带一路"沿线国家石窟文化在语旨方面的评价潜势都较强，在态度资源的利用上都倾向于"鉴赏资源"，在情感资源方面均以"你指向"情感为主。例句如下：

（1）源语：华盖寺石窟……是甘谷县保存最完好的石窟，是天水百里石窟走廊的重要组成部分。

译语：The Canopy Temple Grottoes is the best reserved cave in Gangu County, and is also an important part of the "Tianshui Baili" Grottoes Corridor.

语料多使用夸张的和具有劝导性的词汇如"保存最完好的"（the best reserved）、"重要组成部分"（an important part）并结合鉴赏性词汇"famous""beautiful"等。

（2）源语：在天水麦积区火车站前搭乘34路麦积山旅游专线车，车程约1小时，每7分钟即有一趟。可以在大门口购买门票时再买10元的观光车费用（单程）送到离石窟很近的地方，也可以徒步30分钟缓坡到达。

译语：Take Maiji Mountain's special tourist bus No. 34 at Tianshui Maiji rail station, with 1 hour drive, buses going every 7 minutes. You can pay RMB 10 extraly to buy a single ticket for sight-seeing bus when you buy your admission tickets. By the sight-seeing bus, you can be taken to the place very close to the caves. It takes 30 minutes' walk to there through a gently sloping road.

多用祈使句来实现呼唤功能。游客直接从祈使句的核心动词成分开始理解，按照不同的句子语境去体会祈使句的功能指向，更能成功完成交际目的。

（3）源语：石窟完全被雕凿在悬崖绝壁上，游客必须攀爬悬空栈

---

① Suzanne Eggins, *An Introduction to Systemic Functional Linguistics*, London: Pinter, 1994, p. 78.

道才能参观,可以带手电筒看壁画。

译语:As the rock caves were completely carved in a cliff, you have to climb the suspended plank road for your visiting. You are allowed to take electric torches with you to view frescoes.

汉语为主动语态可译作被动语态。源语中的词类、句型和语态等进行转换使译文更符合目标语的表述方式、方法和习惯。

(4)源语:裸露的崖壁也是游客经常觅奇的景点之一。最宏伟壮观的是由"五峰"和罗汉沟群峰共同构成的"十八罗汉朝玉帝"的景象。其景象的具体构成为:东、西峰和玉皇峰三峰参列,玉皇峰处于正中;宝盖峰和献珠峰与三峰比列,宛若仙童侍立;另有罗汉沟的群峰似具若揖若拜之势,故有"十八罗汉朝玉帝"之美称。

译语:The exposed cliffs are also one of the scenic sites where tourists often seek marvelous spectacles. The most magnificent and spectacular one is the sight called "Eighteen Arhats worship the Jade Emperor", which was presented by five peaks and a group of peaks in Arhat Ravine as follows. The three peaks (the East, the West and the Jade Emperor) participate in the parade with the last one being in the right center, accompanied by Baogai Peak and Xianzhu Peak as their side parade, seemingly like fair-children standing and waiting for the Emperor. While other peaks in the Arhat Ravine facing the Jade Emperor Peak are in bowing-like posture and worshiping-like posture, which therefore was enjoyed this laudatory reputation—"Eighteen Arhats worship the Jade Emperor".

从态度资源上看,十一组语料多使用名词、代词、过程动词、数字等来描述景点。分清主从句进行组合,根据需要利用连词、分词、介词、不定式、定语从句、独立结构等把汉语短句连成长句。

(5)源语:"麦积烟雨"是麦积山石窟的一景。麦积山海拔1617米,在下雨天您能见到麦积山"头顶戴帽子"的美景。

译语:"The Misty Rain of Maiji Mountain" is a scene of the Maiji Mountain Grottoes. The mountain is 1617 metres above sea level, so, on a rainy day, you can enjoy the extremely beautiful scenery of the mountain like wearing a hat on its top.

"你指向"的大量使用增强了文本的对话性,十一组语料多把"您"用作主位,让读者直接参与对话中。描写也更加直白、简单。

三 语式对比分析

语式是描述语言与情景在空间和人际距离方面关系的参数。据埃金斯,这一情景变量主要用来区分口语和书面语的言语特征。口语依赖语境,句子结构松散、动态,使用日常词汇,句子的语法不标准,词汇化密度低。书面语不依赖语境,多使用纲要式结构的句子,使用"声望"词汇,句子语法标准,词汇化密度高。当然,这是对位于语式连续体两极,即典型口语和书面语言辞特征的概括,而实际话语中的多数是介于两极之间,也就是说往往既有口语体又有书面语体特征,差异只是多寡大小而已,即混合语体。① 示例如下。

源语:仙人崖有许多关于仙人的传说,游客游览时可以在天然景观中寻觅。相传南崖燃灯阁有天然仙灯,每当夏秋深夜,天然磷光与阁中的油灯和烛光浮动辉映,人传是神仙携灯往来,故有"仙人送灯"之说。

书面语介绍:There are many immortal related legends as to the Immortal Cliff Grottoes, which you can search from the natural landscapes. It was said that there were some natural immortal lanterns in a burning pavilion of the South Cliff, where natural phosphorescence, the oil burning lanterns and candle light in the pavilion would shine floatingly with addition to each other's splendor, which referred to the immortals "coming and going" each with a lantern in a hand based on the legend, which is so called "Immorzals have brought lanterns" (guides/advices).

---

① Suzanne Eggins, *An Introduction of Systemic Functional Linguistics*, London: Pinter, 1994, p. 78.

口语导游词：There are many legends related to the immortals. So you can find them in the natural landscapes. The saying goes that there were some natural immortal lanterns in a burning pavilion of the south cliff, where natural phosphorescence, the oil burning lanterns and candle light in the pavilion would shine closely. Based on the legend, people say that it is the immortals "coming and going" each with a lantern in a hand. So it enjoys the fame "Immortals have brought lanterns".

十一组语料均是介于口语和书面语两极之间的混合语体，既包含口语特点又包含书面语特点。汉语重构语境的口语倾向通过英语书面语介绍和口语导游词转换更加清晰。

十一组语料中除了"显圣池石窟群""摸子泉""仙人送灯"等少数短语的翻译属于隐性翻译之外，基本上是属于显性翻译的语篇。虽然通过分析发现，语篇中出现了少数的信息不匹配和错误，但是正如豪斯在其翻译评估模式的阐释中指出的，"少数的不匹配与错误的出现是不可避免的"①。因此，十一组语料的译文中的不匹配现象不会影响语篇的概念功能、人际功能及语篇的质量。

---

① Juliane House, *Translation Quality Assessment: A Model Revisited*, Tübingen: Gunter Narr Verlag, 1997, pp. 1-23.

主要参考文献

Basil Hatim and Ian Mason, *Discourse and the Translator*, Shanghai: Shanghai Foreign Language Education Press, 2001.

Bronislaw Malinowski, "The Problem of Meaning in Primitive Languages", In C. K. Ogden and I. A. Richards (eds.) *The Meaning of Meaning*, London: Rout-ledge and Kegan Paul, 1923.

Juliane House, *Translation Quality Assessment: A Model Revisited*, Tübingen: Gunter Narr Verlag, 1997.

John Rupert Firth, "Personality and Language in Society", *The Sociological Review*, Vol. a 42, No. 1, January 1950.

M. A. K. Halliday and Ruqaiya Hasan, *Cohesion in English*, London: Longman Group Ltd., 1976.

Pauline Robinson, *ESP (English for Specific Purposes)*, Oxford: Pergamon Press, 1980.

Suzanne Eggins, *An Introduction to Systemic Functional Linguistics*, London: Pinter, 1994.

董广强等:《石窟走廊》,《文化天水》2006年12月18日。

侯维瑞编:《英语语体》,上海外语教育出版社1988年版。

(晋)皇甫谧:《帝王世纪》,辽宁教育出版社1997年版。

廖七一等编:《当代英国翻译理论》,湖北教育出版社2001年版。

刘雁翔等:《天水伏羲文化资源及旅游开发论析》,《天水师范学院学报》2006年第4期。

刘雁翔:《天水三国遗迹丛考》,《天水师范学院学报》2004年第

4 期。

徐日辉：《三国文化与天水旅游经济发展研究》，《天水师专学报》1996 年第 1 期。

萧易：《甘肃石窟——佛从西来相自东传》，2015 年 10 月，国家地理中文网（http：//www.nationalgeographic.com.cn/science/archaeology/4328.html）。

司显柱：《功能语言学与翻译研究——翻译质量评估模式建构》，北京大学出版社 2007 年版。

王洪宾总编：《天水市志》（下卷），方志出版社 2004 年版。

杨仲杰：《天水旅游景点分布及发展规划的基础研究》，《甘肃科技纵横》2005 年第 3 期。

雍际春：《秦文化与秦早期文化概念新探》，《西安财经学院学报》2007 年第 4 期。

雍际春：《论天水秦文化的形成及其特点》，《天水师范学院学报》2000 年第 4 期。

王宗光：《甘肃石窟文化综述》，《西北民族学院学报》（哲学社会科学版）2002 年第 4 期。

附 录

天水"五大文化"补充英语语料

(一) 天水伏羲文化

1. Fuxi Temple

The Fuxi Temple, originally named the Taihao Temple, is popularly called the Renzong Temple. Located in the Fuxi Road, West Pass of the city proper of Tianshui Municipality, it is one of the state-preserved key cultural relics announced by the State Council in 2001.

Fuxi is the first of the legendary Three Sovereigns. A story is going around that Fuxi had a snake's body and a man's head and was born in Chengji of Longxi. The ancient Chengji had a very vast area and its center was in the area under today's Tianshui municipality's jurisdiction, so the City of Tianshui is always called "Hometown of Legendary Ruler Fuxi". As a great tribe head, his main contributions are—firstly drawing the Eight Trigrams (eight combinations of three whole or broken lines formerly used in divination), inventing tools of fishing and hunting, working out the rites of marriages, establishing the calendar, producing characters, drilling wood to make fire and making *qin* (a seven-stringed plucked instrument in some ways similar to the zither) to play music. So Fuxi is always looked upon as the human ancestor. Among the people he is popularly named "Ren Zong Ye", which is a worshipper's form of address for "the human ancestor".

The Fuxi Temple was firstly constructed in the year of Chenghua 19 of Emperor Xianzong in the Ming Dynasty (that is 1483 AD). It has been reconstructed 9 times and has formed the broad building complex. After the ninth reconstruction in the 11th to 13th year of Emperor Guangxu of the Qing Dynasty (1885 – 1887 AD), it covered an area of 13,000 square metres. The existing area now is 6,600 square meters. There are 76 old and new rooms altogether. The whole building complex faces south. Such ancient buildings as the memorial archway, the entrance door, the inner gate, the Xiantian Hall and the Tai Ji (the Supreme Ultimate, the Absolute in ancient Chinese cosmology, presented as the primary source of all created things) Halls are arranged along the vertical south-north axis in proper order, solemnly and magnificently. There are four rows of houses and four yards, connecting one and another, high, deep and remotely. And wing rooms and the corridor housing stone tablets are symmetrically distributed along the lateral axis, having distinctive Chinese traditional architectural style. There were originally 64 dark green cypresses in the Fuxi Temple, which were planted according to the Sixty-four Hexagrams. Now there are only 37 sturdy, tall and straight cypresses. Their thick foliage seems to blot out the sun. Since Fuxi is the first sovereign that the ancient time said, the building complex appears the model of palatial architecture.

The Xiantian Hall is the main building of the Fuxi Temple building complex, which is located right in the middle of the back of the middle yard. In the Hall the holy statue of Fuxi is more than 3 metres tall, the whole body is yellow, green leaves like scales drape over his shoulders, his hand holds the Eight Trigrams on the open palm, and two feet step on the raised grain. The whole statue is tall and strong in posture and appears wise, bright and touching.

In the Fuxi Temple there are 17 ancient tablets, 4 newly-built tablets. The tablet inscriptions are mainly written by famous local officials or well-known calligraphers. Many horizontal inscribed boards hung on the halls such as "*yutiandizhun* (Fuxi is level with the heaven and the earth)", "*kaitianmingdao* (creating heaven and making people know the Tao)", "*yihuakaitian* (the Eight Trigrams make the civilization come into being)", "*kaitianliji* (creating heaven and making norms)", "*wenmingzhaoqi* (the beginning of the civilization)", "*daoqihongmeng* (the Tao makes the people shake off the ignorance)" and "*xiangtianfadi* (taking the heaven as standards and the earth law)" etc. are brief in writing and profound in meaning, directly pointing to the old and mysterious fountain of the Chinese traditional culture.

In recent years, on each birthday of Fuxi on the sixteenth of the lunar January and the birthday of the dragon on the thirteenth of the lunar May, the local government will hold holy and solemn public memorial ceremony in big scale in the Fuxi Temple. Now the activity has formed a characteristic brand of the tourist culture and is attracting numerous home and overseas Chinese to come to the City of Tianshui to seek their ancestors, searching for the source of the Chinese civilization.

Fuxi Temple, also called Taihao Gong, is the biggest of its kind in China in memory of a legendary figure named Fuxi who is known as the ancestor and a great sovereign in many Chinese legends. Fuxi was said to be half human and half snake. The snake was a popular totem of the time and is the origin of the dragon. In addition, Fuxi was born here in Tianshui and that's why we have a temple for him here. The temple is a Ming Dynasty's construction that, despite renovations in the Qing Dynasty, still retains its basic Ming format. The temple was completed in 1490 AD during the reign of Emperor Hongzhi of the Ming Dynasty, and covers a total area of 6000 square metres.

Facing the street, the temple consists of three rows of buildings with two temple gates, ranging from south to north include the Archway, Moon Terrace, Tablet Tower, Main Hall and other buildings. The buildings are symmetrically laid out in regular order. The Main Hall is named the Xiantian Hall. In the middle of it sits the statue of Fuxi. On his right is a queerly shaped dragon-horse with wings, which is about to fly while on the left is an eight Trigram's carried by the dragon-horse to come out from the river. Legend has it that his acute observation of nature inspired him to come up with eight Trigrams that were believed to explain all the laws of the world. But apart from being a philosopher, Fuxi was also a great inventor. It's said Fuxi developed the net, allowing people to catch fish and wild animals. It's also about this time that the domestication of animals takes place. Fuxi was obviously a busy man. The list of his achievements goes on and his reign marked the dawn of civilization for the people of the time. But his most incredible claim to fame is his legendary status as the ancestor of the Chinese people. He apparently married his own sister Nvwa and started populating the planet. What Nvwa couldn't produce herself, she made from clay. It's really difficult for people today to understand the legend of a brother-sister marriage. Actually a lot of folklore has a strong cultural background. Fuxi and Nvwa were not real people. We believe they are the names of two ancient Chinese tribes. Fuxi-Nvwa account reflects the earliest form of marriage in human society—marriage between brothers and sisters. At that time, there were actually such unions. It's a roundabout reflection and a mysterious interpretation of time.

  Sixty-four cypress trees used to grow in the temple's courtyard. Now there are just 37 left. They were planted according to points dictated by the Eight Trigrams. Many local people still believe these old trees have the power to cure and heal. Actually the idea of old trees having supernatural powers is a common theme in Chinese superstition, so it's easy to understand that these trees have earned this reputation. Every 16th of the first month in the lunar calendar is said to be the birthday of Fuxi, and on that day, people in Tianshui come here one after another to pay homage to him, the ancestor of the Chinese nation.

2. Nanguo Temple

Nanguo Temple is located in the Huiyin cols about 2 kilometres to the south of Tianshui City with the Xi River before it and green hills behind. Nanguo Temple has become one of the most famous sites in the city not only for its beauty and quietness but also because of the scholar trees of the Tang Dynasty and Chinese cypresses of the Han Dynasty, and also because of great poet Dufu visited it and wrote a poem about it.

No exact historical material proves when Nanguo Temple was built. But we know it was first built in the Sui Dynasty. In 759 AD of the Tang Dynasty the sage poet once visited the Temple and wrote the lines:

On the hill stands the Nanguo Temple,

the Spring named Beiliu winds down.

In the courtyard grow old trees,

below the hill flows the famous Spring.

Under the big stones bloom autumn flowers,

evening glow shines upon the bell.

Hardly can I restrain thinking from the sad life,

chilly wind blows to the accompaniment of the dreary future.

The Sage poet's eulogy to the Temple adds rich historical humanity to the spot.

In the Song Dynasty the Temple was named Miaoshengyuan. In the fifteen year reign of Emperor Qianlong in the Qing Dynasty (1750 AD) the Emperor gave it the name "the Temple of Guarding the Country".

The most recent buildings in the Temple were built in the Qing Dynasty and have been kept intact. In the center of the Temple there are three memorial archways which link three courtyards—the west, middle and the east courtyards.

The middle courtyard consists of two parts, the front and rear countyards. In the rear courtyard there are east and west watching towers, the bell and drum tower and the east and west temples. In the years of Emperor Guangxu's reign (1875 – 1908 AD) to memorialize the great poet Dufu, the east temple was rebuilt as Du Shaoling Temple where the statue of Dufu is enshrined. In the rear courtyard are the Tianwang Temple and two temples on its sides. In the east courtyard are the Guanshen Temple, Qinchi Temple, Guanyi Temple and Shengmu Temple. In front of the Guanyi Temple is a well in which the constant supply of water is clean and sweet. So the well got the name "the well of Spirit", namely Beiliu Spring in Dufu's poem. In recent years two other sights have been added to Nanguo Temple. They are the stele of Ermiaoxuan (two wonderful things combined together) inside and the memorial pavilion of General Dengbaoshan outside the monastery.

The old cypress on the south mountain is one of the eight scenes which have been in Qinzhou since ancient times. The most beautiful scene of Nanguo Temple is this old tree. In front of the west memorial archway there are two old scholar trees, which are about 25 metres high and 6.8 metres round. The leaves of the trees are very exuberant and they are over 1000 years old. Their popular names are scholar trees of the Tang Dynasty. In the east of the courtyard of the old cypress is about 2300–2500 years old. Its local name is cypress of spring and autumn, namely the old tree in Dufu's poem. The most surprising thing is that the cypress holds a parasitic Chinese hackberry in its branches. This tree and the other two trees—an euonymus and an old scholar tree whose shape on the top is like a dragon claw are all three uniques.

Recently, the local government has decided to build a forest garden around Nanguo Temple and the whole Huiyin Mountain. Now it has been on a scale. Nanguo Temple is surrounded with green trees almost all the year round and the air here is very fresh. Looking from the mountain, the whole city is in a clear sight. The Temple has become an ideal place for people to yearn for old times and enjoy quietness, and it is also an ideal place to spend free time and foster one's pleasant feelings and reasonable character.

The Stele of Ermiaoxuan

It's in the east courtyard of Nanguo Monastery. Sculptors who copied great calligraphers—Wang Xizhi and others' calligraphy—sculptured the great poet Dufu's poems on a stele. Both the great calligrapher's calligraphy and the great poet's poems are combined together, for which it's named "Ermiao".

During the thirteen year regime of Emperor Shunzhi in the Qing Dynasty (1656 AD), a great poet Songwan contributed some money to repair Dufu's hall in Yuquan Temple and engaged Zhang Zhenyan, and Zhang Zhenxin who were good at copying great calligrapher Wang Xizhi's calligraphy and sculpturing Dufu's poems on 36 steles, and then built a pavilion in which the steles were put on display. But we don't know why the steles were missing only after one hundred years. In the 1990's Mr. Zhouheng donated the book of rubbings of Dufu's poems, which he collected and kept for a long time in his hometown. The book of the roll is 0.24 metres wide and 15.16 metres long. At the beginning is the statue of Dufu and Songwan's praises on the statue which were written in Lishu, an ancient style of calligraphy current in the Han Dynasty (BC 206-AD 220), and then the main body of the book in which were collected Dufu's 60 poems written in Gansu. The last part of the book is postscripts of Dang Chongya and another five persons and "postscript of Dufu's poems sculptured on steles" written by Songwan.

In 1998 the department concerned of the city chose a place in Nanguo Temple and built a corridor of "Ermiao". The stele, 35.6 metres long and 4.36 metres high appears refined and grand. The style of calligraphy is either Kaishu (regular script) or Caoshu (characters executed swiftly and with strokes flowing together). The strength when writing with a brush matches well the layout of Chinese characters, as if alive and are full of vitality.

Now there are 117 protected poems by Dufu in Gansu, half of which were sculptured by Songwan' men, so the sculpture on the stele is very valuable for studying calligraphy and Dufu. Beside the corridor the statue of Dufu was built as a memorial.

In the spring of 2002, when buildings were under construction in Wenmiao (a market in Tianshui City), the builders dug up a stele of varied poems by Dufu on which 40 poems were sculptured.

The stele is 2 metres high and 1 metre wide. Now stands beside the stele of "Ermiaoxuan". The stele built in the nineteenth year of Chenghua in the Ming Dynasty (1483 AD) is 170 years earlier than that of Songwan and shines more brilliantly in the other's company. It provides new and valuable material for studying Dufu.

3. Yuquan Taoist Temple

The Yuquan Taoist Temple is located at the foot of Tianjing Mountain to the north of Tianshui City. It is the center of the Taoism activities in the area of Tianshui. The Yuquan Taoist Temple, also named the Jade Spring Taoist Temple, is so named because in it there is a spring whose water is cool, sweet, blue and transparent. It is 1 kilometre from the central square of Tianshui Municipality. It overlooks the Qinzhou District to the south and to the north of it are green hills. In the Yuquan Taoist Temple, there are many beautiful buildings, ancient trees and dark green cypresses. And it is one of the eight famous scenic spots in Qinzhou for the Immortals Cave in the Yuquan Taoist Temple.

The Yuquan Taoist Temple was firstly constructed in the year of Zhiyuan 13 of the Yuan Dynasty (1276 AD). It is recorded that Liang Zhitong, the disciple of Qiu Chuji, a Taoist priest of Quan Chen Tao, wandered about the country and came to Tianshui. He adored the peace of the

Tianjing Mountain, so he constructed the Taoist temple to achieve the true peace of mind. This is the beginning of the construction of the Yuquan Taoist Temple. In Dynasty of Yuan, Ming and Qing, there were new buildings constructed in it. To the end of the Qing Dynasty, it had formed a huge Taoist building complex with over 80 buildings. At that time, temples, pavilions, bridges, towers, caves and memorial archways were all situated at the foot of the mountain and made use of the mountain momentum, ingeniously scattered on hills and streams. In the several tens of years since the end of the Qing Dynasty, more than half ancient buildings were damaged and destroyed. In 1981, the local government organized labor power to make the overall repair of it. The present Temple is the result of that repair.

The building complex of the Yuquan Taoist Temple is scattered from the foot of the mountain to the half-mountain. There are dozens of halls, temples, caves, gates and bridges. These buildings go up along the neat stone steps. They are in proper sequence the Tongxian Bridge, the Taiyang (the Sun) Temple, the Qinglong (Blue Dragon) Hall, the Baihu (White Tiger) Hall, the Yuhuang (Jade Emperor) Hall and the Sanqing Hall. On the two sides of the central axis, there are the Gaozu Temple, the Sanguan (Three Officials) Hall, the Li Du (Li Bai and Du Fu, two greatest poets in the Tang Dynasty) Memorial Temple, the Cang Jie Palace, the Wenshu Hall, the Wenchang Palace, the Beidou (the Big Dipper) Palace, the Yuquan (Jade Spring) Pavilion, the Sangong Ancestral Temple, the Tianjing Tower and the Xuansheng Pavilion, etc. Among them especially the Yuhuang (Jade Emperor) Hall, the Sanqing Hall and the Xuansheng Pavilion are the most magnificent.

The Yuhuang (Jade Emperor) Hall is the central building of the Yuquan Taoist Temple. It is located inside the pailou (decorated archway) with four posts and three doors. Its horizontal is "*renjiantianshang* (the heaven on earth)". The hall was constructed in the year of Zhiyuan 26

(1289 AD). In the Dynasties of Ming and Qing, it was rebuilt. Now it still has the architectural style of the Ming Dynasty. The main hall is covered with green tiles on the roof. Its ridge is built with brown tiles. On the main ridge are dragons. In the middle of it there is a precious vase. In the hall the statue of the Jade Emperor is enshrined.

Going up from the Jade Emperor Hall, you can reach the highest building of the Yuquan Taoist Temple, the Sanqing Hall. The Sanqing Hall is so named because in the hall the highest gods of the Taoism are enshrined. They are the Yuanshi Supernatural being, the Lingbao Supernatural being and the Daode Supernatural being (Most Exalted Lord Lao, a Taoist deity, identified with Lao Zi). It was established in the year of Zhiyuan 13 of the Yuan Dynasty (1276 AD). In the Dynasties of Ming and Qing, it was rebuilt. The main hall has a double-eaved saddle roof. Its three sides are surrounded with 16 huge crimson posts. Its frame is magnificent. On the front of the hall hung the antithetical couplet written by the famous scholar Mr. Huo Songlin:

The Jasper Hall relying on Sanqing, the one gave birth successively to two things, three things, up to ten thousand (i. e. everything);

The Jade Spring penetrating the subtlety of the Taoism, the ways of earth are conditioned by those of heaven, the ways of heaven by those of Tao, and the way of Tao by the Self-so.

At the northwest corner of the Yuquan Taoist Temple is the Beidou (the Big Dipper) Tower. Going down from the tower along the stone path, you can reach "the Jade Spring". On the spring there is a pavilion with an octagonal pinnacle, commonly called "the Bagua (the Eight Trigrams) Pavilion". The spring has a long time. Its water is not dry all the year around. It had already been recorded in the Yuan Dynasty.

The Yuquan Taoist Temple has many cultural relics and historic sites that are rich in historic value. The tetrahedral *daoliu* (the spreading order of

Taoism) tablet of the Yuan Dynasty now is in the Xuansheng Pavilion. On four sides of the tablet there are characters, which record and narrate matters of the Quan Zhen Tao of the Taoism. Up to now these characters have gone through more than 700 years, but scripts are still clear as they were. The tablets with poems written by Zhao Mengfu are now in the corridor of tablets with poems. There are 4 tablets in all (one of them is incomplete now). On them are 4 *wuyanjueju* (a poem of four lines, each containing of five characters with a strict tonal pattern and rhyme scheme) written by poets of the Tang Dynasty. Zhao Mengfu, the great calligrapher of the Yuan Dynasty, wrote these 4 *wuyanjueju* on tablets. The scripts alternate with running hand and grass scripts, and the technique of calligraphy is mellow and full. These calligraphy is natural, beautiful, smooth, moving and forceful, which are treasures seldom seen all over the country. Now there are 50 ancient and valuable trees, of which more than 10 are ancient cypresses being more than 1,000 years old. These 10 are all valuable fragrant cypresses.

On each ninth of the lunar January, the Yuquan Taoist Temple will hold the temple fair, which is called "making a pilgrimage to the temple". The temple fair has now become an important mass activity famous in Gansu Province.

4. Hu's Folk Residences

The Hu's Folk Residences, also named the Southern and Northern Residences, are situated on the Minzhu Road, the central street of the city proper. The Residences are located on the north and south of the road, the street in the middle. The Residences are the mansions of Hu Laijin and Hu Xin, who were "father-son country worthies" of the Ming Dynasty. In 2001 the State Council announced them the unit of state-preserved key cultural relics.

Hu Laijin, styled himself Zhongzhang, also known by his literary name Dongquan ("Eastern Spring"), is a native of Qinzhou of the Ming

Dynasty. He was a *juren* (a successful candidate in the imperial examinations at the provincial level in the Ming and Qing Dynasties) of the provincial examination (under the Ming-Qing civil service examination system, the examination for the selection of *juren* out of *xiucai*, held triennially in the various provincial capitals) in the year of Jiajing's reign of the Ming Dynasty (1558 AD). In the capacity of *juren*, he was promoted to the county magistrate of Daxing County. During his tenure of office, he was honest in performing his official duties, not fear power and influence, fair in meeting out rewards and punishments, and won the love of all the people. Later, he successively held some official posts of the Guizhou and Shanxi Provinces, etc. After he died of illness, he was imperially mandated Zhongxiandafu (a senior official in feudal China). His statue was put in the country worthy memorial temple to solemnly offer sacrifices. The Southern Residence is the residence of Hu Laijin, which was built in the years of Jiajing to Longqing of the Ming Dynasty (1522-1567 AD). The residence facing north, is a compound with houses around a square courtyard and has three rows of houses. The gate is supported by two posts and has a gabled roof. On it there are three big vigorous and forcible characters— "*Fuxiandi* (the mansion of an official posted as *Fuxian*) ". Inside the gate there are a small yard and a screen wall. In the east and west there is a festoon gate. Entering into the gate, you can see a *siheyuan* (a compound with houses around a square courtyard). In the east and west there are wing-rooms, in the south five main halls. These rooms have single eaves and suspension roofs. In the north there are five rooms. In the southwestern corner there is a small door. Entering into the door, you can see another small *siheyuan*. Here is a family hall for worshipping Buddha, a study and a drawing room.

Hu Xin is the son of Hu Laijin. He was a *jinshi* (a successful candidate in the highest imperial examinations) in the 17th year of Emperor Wanli's reign of the Ming Dynasty (1589 AD). At first he was posted the head of the

Linfen County of the Shanxi Province. Later because of his official achievements he was promoted to higher posts. He had frankly memorialized the emperor for many times, winning the praise of "Northern Hai Rui (an ancient official in the Ming Dynasty famous for frank memorialization)". He wrote a book named *Yufencao*, in which he made every effort to state the ills of the times. The Northern Residence, his residence, was built in the year of Wanli 43 of the Ming Dynasty (1615 AD). It is square. Its gate faces the main street. Outside the gate stand two stone lions. Inside the gate there is a screen wall. The whole residence is made up of 6 *sanheyuans* (a compound with houses around a courtyard except the front) and *siheyuans* of varying sizes. The hall tower in the main hall in the second eastern yard is the main building. The hall tower is five rooms wide and three rooms deep. With the post and panel structure, it has double-eaved roof, which is two-storied, and has a gabled roof. It is magnificent and gorgeous. At present the Southern and Northern Residences are the folk residences of the Ming Dynasty which are most completely preserved in Tianshui Municipality. It has relatively high research value of the architectural art.

5. Guatai Hill

The Guatai Hill, also called Guatai, Xitai and Xihuangtai etc., is situated in the west of the Weinan Township of the Maiji District. It is around 30 kilometres away from Tianshui Municipality. "Guatai of Fuxi" is one of the ten famous scenic spots in Qinzhou.

The Guatai Hill is 1,363 metres above the sea level. The relative altitude is 170 metres. It is the remained terrace because of the long-term erosion of the Wei River to the bedrocks. On the northern side rocks are exposed, while on the southern side the hill is covered with the loess. Its shape is like a dragon's head, towering, tall and straight. The Wei River is come from the west. In the Sanyang Plain it winds its way to the east. It forms a huge "S" shape between the Guatai Hill and the Horse Mouth Hill in the eastern narrow. The southern and northern mountains are out-bow-shaped, like embraced, also like shut. The whole Sanyang Plain is like a giant Trigram of the Supreme Ultimate (consisting of a wavy or double curved line bisecting a circle, one half of which is white and the other black). The dividing line of *yin* and *yang* (in Chinese philosophy, the two opposing principles in nature, the formeris feminine and negative, the latter is masculine and positive) is the Wei River. The peculiar geographic terrain is completely identical with the Eight Trigrams. It is said that on the terrace Fuxi, taking a broad view of the Sanyang Plain, realized the Eight Trigrams.

According to the textual research, in the period of the Yangshao Culture (a Neolithic culture characterized by a fine painted pottery; named after Yangshao, Henan Province, where remains were first found in 1921). 5000-7000 years ago, the Guatai Hill area was a region where people of a certain ethnic group live in compact communities, where ancients labored and lived. In the Sui Dynasty a temple was built on the Guatai Hill (at that time it was called Bailu Hill—White Deer Hill, because on the hill deer were always seen). In the Song Dynasty, a fortress was built. In the Jin Dynasty a monastery was built and for a time it was the center of the activities that were held to offer sacrifices to Fuxi. Although in the Dynasties of Ming and Qing the Guatai Hill was sometimes restored, sometimes abolished, it always had many worshippers and was the sacred hill in the mind of the common people. During the Great Proletarian Cultural Revolution (1966-1977 AD), the buildings in the temple were all destroyed. Since the eighties of the twentieth century, the Fuxi Temple on the Guatai Hill has been rebuilt. Such buildings as the Xiantian Hall, the Wumen Gate, the east and west wing rooms and the Clock and Drum Tower, etc. were successively built.

The wonder of the Guatai Hill lies in the spirit of Fuxi and the scenery of the Sanyang Plain. Standing on the Guatai Hill, you can look as far as your eyes can see and give free rein to your thoughts and feelings, reaching the end of the amusement of seeing and hearing. The Sanyang Plain, where the Guatai Hill is, is a long ring-like plain, which is about 30 kilometres long. Its vastness and richness is rare in the area of the central and south of the Gansu Province. In the area of the plain there are three townships of the Maiji District: the Weinan Township, the Zhongtan Township and the Shifo Township. Many villages and households are densely scattered on the two banks of the Wei River. Since the ancient times, "The Autumn Sound of the Wei River" is one of the eight famous scenic spots in Qinzhou. The best observation point of the grand and beautiful scenery is the Guatai Hill. In autumn, you can climb on the Guatai Hill, hearing the autumn sound of the Wei River, seeing the mountains and the river, thinking the great virtues and the holy behavior of Fuxi, showing the reflections on the things from ancient to modern times.

Facing the Guatai Hill across the river, there is a Dragon Horse Cave. The Cave is deep and in it there is a gurgling spring. The cave appears cool and distant. When it has dense fog, the cloud and mist is full of the cave, giving the people the illusion of the Dragon Horse haunting. At the border of the Wei River and the beach ahead to the side of the Guatai Hill, there is a big stone. The big stone is about 5 metres wide and 6 metres high. The outside of the stone is solid and the inside is empty. It is not square or not round. It is like a post and also like a bamboo shoot. When the water rises, the torrent washes the stone and the trace of the stone goes into hiding, and the water splashes in all directions. When the water falling, the stone coming out from the water, the setting sun shining on the stone, the lights of five colors appearing, it is just like the original Trigram of the Supreme Ultimate. This is the famous wonder of the Fenxinshi Stone (the stone is divided from the center).

6. The Double Yulan Hall of the Ganquan Town

The Double Yulan Hall of the Ganquan Town is situated in the Taiping (peaceful and tranquil) Temple in the Yulan Village of the Ganquan (Sweet Spring) Town in the Maiji District. It is 15 kilometres away from Maiji and the Maiji Mountain Grottoes each. It is so named because in the temple there are two tall magnolia (called "yulan" in Chinese) trees standing side by side.

The Taiping Temple, also named the Ganquan Temple, is so named because in the temple there is a clear, sweet and mellow spring. It is recorded that in the Tang Dynasty there were about 200 permanent monks in the Taiping Temple, which shows that the temple had many worshippers. In the year of Qianyuan 2 of the Tang Dynasty (759 AD), when the "poet-sage" Du Fu resided in Qinzhou, he visited the temple and composed the poem "the Spring of the Taiping Temple". In the poem there are lines like "fetching the spring water to supply the monks from all directions; the spring water is sweet and pleasing like milk". Originally in the temple there was a 3-room main hall, 5-room eastern and western chanfang (Buddhist monks' living quarters) each, a 3-room Tianwang (Heavenly King) Hall, an octagonal pavilion, a theatrical stage, a clock tower and an iron bell made in the Tang Dynasty. Later the temple was damaged, there being only a hall facing east. It is the "Double Yulan Hall". Since the nineties of the twentieth century, after raising money in many ways, the local masses have begun to rebuild the Taiping Temple. After a few years, there is a success. Now in the newly-completed Taiping Temple, besides the newly-built "Double Yulan Hall", there is still a precious Hall of the Great Hero (the main hall of a Buddhist temple, in which Sakyamuni is the central figure of a triad enthroned upon lotus pedestals, with the two others being usu. Ananda and Kasyapa, his two favorite disciples), a Shengmu (a female deity) Palace and a Guansheng Hall. Besides, there is still an octagonal spring pavilion. Its horizontal tablet is "Ganlu (Sweet Dew) Spring".

The double magnolia trees are the main sight of the Taiping Temple. In the temple there are two magnolia trees side by side. The distance of the two trees is 3 metres. The tree trunks reach to the sky and the trees have luxuriant foliage. The arm span of the trees is about 2 metres and the trees are about 25 metres high. The color of the flowers on the left tree is white, the right is red. In the seasons of Qingming (the 5th of the 24 solar terms) to Grain Rain (6th solar term) of every year, the flowers of the two trees come into bloom together. Many many flowers are set on the branches, bursting into bloom, attracting bees and butterflies. The sweet scent of flowers can be smelt several hundreds metres away. The flowers can be in full bloom for half a month. According to the survey, the age of the two trees is 1,200 years old. They were planted about in the Late Tang Dynasty. So old and tall magnolia trees are rare even in the whole country. In 1954, Mr. Deng Baoshan (born in 1894, died in 1968, the native of Dengjiazhuang Village of the Maiji District of Tianshui), the former head of the Gansu Province, wrote an antithetical couplet to praise the two magnolia trees and the deep affection relationship between Du Fu and Qinzhou. Later Qi Baishi was asked to write the horizontal tablet "Double Yulan Hall". The antithetical couplet and the horizontal inscribed board are hung on the hall behind the two magnolia trees.

7. Dragon Garden of the Maiji District

The Dragon Garden of the Maiji District, situated on the south side of the Wei River in the Maiji District, Tianshui, is a humanistic landscape newly built by the economic-technical development zone of Tianshui in the nineties of the twentieth century.

After Maiji District set up the economic-technical development zone of Tianshui, according to the historical materials and folklore of Tianshui, four gardens were planned, designed and built by financing. They are the

Dragon Garden, the Black Ox Garden, the Horse Garden and the Sanyang-kaitai which means with three "yang" (goat) beginning prosperity—the New Year ushers in a renewal and a change of fortune (from the *tai* hexagram of the *Book of Changes*, which in calendrical lore is correlated with the first month and whose three unbroken lines underneath three broken ones, are three strokes of yang "positive force", often said as a wordplay on the homophonous *yang* and *yang* "goat") Garden. Of them the Dragon Garden is of the grandest scale. The Dragon Garden is a building complex in the style of the ancients to carry forward the culture of Fuxi and to commemorate the historical celebrities of Tianshui. It is also the place to centrally show and watch the literary grace of the dragon. Tianshui is the native place of Fuxi. Fuxi looked up to observe the sky and looked down to investigate the earth, drawing the Eight Trigrams, knitting the net, creating characters, promoting marrying, and laying the foundation of the Chinese civilization. He is the earliest ancestor of the human beings. It is said that Fuxi had a snake's body and a man's head, so the totem of the dragon became popular. Fuxi is respected as the dragon ancestor of *Huaxia* (an ancient name for China). The descendants of the Chinese nation are also praised as the descendants of the dragon. Tianshui is the important birthplace of the dragon culture. This is the cause of building the Dragon Garden.

The Dragon Garden faces east, covering an area of 13 mu (about 8,666.7 square metres). The main buildings are the Chengji Hall, the double-eaved bicyclic pavilion, the stone memorial arch with a dragon's head, the white marble *huabiao* (ornamental columns erected in front of palaces, tombs, etc.), the bronze dragon horse and the gate with a saddle roof about 50 chi (about 16.6 metres) wide. The main body is the Chengji Hall. It is the building with double-eaved roof with the designs of the Ming and Qing Dynasties about 90 chi (30 metres) wide. It is 45 metres long, 27 metres high and 13.6 metres deep. The dougong (a system of brackets inserted between the top of a column and a crossbeam) of the hall eaves is lifted up with 9 tall white marble dragon posts, in outstanding manners. Two dragon walls are set in the solemn and respectful hall. Besides, in it hangs the relief showing the humanistic time of Tianshui and are on display 19 bronze statues of the sages in past dynasties of Tianshui since Fuxi. These sages are—Fuxi, the legendary ancestor of the Chinese people; Shi Zuoshu, a Confucian; Ji Xin, *Zhongliehou* (a marquis); Li Guang, the flying general (courageous and skilful general or soldier in battle); Zhao Chongguo, *yingpinghou* (a marquis); Duan Huizong, a *duhu* (an official name) in the Western Regions (a Han Dynasty term for the area west of Yumenguan, including what is now Xinjiang and parts of Central Asia); Jiang Wei, the famous general of the Shu Han Dynasty in Three Kingdoms; Fu Jian, the king of the *Qianqin* (a kingdom); Jiang Mo, the famous general of the early Tang Dynasty and the *cishi* (provincial or prefectural governor) of Qinzhou; Li Shimin, Emperor Taizong of the Tang Dynasty; Quan Deyu, the famous chief minister of the Middle Tang Dynasty; Wang Renyu, the talented scholar of the Five Dynasties; Liu Qi, the famous general against the aggressive Jin Dynasty; Xia Jinghe, the subject who criticized the emperor's faults frankly in the Ming Dynasty; Hu Zuanzong, known by his literary name Niaoshushanren; Hu Xin, a senior official in the Ming Dynasty; Ren Qichang, an outstanding literary figure in the Longnan Prefecture; Zhang Shiying, the educator in the Late Qing Dynasty; An Wei Jun, a man of iron of the Gansu Province, etc. Although these sages have passed away, their spirits will last forever.

(二) 天水大地湾文化英语语料

1. Dadiwan Ruins

The Dadiwan Ruins is situated on the east side of the Shaodian Village of the Wuying Township in the northeastern of the Qin'an County of Tianshui. Being 102 kilometres away from the city proper of Tianshui, it was classified as the state‑preserved key cultural relics by the State Council in 1988.

The Dadiwan Ruins is located on the second and third step land and hilly area with gentle slope on the south bank of the Qingshui River, the branch of the Hulu River. The total area is 1,100,000 square metres. The Ruins began to be excavated in 1978. Up to 1984, the area excavated had been 13,700 square metres, the house ruins unearthed had been 238 square metres, pits 357 square metres, tombs 79 square metres, kilns 38 square metres, the tops of a kitchen range 106 square metres, ditches used to protect and drain off water 8 square metres. Various kinds of pottery wares, decorative wares and living implements made of bones, stones and freshwater mussels had been 8,034 square metres. In 2001, in the 15‑day general survey to the area on the east side of the protection scope of the Dadiwan Ruins, 46 important cultural relic areas were found and recorded. The total area of the Ruins is possible to be expanded to 2,800,000 square metres. The Dadiwan Culture was 4800‑7800 years ago. It can be divided into five periods: Dadiwan Period Ⅰ; the early, middle and late periods of the Yangshao Culture (a culture of the Neolithic period, relics of which were first unearthed in Yangshao Village, Mianchi County); and the period under the level of Changshan Culture of Dadiwan. The scale is so big and the connotation is so rich that it is rare in the time of the Chinese archaeology.

In the early period, the houses in the Dadiwan Ruins were mainly semi‑paintpot round. In the middle period, the houses built on the level ground appeared, the area of the houses became larger and the floors were plastered with Liaojiangshi mud. In the late period, the palace hall‑styled houses with complex structures appeared. For example, the ruins of the big house No. F901 was built about 6000 years ago. The total area is 420 square meters. It is made up of the main room, the eastern and western side rooms, the back room and the adjacent accommodation in front of the door. It is the place where the primitive tribe alliance discussed official business together. The floor of it is the concrete of Liaojiangshi mud and artificial ceramsite light aggregate. The hardness of the concrete balances the cement No. 100. It is the house building with the largest area and the highest technological level in the prehistoric times found in China today. In the floor of the house No. F411, there is still a quite vivid ground painting. It is the earliest primitive ground painting found in China today.

The Dadiwan is the important birthplace of Chinese painted pottery culture. Many painted potteries were unearthed in Dadiwan. Of them there are two most valuable ones. One of them is a big colored pottery basin with the round bottom and tortoise-lines. Its bore is 50.2 centimetres. The other is a head-shaped colored pottery flask. It is 31.8 metres high.

In the Dadiwan Ruins, there are many agricultural production implements unearthed. They are stone axes, stone knives and pottery knives. The construction of the big bag-shaped kilns used to store articles, the appearance of many storage implements such as the big pottery jars, pottery pots, etc., and the discovery of the earliest farming samples in China, charring millets and rapeseeds, all show and reflect that the economic formation at that time was the sedentary type taking the farming as the main living means.

2. Xingguo Temple

The Xingguo Temple, situated in the north street of the county of the Qin'an County, is a group of building complex built in the Yuan Dynasty. With simple and unsophisticated style with odd appearance, it is rare in the country. In 2001, the State Council lists it as the state-preserved key cultural relics.

The Xinguo Temple began to be built in the year of Zhishun 3 of the Yuan Dynasty (1332 AD). Later it has been rebuilted for many times. Now there exists the gate, the clock tower, the Tianwang (heavenly king) Hall, the main building and the Bore (the highest wisdom) Hall. The Bore Hall faces west. It is three rooms wide, 11.7 metres long and two rooms, 8 metres deep. The roof is single-eave saddle roof. It is covered with gray tube flat tiles. The figures of flying dragons and peonies are carved on two sides of the main ridge. The dragons' mouths are carved at the two ends of the main ridge. The two dragons have glaring eyes and curly tail, vividly opening their mouths to swallow the ridge. The glazed beast face is decorated right in the middle of the main ridge. A big red pearl is put on it. The animals are put on the two sides. The auxiliary steps of the main hall are supported with 6 eaves posts. The 2 eaves posts in the middle are perfectly round and very large. The post heads are like inverted basins. The lower parts of shafts are simple round post bases. The structure of beam mount uses the components of sloping beams firstly created in the Yuan Dynasty. In the hall there is no big posts. There are only 4 small posts with the diameter of 15 centimetres below the sloping beams, which shows the excellence of the architectural skills. On the hall hangs the horizontal tablet "bore" written by Hu Zuanzong. The two characters, bold, simple and unsophisticated are rare good calligraphical works. The Bore Hall of the Xingguo Temple is vigorous, firm and harmonious in the whole. The outline of it is stable and graceful. Although it has gone through rebuilding many times, the structure of the beam mount and the style dougong (a system of brackets inserted between the top of a column and a cross beam) still keep the features of the buildings in the Yuan Dynasty. It is the ancient building with wood structure. In the Gansu Province, it is built in earlier years and it is better preserved.

(三) 天水秦文化英语语料

1. The Qin Tomb on the Pastureland of Grazing Horses

The pasture-land of grazing horses which is located about 20 kilometres east of Maiji Mountain and 10 kilometres west of Stone Gate is said to be the place where the forefather of the Qin people—Yingfeizi herded horses for the Zhou Dynasty emperor. In 1986 a group of tombs of the Qin and Han Dynasties were unearthed here. In 1993 it became a provincial forest garden. From then on the pastureland became a special scenic spot with both man-made and natural characteristics.

The Qin Tomb is located at the source of the Dangchuan River, which belongs to Maiji District of Tianshui City. It is the tomb ruins of Qin people in Late Warring States Period, covering an area of around 10000 square metres and has over 100 tombs. Among 14 unearthed tombs, 13 are tombs of the Qin Dynasty, while one is of the Han Dynasty. Over 400 historical relics have been found including wooden maps, 7 maps on 4 wooden planks, 460 bamboo slips, 2 paintings on a plank of wood, 28 pieces of pottery, 11 pieces of lacquer ware, copper ware and brushes.

Of the unearthed historical relics, the most valuable are the wooden maps, which are given the number M1. These seven maps were drawn on four planks of wood of the same size using a carpenter's ink marker. Six of the seven maps are complete, while one is unfinished. The lines and characters on the maps are very clear. Scholars believe the six complete maps are about Qin County and Gui County as well as other nearby districts, products distribution, the river systems of the Wei River and Jialing River. The area on the maps relate to 3 districts of Tianshui City, Pingliang, Longnan in Gansu Province and Guyuan in Ningxia. This area is the main area where Qin people were active in the Spring and Autumn Period. It has been proved that these maps were drawn in 300 BC. They are the earliest maps in China and have an important place in cartography and the time of science and technology both in China and abroad. In addition 460 bamboo slips found in Qin tombs can be divided into three parts according to their contents. They are "*Record of the person in this tomb*", A "*The Sun and Moon*" and B "*The

Sun and Moon". The maps, bamboo slips and "The Sun and Moon" found in the pastureland provide us with true historical information about politics, economy, traffic, nature and products in Tianshui area where the mother town of Qin people has been since the Warring States Period.

2. The Old Town of the Gui County

The Old Town of the Gui County is situated in the center of the city proper of the Qinzhou District of Tianshui Municipality.

Before the people of the Qin State formally governed the area of Tianshui, the residents in Tianshui were the people of the Qin State and the West Rong. In 688 BC, Duke Wugong of Qin sent armed forces to suppress the West Rong and conquered the Guirong and Jirong. After that, he established the Gui County and Ji County in their living region, making effective management and administration. Of the two counties, the management scope of the Gui County is the area of the eastern part of the Tianshui Prefecture.

In 280 BC, the Qin State established the Longxi Prefecture in the west of the Gansu Province. The Gui County is in the jurisdiction of the Longxi Prefecture. After the Qin State unified the Six States, the Gui County was renamed the Shanggui County. In the seventh year of Taikang of the Western Jin Dynasty (286 AD), the seat of the Qinzhou was moved to the Shanggui from the county seat of the Ji County. From then on, the position of the Shanggui County has fixed as the center of the politics, economy, culture, military affairs and communications of the Tianshui Prefecture in the west of the Gansu Province.

According to historical records, the seat of the Shanggui County was on the side of the Luoyu River, which is on the north of the Xi River and on the south of the Fenghuang Mountain. The position is right in the center of the Qinzhou District of Tianshui Municipality now.

3. The Old Town of the Mianzhu

The Mianzhu, also called Juyao, Yaozhu, Yao, Yaoshu and Shuyao, is an ancient nationality with a long history. The history called it a section of the West Rong. In the periods of the Spring and Autumn and the Warring States, they lived in the area of the present-day Tianshui of the Gansu Province. Later it was destroyed by the Qin State. In the Han Dynasty, the name of this nationality was used to name the place, where they lived and multiplied. The Mianzhu Circuit was established, in the jurisdiction of the Tianshui Prefecture. According to the records of the Tang Dynasty, the old town of the Mianzhu Circuit was 56 li to the north of the Qinling County (established in the Sui Dynasty, the seat of which is in the present-day Boyang Township of the Maiji District) of Qinzhou. According to the textual research of historians, the place is the Linjiahe Village of the Jiahe Township in the southwest of the Qingshui County. In the Northern Wei Dynasty, the Mianzhu County was established. The seat of it was in the northern level ground of the present-day Shetang Town. The "Mianzhu Water" recorded in the *Shuijingzhu* written by Li Daoyuan still exists now, is just the Chouni River, the branch in the lower reaches of the Niutou River, which is the branch of the Wei River.

The east of the old town of the Mianzhu County borders on the Qingshui County. On the north of it is the Gui Mountain. On the south of it is the Wei River. Around it are mountains and rivers. It occupies a high position, having a southern exposure and having an open terrain. It is the vital communication gateway in ancient times.

4. Cemetery of Zhao Chongguo

The Cemetery of Zhao Chongguo is situated on the first terrace on the northern bank of the Niutou River, 1 kilometre in the northwest of the county town of Qingshui. It is one of the Province-preserved key cultural relics.

Zhao Chongguo (born in 137 BC, died in 52 BC) is a native of Shanggui of Longxi. He is a famous general in the Western Han Dynasty. Being brave and cool-headed, he had the great strategies of the commander-in-chief. In the battles against the Xiongnu (an ancient nationality in China), Qiang (an ancient nationality in China) and Di (an ancient nationality in China), he correctly appraised the situation and won every battle. So his august name was widely known. The emperor bestowed on him the title of Hou General. After Emperor Xuan of the Western Han Dynasty succeeded to the throne, he was conferred the title of Yingpinghou (a marquis) because he had made contributions to assist the emperor in governing the country. The major reason why Zhao Chongguo left the illustrious name in the time is that he put forward the strategy "soldiers work as farmers in time of peace and act as fighters in case of war, which is favorable both to farming and fighting". The strategy was called "tuntianfa (having garrison troops or peasants open up wasteland and grow food grain, a policy pursued by feudal rulers since the Han Dynasty)". The spread of "tuntianfa" in the Western Han Dynasty played a very important role to win the final victory of the battle against Qiang, to keep the stability of the borderland of the northwest China and to develop the farming in frontier regions. After Zhao Chongguo died, the "tuntianfa" was used extensively in the practice by the statesmen and strategists in the past dynasties and it exerted a huge influence in Chinese history.

The tomb of Zhao Chongguo was initially built in the Han Dynasty. In the Song Dynasty, the sacrificial fields were purchased. Many pines and cypresses were planted and the sacrificial hall was also built. In the years of Emperor Jiaqing and Emperor Daoguang in the Qing Dynasty, the imperial edict instructed to repair it on large scales. The existing gravestone now is all the remains of the gravestone made in the Qing Dynasty. In the grave zone, there is a mound tomb now. The tomb slightly appears like a circular cone, 2.5 metres high, 18 metres in girth. In the grave zone, there is lush green grass and it is silent and still. In front of the tomb there are two tablet pavilions, in which stand two stone tablets: one was made in the 13th year of Emperor Jiaqing of the Qing Dynasty (1808 AD), on which are written "The tomb of Zhao Chongguo, the Hou General in the Han Dynasty, Yingpinghou"; the other was made in the 15th year of Emperor Daoguang (1835 AD), on which are written "The Tomb of the Deceased General in the Han Dynasty, Yingpinghou".

In recent years, the government of the Qingshui County moved some graves of the Song Dynasty and stone inscriptions made in the Dynasties of Tang and Song to the grave zone and expanded the area of the grave zone, opening up it as the Cemetery of Zhao Chongguo. The Cemetery attracts numerous people to come to tour and visit.

5. Huashi Cliff Natural Scenic Spot

The Huashi Cliff Natural Scenic Spot is situated in the southwest of the Tuzhai Village of the Longdong Township of the Qingshui County. It is 22 kilometres away from the county town of Qingshui. It is 5 kilometres away from the Yao'ai Village of the Yuanlong Township of the Maiji District. It is the juncture of the Qingshui County and the Maiji District, also is a scenic spot where Buddhism and Taoism coexist.

The Huashi Cliff overlooks the Wei River on the south. The Longhai Railway and the national road No. 310 pass from the place not far away from the foot of the hill. Here there are deep and quiet gullies, luxuriant forests and dense grass. The cliffs have five-color appearance, so it is called Huashi (Colored Stones) Cliff. Because there are many peaks, ridges, flowers and trees. These have a riot of color, so it is also called the Wanzi (many colors) Hill. In the gullies there are many odd stones, pines, cypresses, clear springs and flying waterfalls. There is not only the "warm water", which does not freeze in winter, but also the "cold water", which becomes very long icicles in winter. When it is raining or when it is humid, clouds and fog wind the Huashi Cliff, which is a scene of freedom, nature, quaintness, elegance and a little desolation.

The time of development and construction of the Huashi Cliff is relatively long. It is said that there were temples before the Tang Dynasty. The existing halls were mainly built in the Ming and Qing Dynasties. Of them two are grottoes made in the Ming and Qing Dynasties. Besides, there are some painted sculptures, wall paintings and horizontal inscribed boards made in the Ming and Qing Dynasties. According to the terrain, the Huashi Cliff can be divided into the eastern cliff and the western cliff. On the whole the buildings built according to the lie can be divided into five parts: the Stone of Patching the Sky, the Needle-grinding Hall, the Great Hall Courtyard, the Yuhuang Top and the Leiyin Cliff. There is a legend that Nvwa (a creator-goddess who patched with stone blocks the holes in the sky made by Gonggong, the Spirit of Water, in a conflict with Zhuanxu, the Spirit of Fire) melt down stones to repair the sky and left behind a stone here. There is also a legend that the Tang monk passed here on the way to go on a pilgrimage for Buddhist scriptures and fought with the yellowwood wolf.

There is an odd stone in the middle of the Huashi Cliff, called the Stone of Patching the Sky. It is over 30 metres high, more than 10 metres wide. So huge a stone is inserted below the cliff just as it flew here. It is striking and mysterious. Three Chinese characters "The Stone of Patching the Sky" were written by Mr. Mao Huimin, a contemporary, each of which is 9 square metres. These characters are simple, ancient and handsome and have a broad tolerance. They are the most wonderful inscriptions on precipices in the area of Qinzhou.

6. Malu Natural Scenic Spot in the Guan Mountain

The Malu Natural Scenic Spot in the Guan Mountain is situated in the area under the Malu Tree Farm's jurisdiction of the Hui Autonomous County of Zhangjiachuan. It covers an area of about 18.1 square kilometres. On the west of it is the Malu Township of the county; on the east is the Long County of the Shaanxi Province; on the south is the Qingshui County. The scenic spot is the southern remaining mountain range of the Liupan Mountain. It is the temperate humid climate. The vegetation is intact. The spring and autumn period is short. In summer it is cool and in winter it is cold. The annual precipitation is 700 millimetres or so.

In the scenic spot there are many greenish ridges and peaks. The water is green and the forests are luxuriant. There are many jagged rocks of grotesque shapes. All of these form the clear, secluded, beautiful, refined, grand, rare, dangerous and high view of the mountains and rivers. The main natural scenic spots are the Five Dragons Mountain, the Old Dragon Pool, the Cliff of Cutting the Snake, the Small Maiji, the Five Fingers Mountain, the Bluestone Precipice and the Stone Figure Peak, etc. It is rich in water resources. The streams in the Malu River, the Sangu Water, the Gully of the Disordered Wood Farm and other gullies run all the year round. The water in them is so clear that you can see the bottom. The humanistic scenic spots are the remains of the Yunfeng Temple of the Five Dragons Mountain, the Trigram of the Tai Ji Ba Gua on the Foye (Buddha) Cliff, the stone with footprints of Erlangshen and the Horse Post, etc.

Being a natural paradise of animals and plants, the scenic spot is rich in animal and plant resources. According to the statistics, there are 36 families and 102 species of plants, of which 78 are arbors, 22 are bushes and 2 are vines. Besides, there are more than 20 woody, herbal and animal medicinal materials. There are also many animals, of which the beasts are the musk deer, the leopard, the yellow weasel, the otter, the badger, the wolf, the wild boar and grass hare, etc.; the birds are the sparrow hawk, the golden pheasant, the pheasant and the magpie, etc.; the fishes are mainly the salmon of the Qinling Mountains.

Here was the only way that must be passed from the Shaanxi Province to the Gansu Province of the ancient Silk Route. In the past it was called the Ancient Pass of the Guan Mountain. The pass was a place of strategic importance. In the lofty Guan Mountain, ancient trees towered to the skies, roads were dangerous and twisting up, and water from the mountain murmured. All of these have passed away. Nowadays, the Tianbao Road crosses the scenic spot. In addition it has the good position—it borders on the Guanshan Grassland of the Long County, which is a gold tourist spot developed by the Shaanxi Province in recent years. All these have made the scenic spot one of the popular tourist attractions containing great development potentialities.

7. Xuanhuagang Kubba

Xuanhuagang Kubba, situated at the Beishanchawan Village in Zhangjiachuan Hui Autonomous County, is a memorial place of Islamic "Jahariyah" school.

Arabic "Jahariyah" – public and loud, means to praise God loudly. Inside it, Xuanhuagang Kubba Remains of four founders of "Jahariyah" were buried and it was the "Zhe" Islamic base of the founders of seventh generation of Mayuanzhang and his young brother Mayuanchao. Mayuanzhang was a grandson of the fourth generation of "Zhe" school founder Maminxin during the Emperor Tongzhi of the Qing Dynasty (1862 – 1874 AD). "Zhe" school was cruelly suppressed by the Qing government and few people survived. Mayuanzhang and his brother escaped from Yunnan to the North Mountain of Zhangjiachuan and did activities of "Zhe" school secretly. The eighth year of Emperor Guangxu of the Qing Dynasty (1882 AD), Mayuanzhang sent someone to buy with a lot of money. Mahualong and other three people's bone of the heads and buried there. Later, Mayuanzhang and his brother preached the sermon here. The fifthteenth year of Emperor Guangxu of the Qing Dynasty (1889 AD) the arched roof (the dome) was built above the tomb of Mahualong, which was called "Kubba" (in Arabic language this kind of arched roof is called "Kubba"). This sort of building started to be built on a large scale in the fourth year of Minguo (1915 AD). After three years of expansion, Xuanhuagang covered an area of 13200 square metres. The dome like structures of the four founders of Mahualong, Mayuanzhang, Majincheng and Mayuanchao were built one by one, hence Xuanhuagang became the mecca of "Zhe" school in China.

The buildings of Xuanhuagang were spacious and bright and carved meticulously, part of the buildings were the tombs of the founders, part of which were halls of preaching and the other buildings were the rooms for people and relatives to live in. During the Cultural Revolution most of the buildings were destroyed. The government of Zhangjiachuan has recently raised RMB 2.5 million, and some of the buildings have been restored.

Xuanhuagang Kubba is an influential place of Islam in the northwest. Every year big religious activities have been held here and people who take part in the activities come from thirteen provinces and areas.

8. Qinting Site

Qinting site, situated at Waquan Village, which is in the south of Zhangjiachuan Hui Autonomous County, is an ideal place to build a city for its space, mountain and water around it. Because many years passed, no trace of the old city can be seen.

Qinting—old name "Qin" was an important base in hard times of its development. Qinfeizi was granted a piece of land in Qin City by King Xiao of the Zhou Dynasty for his hard work of herding horses. Five generations from Feizi, Qinhou, Gongbo, Qinzhong and Zhuanggong lived in Qin City and it was the starting point that Qin people built their country. "Qin" also was the first place that Qin people established the city. During Western Han Dynasty (202 BC – 8 AD) Qin City was renamed from "Qin" to Qinting. In the earlier years of the Qin Dynasty, Qinting for its important position of strategy played an important part in the long struggle of Qin people against the foreigners.

（四）天水三国文化英语语料

1. The Site of the Old Battlefield of Jieting

The Site of the Old Battlefield of Jieting is located at about 100 kilometres northeast of Tianshui City. The center place of the battle is at Long County of Qin'an Town. The battle happened in a long and narrow valley as well as the southern hilly land which covered from the eastern Longshanzheng of Zhangchuan to the western Longcheng County of Qin'an. The valley is about 16 kilometres long and 3 kilometres wide. The area of the battlefield is about 48 square kilometres.

Jieting is also named as Jiequanting, which came from Jieqian County in Western Han Dynasty (202 BC-8 AD) The old Jieting was located on the famous traffic road of "Guanlong" road which was linked through east to west. The old Jieting was a very important site from which one could reach Jingning to the north, arrive at Tianshui to the south, go to Lanzhou to the west and get to Guanzhong to the east, and it was a strategic place which Kingdoms of Shu and Wei struggled for. In the valley there is a hillock about 500 metres high and 1000 metres long, which is situated in the south of the Qing River. The locals call it "Xiliangzi" or "Duanshan" because the hillock is a strategic point. Its importance seems as if one man guards the pass, many people can not pass through it.

In the Jianxin sixth year of Shu-Han (228 AD) Zhugeliang started the first attack in order to unite Zhongyuan. Under the pressure of circumstances the soldiers in Nan'an, Tianshui, turned traitors, and Wei Kingdom was afraid and surprised. For resisting the army of Shu Kingdom, the general Zhang He of Wei Kingdom led his army straight to Jieting. The general Masu of Shukingdom didn't obey Zhugeliang's strategic planning, but he believed the rule of military strategy and tactics— "If one was in a favourable position, one could win one victory after another with irresistible force. ", so he ordered the soldiers to pitch camps on the top of the mountain. At last they were surrounded by scheming Zhanghe and lost Jieting without a battle.

The stories of "Lost Jieting" and "Killing Masu" became well-known in Chinese history.

In the area of Longcheng of Qin'an and Longshanzheng of Zhangchuan, all kinds of arms have been unearthed, in addition, there are many local villages named as "Ying" (camp) such as Zhangying, Changying, Wangying and Wuying. All of these show that at that time camps were pitched there.

2. Li Guang Tomb

The Li Guang Tomb is situated on the Stone Horse Plateau in the south of Tianshui Municipality. Black bricks surround the tomb, which appears tall, magnificent, solemn and quiet.

Li Guang, the famous general of the Western Han Dynasty, was born in Chengji of Longxi (now the north of the Qin'an County of the Gansu Province). His life had gone through the reign periods of Emperors Wen, Jing and Wu. Li Guang is upright, just and honest, and he is skilled in horsemanship and marksmanship. In over 40 years' military life, he had experienced more than 70 battles, big or small. *Xiongnu* (an ancient nationality in China) called him "the flying general (courageous and skilful general or soldier in battle) ". In the year of Yuanshou 4 in the reign of Emperor Wu in the Western Han Dynasty (119 BC), he wrathfully cut his own throat in the battlefield because he lost his way in the battlefield and exceeded the time limit.

After he died, it is not known where his remains were buried. The countrymen built his tomb containing his personal effects of the deceased in order to commemorate his heroic achievements, and to express their feelings of admiration. The tomb area originally had a relatively large scale, covering an area of 1,300 square metres, having walls, gates, halls, stone horses and gravestones, etc. Later it declined day by day. Now in the graveyard, in addition to the hemispheric tomb, which is ten metres tall, around 25 metres in girth, there is still a stone tablet tower, 3 sacrificial pavilions, 2 stone tablets and 2 stone horses. One of the stone tablets is the tablet of "The Tomb of Li Guang, a general in the Han Dynasty" rebuilt in the year of Emperor Qianlong 4 of the Qing Dynasty (1739 AD). The other tablet is the tablet of "The Tomb of Li Guang, a general in the Han Dynasty" inscribed by Jiang Zhongzheng. The stone horses were built in the Han Dynasty, bold and unconstrained in shape. The style is simple, unadorned and powerful. Although these horses have gone through many vicissitudes of life and appear worn-out and incomplete, their artistic conception is still enough to move one's heart. The Stone Horses Plateau is so named.

3. Site of the Zhuge Rampart

The Site of the Zhuge Rampart is situated on the east bank of the Luoyu River in the eastern suburbs of the city proper of Tianshui. It is to the south of the Tianbei Road, 2 kilometres from the city town. It is one of the ten famous scenic spots in Qinzhou. Now it is a big mound with the diameter of about 8 metres. Nearby stands a tablet written by the General Zhang Aiping. On it are four Chinese characters "The Zhuge Rampart".

The area of Tianshui in the Three Kingdoms was the front and the strategic passage of the wars between Wei and Shu Han. In those years, in order to go ahead steadily and strike sure blows, Zhuge Liang ordered soldiers to build many defense works in the area of Shanggui, Lucheng and Qishan used to defend, fight and take as the backing when attacking. These defense works were called the rampart. The Zhuge Rampart situated to the east of the city town of Tianshui is commonly called "Xiamucheng Town". For a time it existed side by side with the "Sima Yi Rampart" nearby. The majorities think that the Rampart is the general platform of drilling soldiers, so it is called "*dianjiang* (calling the muster roll of officers and assigning them tasks) Platform of Zhuge Liang". About the origin of the Rampart, there are two legends, one is the Rampart made by accumulating the saline soil, and the other is the Rampart made by accumulating the soil in the shoes. These two legends are both not worth believing.

The Zhuge Rampart was destroyed in the 50s and 60s of the 20th century. According to the memories of the old local men, the original rampart had the small upper part and the big lower part. The upper part was plane. It was more than 3.33 metres high. In front of it, there was a tablet pavilion. Around it there were green pines and cypresses. There is a very interesting thing that at the high noon of the sixth of the lunar June, in the sun, the Rampart had no shadow. So the local people also call it "the Mound Having No Shadow".

4. Mumen Passageway

The Mumen Passageway, the site of the ancient battlefield of the Three Kingdoms, is situated in the Mumen Village of the Mudan Township, 41 kilometres to the southwest of Tianshui Municipality. It is here that in 231 AD, Zhuge Liang worked out a plan to kill Zhang He by shooting arrows, a senior general of the Kingdom of Wei.

The Mumen Passageway is commonly called Xiamen. The terrain here is strategically situated and difficult of access. There is a piece of empty land of the river valley between two mountains about 333 metres high, which is only 50 metres wide and about 500 metres long. In the deserted valley, there is river water from the valley rushing down south into the Xihan River. On the bank of the river, there is a winding path running down from north to south, forming the natural gateway. The gateway is one of the main passages from Jieting and Shanggui to Qishan. In the year of Jianxing 9 of the Shu Han Dynasty (231 AD), Zhuge Liang, the chief minister of the Shu Kingdom, secondly launched the offensive from Qishan and won a completely victory. Unexpectedly, he was recalled by Liu Shan without reason. When they retreated to Hanzhong, Zhuge Liang sent the senior general Wei Yan to lead 10000 soldiers with bows and arrows to wait in the Mumen Passageway to prevent the attack of the soldiers of the Wei Kingdom. Zhang He, the senior general of the Wei Kingdom, was lured by Wei Yan into the Mumen Passageway and killed by arrows because he didn't take the advice of Sima Yi and hurriedly pursued and advanced rashly since he was anxious to gain victory. There are such battle sites as the Ambush Bend, the Bend of Tying Horses and the Zhang He Level Ground, etc. In recent years, in order to commemorate Zhuge Liang, the ancient prominent statesman and strategist, and the local people built the Memorial Temple of Wuhou (a marquis for Zhuge Liang).

5. Jiangwei's Tomb

Jiangwei's tomb, situated at Jiangjia village, Liufeng Township, 10 kilometres east to Gangu Town, is the tomb of Jiangwei's clothes. The old tomb was destroyed. In 1988 the new tomb was rebuilt at the original site by Gangu government. The tomb facing the north is 1.2 metres high and 6.2 metres around, it symbolizes that Jiangwei left home at the age of twelve and joined the army, and devoted himself to the country at the age of 62. In front of the tomb there are nine steps which mean Jiangwei's great achievements in the nine battles attacking Zhongyuan (Zhongyuan refers to middle and lower reaches of the Yellow River). Above the steps there is a smooth slope on which was written "Great Ambition" which sings praises of Jiangwei's great ambition and lofty quality. The height above sea level of the place where Jiangwei's tomb was situated is 1260 metres which is over 60 metres higher than Jiangjia Village. The Wei River is in front of the tomb and behind it are mountains.

In addition, Jiangwei's temple was built at a higher place behind Jiangjia Village. In front of the temple there stands a monument written

"Jiangwei's Hometown" by General Yangchengwu.

Jiangwei who was a famous general in Three Kingdoms times styled himself Boyue. He was from Ji County (now it is Gangu County) and his native place was at Jiangjia Village, Liufeng Township. Jiangwei joined Wei Kingdom army in Tianshui county and submitted to Shu-Han when Zhugeliang first attacked Wei Kingdom. Later, because of his military ability he was regarded highly by Zhuge Liang. He was ever appointed one after another the head of storehouses, the supervisor in the army, the general who led the army to attack the western army in China and the highest official in Liangzhou. In 228 AD Jiangwei submitted to Shu-Han at the age 27 until he committed suicide at Jiangmen when he was 62 years old. He assisted loyally Zhuge Liang more than 30 years in order to unite the middle and lower reaches of the Yellow River. He was such a person that he thought deeply and planned carefully and accepted the task when his country was in a difficult condition. In all his life he lived a simple life and had no money. He set a good example in being loyal, brave, honest and upright.

6. The Old County of Ji

The old county of Ji is situated to the south of Gangu County. The residents of Tianshui were Qin people and the western people in China before Qin people governed Tianshui City. In 688 BC Duke Wu of Qin Dynasty attacked the west part of China and conquered the army of Gui and Ji, and then set up Gui County and Ji County. Both counties were governed and managed efficiently by Qin people. The governed area of Ji County was the present western area of Tianshui.

In 280 BC Qin people established Longxi County in which included Jin County. In 114 BC Ji County was separated from Longxi and was governed by Tianshui County. At the beginning of setting up, the area of Ji County was much bigger, later because more counties were set up, its area was becoming smaller and was about as big as present Gangu County. During Qin and Han Dynasties, Ji county was once the center of Tianshui area and even the center in Gansu. In Eastern Han Dynasty Tianshui County was renamed Hanyang County. In 74 AD the government of Hanyang County moved from Pingxiang to Ji County. In 265 AD Qin perfecture was established in the area of Tianshui and Ji County became the seat of the government. In 286 AD, the government of Qin County was moved from Ji County to Gui County. From then on, Ji County has been an administrative area of county although the name of the county was changed. Now Ji County is named Gangu County.

(五) 天水石窟文化英语语料

1. The Famous Scenic Area of Maiji Mountain

The famous scenic area of Maiji Mountain which is located at about 45 kilometres southeast of Tianshui City, belongs to the east part of the northern branch of the western Qinling mountains, crosses the Wei River in the north, and links the Jialing River in the south. It is one of the 44 national important scenic areas first announced by the State Council in 1982. It was evaluated as a 4A scenic area by the State Travel Bureau in the year 2000.

The whole area consists of five parts. They are the Grottoes of Maiji Mountain, the Immortal Cliff Grottoes, Stone Gate, Winding Stream and Jieting Yangtze. These five parts cover an area of 215 square kilometres and cross the Yellow River and Yangtze River and are in the shifting region of north and south climate. 76% of the spot is covered by forest. There are very rich plant resources, many kinds of animals, different geological forms and various historical sites. The area is beautiful because the natural scenery combines with manmade scenes. There are 35 small tourist areas and 180 scenic spots, including a national preservation unit of cultural relics, a plant garden of united international preservation and three provincial level forest gardens.

2. Scenic spot of Maiji Mountain

Maiji Mountain is known locally as Maiji Mountain Cliff. Wang Renyu, a native of Tianshui in the Five Dynasties stated in *Chat in Yudang* "Maiji Mountain crosses the Qin and Wei Rivers to the north and approaches Liangdang to the south, it is about 250 kilometres in length, half way along which protrudes a stone of 80 million feet high, which resembles a stack of wheat straw, hence calling the name Maiji.

The Maiji scenic spot with its many ranges of green hills has pines and bamboos and clear water flowing everywhere so it has been so called since ancient times—the best place of forests and springs in Qinzhou. In spring it looks green and in summer there are wild flowers everywhere. In autumn the scene is one of white clouds and red leaves and in winter the trees are covered by snow, so that it looks beautiful in every season. One of the eight beautiful scenes of Qinzhou is the mist and rain of Maiji Mountain.

Wuxichuan, a poet of the Qing Dynasty wrote in his poem "the most beautiful scenery is the one after autumn rain and the mist at dusk". Climbing "the tower of scattering flowers" on Maiji Mountain Grottoes, you can overlook the sea of forests, like a beautiful painting full of great power and grandeur.

The Grottoes of Maiji Mountain form a main tourist spot among the scenic spots of Maiji Mountain. Around it there are many natural and man-made scenic spots, such as the Plant Garden, Diaochao Valley, Arhat Cliff, Xiangji Mountain, Tianchiping, Yanshan Waterfall and XiaGate etc.

3. The Grottoes of Maiji Mountain

Maiji Mountain, which is located in the Maiji District of Tianshui City, is 45 kilometres to the southeast of Tianshui city and 30 kilometres away from its railway Stop. Maiji Mountain, surrounded by many Mountains belongs to the north of the western range of the Qinling Mountains and is 1671.4 metres above sea level and 142 metres high itself.

The Grottoes of Maiji Mountain form an important place of preservation of cultural relics, first nominated by the State Council in 1961.

After the opening of the Silk Route, building of Maiji Mountain was started in the Later Qin Period of the Sixteen States (384-417AD). As the saying goes "To pile up a Maiji cliff cut down all trees on the south mountain", we can see that the project was a major one. In Xiqin an eminent monk Tanhong and a famous Buddhist monk Xuangao lived on Maiji Mountain, giving lectures which attracted over 100 monks. From this we know that Buddhism was very active at that time. After the Northern Wei Dynasty, cliffs and pavilions came into fashion so Maiji Mountain was carved and many different images were made there. The art style was maturing. King Wen's first wife—Queen Yifu once became a nun here and was buried in the shrine of the mountain after her death. In the Northern Zhou Dynasty (557-581AD) Li Yunxing, the general military official of Qinzhou built a pavilion of seven Buddha for his dead father, about which the writer Yuxin once wrote an article. In Sui Dynasty, Emperor Yangjiang gave an order to bury Buddhist relics all over the country, so a Buddhist relic was buried on the top of Maiji Mountain. At present a stupa 9.4 metres high still stands. After that the cliff was carved again and repaired in the Tang, Five Dynasties, Song, Yuan, Ming, and Qing Dynasties. Although earthquake and fires destroyed it in the course of the time, 194 niches, over 7800 clay sculptures, stone carvings, about 1000 square metres wall painting and 8 cliff pavilions have survived. It has become one of the most famous grottoes in China and with the beautiful name of "Oriental Museum of Sculpture". The Grottoes of Maiji Mountain afford us valuable research materials of Chinese national sculptures, paintings, crafts, architectures, and religions.

The niches in Maiji Mountain are carved at least twenty to thirty metres above ground. Some are even chiseled in cliffs seventy to eighty metres high. The niches are close together like beehives. The largest one is 31.7

metres in width, but the smallest one can hold only one person. Wooden walkways built along the face of the cliff lead to each niche, and can have dizzying and frightening effect.

Owing to the amount of rain in Maiji area, many wall paintings have come off, but the clay sculptures are in good condition. Some are like new, some are as strong as fired pottery, and from this we can see the superb skill of ancient artists in clay making. Their specificities of art shapes differ from the style of the sculptures and carvings in different time have great difference. The earliest human sculptures hold their heads and chest high showing us their fathomless and solemn silence. However after the middle era of the Northern Wei Dynasty the models are more fresh, delicate, mild and pretty. They are filled with the rich flavor of life and human interest. From the slim figures of the Northern Wei times to the plump ones in Sui and Tang Dynasties, we can see the changes in the ancient art of sculpture and carving in China.

Tour Guide Speech of Maiji Mountain Grottoes

Dear my friends, Welcome to Tianshui!

The climate of Tianshui is suitable for the survival of mankind. That makes it become a cradle of the Chinese nation. As we know, Fuxi and Nvwa who are the Chinese ancestors lived here. They created the early period of Chinese culture. For the suitable climate, there are many wonderful attractions. This time we will go to Maiji Mountain, and visit Maiji Mountain Grottoes.

Maiji Mountain is located 50 kilometres far from Tianshui just to the south of Maiji Village. It is only 142 metres above the ground, but the altitude of about 2,000 metres above the sea level. It is a single and distinct peak of the Xiaolong Mountain of Western Qinling Range. Since it looks like a huge wheat straw pile from afar, it is called Maiji Mountain (the Wheat Straw Pile Mountain). The flouring various plants with clouds wrapping them in a blanket of mist create one of nature's most majestic sights. In the late of the Western Han Dynasty, it became the palace of Kui Xiao who is a famous general of Tianshui. The Maiji Mountain Scenic Area was listed as a famous resort under the state protection by the State Council in 1982. And Maiji Mountain Grottoes are the most important area of it, which rank the second in the four well-known grottoes in Gansu Province. (The four well-known grottoes are Mogao Grottoes, Maiji Mountain Grottoes, Bingling Temple Grottoes and Mati Temple Grottoes.)

The Grottoes of Maiji Mountain are caved in the cliffs, which are in rows 20-30 metres or 70-80 metres above the foot of mountain. That makes them look like a huge honeycomb in the distance. The wide of those grottoes which are linked by some dangerous ways is from about 1 metre to 3 metres.

Maiji Mountain Grottoes were first dug in the Qin Dynasty of the Sixteen States Period (about 384 to 417 AD). And the grottoes were cut and repaired in the successive dynasties of the Northern Wei Dynasty, the Western Wei Dynasty, the Northern Zhou Dynasty, the Sui Dynasty, the Tang Dynasty, the Five Dynasties, the Song Dynasty, the Yuan Dynasty, the Ming Dynasty and the Qing Dynasty. An earthquake which occurred in Tianshui during the Tang Dynasty (734 AD) resulted in collapse of the cliff, and the grottoes were subsequently divided into two sections—the Eastern and the Western with 54 and 140 grottoes respectively, which were called the Eastern Pavilion and the Western Pavilion during the Five Dynasties.

In the Eastern Pavilion, there are the Thousands of Buddhism Corridor, the Throwing Flowers Building, the Upper Seven-Buddhism Pavilion, the Middle Seven-Buddhism Pavilion, and so on. In the Western Pavilion, there are three grottoes which are the most famous. In them, the biggest is the Thousands of Buddhism Pavilion, the second is the Heavenly Cave, and the smallest is the Cave No. 127, which were all cut in 6 AD.

There is a legend associated with the Throwing Flowers Building. It is said that Sakyamuni appeared here to preach. During the first time, there were tens of thousands of disciples in the valley which were under the Throwing Flowers Building. In order to know whether all of them understand the Buddhist thoughts and tenets, the 28 flying aspara threw different kinds of petals to them. If the disciples understood, the petals would not fall, but if not, the petals would fall. It was surprised that all of the petals rose. Now you can throw some pieces of paper, you will find the pieces rise. Do you know why? Because there is an air current which can make some light things rise.

Though Maiji Mountain Grottoes suffered many earthquakes and fires, now there are 194 grottoes, more than 7,200 statues and over 1,300 square metres murals. As the stone of Maiji Mountain is unfit for caving, most statues are clay sculptures, but they are quite exquisite. The sculptures are mainly images of Buddha and his disciples, Bodhisattvas, the Heavenly Kings and Vajras. It is surprised that the sculptures have been preserved well, even though the climate is wet in Maiji Mountain.

Like the earliest sculpture of Mogao Grottoes, the Grottoes of Maiji Mountain were obviously influenced by the Indian style in 30 caves during the Northern Wei Dynasty, the Western Wei Dynasty and the Northern Zhou Dynasty. By the time of the Song Dynasty, the style was changed greatly due to mixing the Indian Culture and the Central Chinese Culture. The sculptures wear diverse countenance looking vivid. And the dress of them is soft and natural. In the late period, the style was continuously improved on the basis of the Chinese current culture. So the sculptures are more vivid than before and full of the interest of worldly life. However, since the Northern Wei Dynasty, almost all of the sculptures bowed their heads, as if they were looking this world. They are the gods, but they look like the human beings.

The Grottoes of Maiji Mountain are of high values for the study on politics, economy and culture in ancient China, even though they are the Buddhist arts. The grottoes embody the Chinese national tradition and consciousness, and also have the characteristic of making the form show the spirit. Especially the sculptures of the Sui and Tang Dynasties are full and rounded, and in the Song Dynasty, they are thin, delicate and pretty. Maiji Mountain Grottoes reflect the evolution of the clay sculptures art in China. They are referred to as "the treasure houses of oriental sculptures".

4. The Plant Garden

The Plant Garden is two kilometres away from the grottoes in the ditch of back cliff of Maiji Mountain. Surrounded by mountains from three sides, it was built according to the shape of the mountain and took good advantage of the mountain water and vegetation. It covers an area of 5500 "mu" (about 3.67 square kilometres) and has over 1800 plants belonging to 146 species, which can be grown in both south and north areas. A large area covered with deciduous trees, broadleaf, conifers and many other kinds of trees forms a lively and colorful scene of national beauty. Entering the garden you will see pavilions, trees and flowers complementing each other and you will hear birds singing, all of which you will find attractive.

Now you can live and enjoy entertainment in the Plant Garden. And it is also an ideal place for meetings.

5. Diaochao Valley

It is situated left in the ditch of back cliff and next to Maiji Mountain. On the face of the cliff there are many caves which look like birds' nests, hence it's named Diaochao Valley. The scenery is very beautiful and the terrain is difficult to access. The east part of the back cliff is like a fan, so it's also named "Three Fans Cliff". Under the cliff and to the north of the valley there are remains of a summer palace, which belonged to Kuixiao who was a separatist in the early years of the Eastern Han Dynasty. When wandering here you will yearn for the past and the silence while you admire the waterfall and listen to the sound of the wind through the forest.

6. Arhat Cliff

It is situated in the southwest of Maiji Mountain Grottoes and faces the distant cliff of evening glow in the distance.

Because of its basket-like shape, the local people give it the name "Youlong Mountain", and because half way up the cliff there are some Buddhistic statues it has the name—Arhat cliff. Above the mount there is a grotto about 40 metres long in which there is a Buddhist statue of Sanshi of the Song Dynasty. It is said that the Buddhist statue of Sanshi was carved earlier than the Maiji Mountain Grottoes. The following saying proves this, "First chisel Monk Cliff, and then cut Maiji Mountain Grottoes."

7. Xiangji Mountain

Xiangji Mountain situated to the right south 2.5 kilometres of Maiji Mountain gets its name from the Xiangji Temple. The snow-covered scene has been famous since ancient times. It is said that it attracted each other with Ruiyin temple on Maiji Mountain. The sound of the morning bells and the evening drums rose subsided here and there were many activities of pilgrimage. Huzuanzong of the Ming Dynasty praised it in his poem "Xiangji Temple in the south, Maiji Mountain to the north, celestials pick agrimonia pilosa, and return with white clouds". Half way up the Xiangji Mountain there is a natural cave named Yuxiang Cave which meanders down and in the cave some parts are wide and some are narrow. Stalactites hang down and make drops fall. It is difficult to know its secret but it is a good place to explore and enjoy the cool air during summer.

8. The Scenic Area of the Immortal Cliffs

It is situated 15 kilometres northeast of Maiji Mountain. The natural scenery in the area is very beautiful because of its great mountains, clear water, precipitous cliffs and dense forest. Its man-made sites are second only to Maiji Mountain. Most temples, monasteries and niches were built either on the high peaks or steep cliffs. Since the Southern and Northern Dynasties, temples and statues were built in every dynasty, but unfortunately most of them have been destroyed and little is left. In 1953 it was appraised by a prospecting team of Cultural Department that the present temples were repaired or rebuilt during the Tang, Song, Ming and Qing Dynasties, and some of the clay statues are works of the Late Northern Wei Dynasty. At present there are 197 statues made in the Bei, Cun, Ming, Qing Dynasties and 84 square metres of paintings. It has long been a famous scenic place of Buddhism, Taoism and Confucianism.

9. The Immortal Cliff Grottoes

The Immortal Cliff Grottoes, which stands 15 kilometres away from Maiji Mountain Grottoes, consists of three cliffs, five peaks and six temples. It is said that a Celestial being lived here, hence it got the name "the Immortal Cliff" Grottoes. Above the cliffs there are green peaks, and temples were built either on the top of the peaks or steep cliffs. There are three Cliffs named according to their situation, East, West, and South Cliff. Five peaks are named separately—Ruhuang Peak, Baogai Peak, Xianzhu Peak, East Peak and West Peak. There are six temples—Mulian, Shilian, Tielian, Hualian, Shuilian and Linying Temple. In the area of Five Peaks and Monk Ditch there are many high and low peaks with different shapes. The general name of the temple was Huayan Temple, which was renamed Lingying Temple by Emperor Yongle in the fourteenth year of the Ming Dynasty.

"Immortals have brought lanterns" is one of the eight scenes in Qinzhou. In ancient times at the foot of South Cliff, there was built a burning pavilion which is one main building in which the statue of burning lanterns is enshrined. In the late evenings of summer and autumn natural phosphorescence, oil-burning lanterns and candle-light shine. People say that celestials come and go with lanterns, hence the story "Immortals have brought lanterns".

The tourist resources of cultural interest here is very rich, such as a slanting roof beam on the northwest corner of the temple which stands on the West Cliff and was built and repaired during the Tang, Song, Ming and the Qing Dynasties. According to the appraisal of the expert it is a relic of the frame of a house in the Tang Dynasty. On the East Cliff there is a Monk's Temple in which statues of Sakyamuni and 18 arhats were molded and enshrined in the Ming Dynasty. Although the Burning Pavilion was destroyed in the year of Qingdaonian, the statues of the Late Northern Wei Dynasty have survived. During the late years of Zhu Zhihong, Wang Shiyong, a warrior, and Wang Liaowang, a great calligrapher of the Ming Dynasty lived in the shadow of the rocky Cave. Biyan Cave under the southeast side of Yuhuang Temple has shrines and wall paintings of the Tang Dynasty.

10. Manshu Temple

Manshu temple, located in the rear plain of Celestial cliff, has a long history. Since the end of the Tang Dynasty and the Early Song Dynasty it has had different names such as Jigu Temple and Jindu Temple. Also because there is a Buddhist belief that the place where Buddha lives has no pollution of common people, it's named Pure Temple. In 1971 Pure Temple was pulled down, and almost all of the inscribed boards and steles were missing. However in the 90s an eminent monk Haizheng from the Buddhist Wutai Mountain followed his master's words to look for a place to preach and built this temple. Many monks in Pure Temple collected RMB 40 million and built a group of buildings. Now it has the same building style as Wutai Mountain.

Pure Temple is surrounded by mountains and the sound of the pine trees blowing in the mountain winds is one of the eight wonders of Qinzhou. Wuxichuang, a successful candidate in the highest imperial examination wrote a poem to praise it:

When building Pure Temple, many pines are around it.

It differs from man's world, so it comes from heaven.

I heard it beautiful long time ago, tried to visit it secretly but not come true.

Look around the distance on the top, but it's already sunset.

The eighteen peaks around Pure Temple form a famous landscape depicting eighteen Arhats worshipping Buddha Wenshu.

Riyue Cave, Xiuxing Cave shadow in the green trees of steep cliffs. The natural Buddhist statues which are formed by jutted up stones are living. Yaowang, Kuanxin, Zhihui and Banruo four springs are very clean and sweet. The Great Monk Temple, the temple of Buddhist scriptures and the memorial gateway have been erected in recent years.

11. The Valley of Stone Lotus

At the intersection of the front and rear Zhujia Plains, streams from both plains flow through the mouth of the Huangjia Valley forming a river. Torrents flow into the valley and splash water on the stones, which have the appearance of lotus flowers. Thus the valley is named the Valley of Stone Lotus. This deep, quiet valley meanders past many strange irregular stones for over 5 kilometres to the Tongke Valley. The waterfall of Guanguan Tan is splendid and the rock depicting a lion playing water is also specially attractive.

The pines and cypresses overhang the cliff. And fish, crabs and otters swim freely in the water.

12. The Scenic Area of Stone Gate

The scenic spot of Stone Gate is 15 kilometres away from Immortal the Cliff, of which Stone Gate is one important site among many natural and man-made spots. The deeper you walk into it, the more beautiful it seems. The beautiful scene resembles Mount Huang after which it is called a small Mount Huang. The scene of moon light at Stone Gate is one of the eight sceneries of Qinzhou. At Pastureland of Grazing Horses about 20 kilometres east to Maiji Mountain and 10 kilometres west to Stone Gate were unearthed a group of tombs of the Qin and Han Dynasties in 1986. In 1993 a provincial forest garden was developed including the gate of the mountain, eight galloping horses and the building for view.

13. Stone Gate Mountains

The name of Stone Gate comes from the fact that both south and north peaks face each other between a bridge linking them. This resembles a gate, hence the name "Stone Gate".

For a long time people praised Stone Gate by referring to one tower, two birds, three rarities, four China firs, five beasts, six treasures, seven flowers, and eight sceneries. One tower refers to a bell-tower on the north peak standing in the tower, you can see coiling incense smoke and hear the sounds of chanting, bell ringing and knocking of wooden fish, all of which have a calming effect; two birds refer to pheasant and parrot; three rarities refer to peaks, pines and stone which have the same characteristics as Mount Huang, so Stone Gate has earned the title "small Mount Huang"; four China firs refer to four types of fir i. e. dragon spruce, metasequoia, fir and Chinese larch; five beasts refer to paradise flycatcher, muntjac, musk deer, deer and rabbit; six treasures refer to daphne giraldii, akebia quinata, valeriana officinalis, pine mushroom, pine nut and zanthoxylum schinifolium; seven flowers are viburum macrocephalum, magnolia, azalea, lilac, phyllostachys bambusoides, sorbaria sorbifolia, spiraea japonica; eight sceneries refer to moonlit night at Stone Gate, celestial bridge surrounded by green plants, high peaks penetrating the sky, crouching tiger on the range, white deer reflecting on the gate, peak like a dragon, the cave of Pangu (creator of the universe in Chinese mythology) and wonderful clouds.

The most beautiful natural scene is a Moonlit Night at Stone Gate. On the 15th of every month, if the weather is clear, the moon rises slowly from between the south and north peaks, which is just like a jade plate in the sky, bright and white. It is one of the eight scenes in Qinzhou. Zhangshiyin, a scholar in the Early Qing Dynasty once wrote a meaningful statement, "The most famous in Gansu". Moreover, the Sea of Clouds at Stone Gate is a very beautiful view.

Stone Gate is a famous Taoist site in Longnan and Tianshui. There once lived Taoists in the Tang and Song Dynasties. Most of the present temples were rebuilt in the period of Emperor Qianlong of the Qing Dynasty. Around the north and south peaks at Stone Gate there are many peaks, which form one mountain after another, and one peak after another. Clouds and fog coil over the peaks on which many pines and cypresses and stones of strange shapes show us their charms.

14. The Scenic Area of the Winding Streams

The sight of the winding stream situated in the heart of Xiaolongshan 20 kilometres to the southeast of Maiji Mountain belongs to Maiji District and the Jialing River system. Here dense forest, wild flowers, strange irregular shapes of stones and clear water show us a very beautiful natural picture. Also because of low population the natural conditions are very well protected.

The spirit of the scene is water. The water in the Winding Stream comes from the Leng River. It meanders from the northeast to the southwest, flowing through narrow valleys or between wide banks. Each place has a different scene so that it gains the name "Eighteen Bends in the Winding Stream". It is about 10 kilometres long and 2 kilometres wide. Wandering along it you can see green mountains, clear water, wild flowers, strange stones and sand beds etc. all of which is too much to absorb.

Winding Stream is also a natural botanical and zoological garden. Here there are many rare flowers and Chinese medicinal herbs such as azalea, magnolia, Chinese herbaceous peony, camellia, peony, codonopsis pilosula, fritillaria, while several rare animals live here, such as sika, antelope, leopard, giant salamander and otter. These plants and animals add vitality to the lively and charming scene.

15. The Scenic Areas of Jieting

The scenic spots of Jieting situated to the northwest of Maiji Mountain belongs to Maiji District. They are 24 kilometres away from the Tianshui Railway Stop and are joined by Stone Gate and Immortal Cliff. The scenic spots are the old town of Jieting, Dongke Valley and the Gorge of Hot Spring.

16. The Old Town of Jieting

It is at the foot of Shenlong Mountain. Both the Gorges of Huangjia and Hot Spring flow from the north and west of it, forming the topographical feature that one side of the town is Shenlong Mountain and other three sides are surrounded by water.

There were several different descriptions of the story of "Ma Su was beaten at Jieting" in the Three Kingdoms. It has been examined by experts and most of them conclude from this description that Jieting is Longcheng in Qin'an County. But Jieting in Maiji District seems to have a connection to the wars in the Three Kingdoms. Some relics such as inscription on tablets and historical books provide the proof. In addition the customs of the people and buildings of Jieting are certain to evoke people's thinking.

17. Shenlong Mountain

Shenlong Mountain, also named Shenling Mountain, or Tielong Mountain, has Jieting Town at its foot. From the foot of the mountain to its top there were built Chongfu Temple, Tianwang Temple, Sanshifo Temple, Lingxiao Temple and Shimu Palace, which are the group of Buddhist buildings. There are some strange places here. It's said that on the top of mountain there are holes from where you can hear buzzing noises. If you throw a coin into it, the coin will be puffed out by an air current. In fact the cause of this phenomenon is that there are many holes in the mountain.

18. Dongke Cottage

Dongke Cottage, located at Liujiahe, Jiezi Town, was the place where a famous poet Dufu once lived and it is one of the eight scenes in Qinzhou. In 759 AD of the Tang Dynasty Dufu abandoned his government post and came to Qinzhou. He lived with his nephew in Dongke Valley which Dufu thought at that time it an ideal place to detach oneself from reality because of its dense forest and bamboo, and especially about ten households lived there. So Dufu wrote a poem to express his feelings for the place. It goes as follows.

Owing to preaching to Dongke Valley, tens of households live there.

Vines climb on the roof of the opposite house, water reflecting shadows of bamboo flows away.

Sow grain in poor soil, plant gourds in the sunny hillside.

A boatman told me the news, not to miss the chance to look at the peach blossom.

But, Dufu left Dongke Valley eventually. In the winter of the same year Dufu came to Tonggu (Cheng County, Gansu Province) because he had not enough food and clothes. To remember this great poet, the later generations renamed Bahuai Village as Zimei Village and built a cottage there. Even now a folk song is common among the local people. "Jiugu pine, Bagu Chinese scholartree, Baishui ravine, Yanwo terrace, the place Dufu lived, the cottage was built."

Now the place where Dufu's cottage used to stand is Zimei Primary School. But Zimei trees stand straight like an embodiment of Dufu's spirit.

19. The Gorge of Hot Spring

It is about 4 kilometres from Jieting Town and an essential from Jieting to Stone Gate. The gorge is about 2 kilometres long with high bare rocks. A waterfall can be seen frequently. From the gurgles in the gorge we know there is rich source of terrestrial heat.

The temperature of the Hot Spring is about 40°C and the amount of the water in one day is 3600 cubic metres. There are 19 gentle chemical elements in the Spring, so after having a bath the skin is very delicate and smooth. The Hot Spring has a special curative effect on some illnesses such as neurasthenia, insomnia, hypertension, heart disease, sequelae of cerebral hemorrhage, arthritis, beriberi and dermatitis.

In the gorge some hotels and bathing facilities have been built. Tourists can enjoy eating, shopping, and entertainment here.

20. Water Curtain Cave Grottoes

The Water Curtain Cave Grottoes is situated in the Lu Ban Gorge of the Zhonglou Mountain, 25 kilometres away to the northeast of the county town of Wushan. Here the lie of the mountain is lofty and grand. The brooks gurgle in the mountains. The mountain flowers are luxuriantly blooming. The scenery is beautiful and attractive. The Grottoes began to be cut in the Late Qin of the Sixteen Kingdoms. Later it was built in the Dynasties of the Northern Wei, the Northern Zhou, Sui, Tang, Five Dynasties, Song and Yuan. Now there are mainly the scenic spots and historical sites of the Water Curtain Cave, the Lashao Temple and the Thousand-Buddha Cave, etc. In 2001, the State Council listed it as the state-preserved key cultural relics.

The Water Curtain Cave is in the cliff on the east side of the Shifu Mountain, which is like an axe in appearance. It is a natural arch cave, about 50 metres long, 30 metres high and 20 metres deep. When in rainy seasons, the spring in the peak and walls of the cave pour out together. The spring water runs from the eaves of the cave, just like the bead curtains shutting the door of the cave. So it is called the Water Curtain Cave. In the cave there are such buildings as the Sisheng (Four Sages) Palace, the Guanyin (a Bodhisattva) Temple, the South Hall and the Bodhisattva

Hall, etc. These buildings are well arranged and have ingenious handicraft. Of them the Bodhisattva Hall is the tallest and the most magnificent. The Hall is divided into two stories. In the Grottoes Cave of the lower story there is a clear pool. The water in it is so clear that you can see the bottom. On the name board of the upper story, there are four Chinese characters "The Evening Rain of the West Hill" written by Mr. Fan Zhenxu, the famous painter and calligrapher. In the upper story there is a statue of the goddess of linen thread in the local folklore. In the cliff surface of the Water Curtain Cave, there preserve the huge Buddhist wall paintings made in the Dynasties of the Northern Wei, Sui, Tang and Yuan. In the cave towers, rocks, springs, sculptures and paintings enhance each other's beauty, just like the natural setting.

The Lashao Temple was constructed in the Dynasty of the Northern Zhou. Also named the Big Buddha Cliff, it is situated on the halfway up the mountain opposite to the Water Curtain Cave. Their distance is only several hundred metres. In the temple there preserves many grotto works made in the Dynasties from the Northern Zhou to Yuan. In the steep cliff surface, there are 3 relief sculptures. The big Buddha in the middle is more than 40 metres high. On the two sides there are two Bodhisattvas in attendance, who have lotus flowers in hand and stand solemnly. The big Buddha sits on the lotus throne. The lions, deer and elephants are carved on the inter-layers of the lotus petals. Some of these animals stand, some crouch. They are symmetrically arranged. The carving of the animals is simple, unsophisticated and vivid. The level of the plastic arts is very exquisite. In the many niches for statues of Buddhas stand the small figures of Buddha made in the Song Dynasty. Since the upper part of the cliff surface sticks out and the wind eaves were built to keep from winds and rains, the statues have been better preserved up to now. Flying clouds and beasts are carved on the end of the eaves and the bronze bells are hung on it. When the gentle breeze blows, the bells dingdong. The figures of Buddha and wall paintings of the Lashao Temple have the trace of the Little Vehicle Buddhism. This is indeed rare in Chinese grotto art.

Going into the gully for 500 metres from the Lashao Temple, you can reach the Thousand-Buddha Cave. It is so named because in the cave a thousand Buddhas were painted on the wall. Originally there were 7 grottoes in the cave. Now the remaining statues and wall paintings on the surface of the sand cliff are full and round and with different shapes. Especially the statue of the Bodhisattva is full and elegant, having a lot of features of the Northern Zhou Dynasty. Some statues have the characteristics of the Western Wei Dynasty. These statues are the important materials to research the early grotto art of China.

21. Wood Ladder Temple Grottoes

The Wood Ladder Temple Grottoes is situated in the Yangping Village of the Mali Township, 35 kilometres to the southwest of the county town of Wushan. It is located in the Shiwei Hill of the Bangsha River valley. In 1981, it was listed as the Province-preserved cultural relics. In 2001, as a part of the Water Curtain Cave Grottoes, it was raised as the state-preserved key cultural relics.

The Shiwei Hill runs from south to north. All sides of it are steep precipices and cliffs. Now on the northern side of the Grottoes there is an iron gate. Through it you can go into the temple. The Wood Ladder Temple Grottoes is dug on the halfway of the Shiwei Hill. It is more than 333.3 metres above ground level. It is said that on the precipice there was originally a tall wood ladder, which is over 10 metres long, through which you can climb up into the grottoes. So it is named the Wood Ladder Temple. The Grottoes began to be built in the periods of Southern and Northern Dynasties. Later in the past dynasties it was built again. In it there was originally 10 halls, 9 caves and 2 towers made of bricks. Now the 2 towers have no remains, there being 18 grotto niches, 4 halls, 78 statues and 234 wall paintings. The area of the paintings is more than 2,100 square metres. Of them the statues in the No. 5, 7, and 9 grottoes are better preserved. The biggest statue is more than ten metres high. The skills of molding are superb and refined. The shapes are simple and unsophisticated. It has higher artistic value.

In the temple there are still such buildings as the Yuhuang Pavilion, the Sanguan Hall, the Wuliang Hall, the Nanhai Bodhisattva Hall, the Thunder God Temple, the Kuixing (the four stars in the bowl of the Big Dipper, or the one at the tip of the bowl) Pavilion, the Big Buddha Pavilion and the Fengpo (the old woman in charge of blowing) Cave, etc.

22. The Grottoes of Giant Buddha

The Grottoes of Giant Buddha is located in 2.5 kilometres to the west of Gangu County which belongs to Tianshui City and 5 kilometres to Gangu Railway Stop, whose name is from the giant Buddha in the middle of the hill. In 2001 it became an important place of preservation of cultural relics. The giant Buddha Mountain, because of its shape like a waving flag, is also named Wen Flag Mountain. The whole mountain from the foot to the peak is 1.5 kilometres high and covers an area of 640 "mu" (about 0.43 square kilometres). It is an important relic of grottoes and ancient architecture mixing together on the Silk Route of Southeast Gansu.

Before the Northern Zhou Dynasty, people began the earliest Buddhist activities and works making statues and cutting niches. Now there are twenty-two niches and the most important one was chiseled in the great Tang Dynasty, which is located in the middle of the hill. The niche is rectangle at the lower part and has an arch roof at the top. There is a big Buddha in it, which is 23.3 metres high, and its shoulder is 9.5 metres wide. Its body is vigorous and magnificent. Its air is solemn and quiet. The eyes are full of wisdom and the face is plump. It is a valuable art treasure. It is the only one grotto of such big Buddha in the east of Gansu Province, which fills in the shortness of big Buddha such as Grottoes of Maiji Mountain, Water Curtain Cave Grottoes and the whole Wei River Valley in the Tang Dynasty. Moreover, the square roof of the grottoes and Buddhist niches with rooms for monks are seldom seen in China. It was fashionable in the Northern Wei Dynasty to chisel niches and sit meditating. The Grottoes of Giant Buddha is an example to study the development of Buddhism in the east of China.

The most of temples were built in the Ming and the Qing Dynasties. They are close together in a row and dotted with temperament and interest. Their modeling is very special and the styles are different. It is very famous since ancient times that undulating hills and white clouds wind around as well as cool wind and lilac are here and there. Its temple fair is on the fourth of April (of Chinese lunar calendar) every year. People from all places come here hurrily to burn joss sticks. So this day has become the important festival in the local.

后 记

自耗时十余年的专著《从独白到对话——背诵式语言输入形式的创造性转换》于 2012 年在中国社会科学出版社出版后,我原以为再不会有写书的想法。主要因为我对自己的作品缺乏客观认识,总感觉是平常教学活动的尝试。后来该书分别于 2015 年获得天水市第四届哲学社会科学优秀成果二等奖和 2016 年甘肃省第十四次哲学社会科学优秀成果三等奖。专家"十年磨一剑,慢工出细活。这才是做学问该具备的严谨学术态度"的评语给了我自信,也产生了动力。

在"一带一路"倡议实施的背景下,即将出版的《大学英语课程教学指南》的内容在原来通用英语的基础上增加了专门用途英语(ESP)和跨文化交际的内容,成果伙伴对话的本著也从通用英语教学转换到专门用途英语教学。尽管伙伴对话在培训学生掌握英语口语导游词方面取得了一些成效,但学生表达时书面语和口语混淆的现象促使我思考改进的措施。本研究先是借鉴目的语国家导游词样本,再分析口语体的特征,最后由学生完成语篇书面语与口语之间的转换。对学生语内转换作业进行校译是最艰巨的工作,需要校译者具备自由驾驭英语书面语和口语的素质。合作者龚金霞于 2003—2005 年赴英国攻读英语教学硕士,其海外留学的优势刚好弥补了我文体方面的不足。

本著的完成得到各方面的大力支持。相继于 2015 年立项的天水师范学院教学研究一般项目"基于工作项目的高级涉外旅游从业人员跨学科合作教学研究"、2016 年外教社—甘肃省普通高等学校英语教学改革研究一般项目"基于伙伴对话的跨学科旅游英语实践"和

后　记

2016年度甘肃省社科规划项目"'一带一路'语境下天水地域文化的双语构建研究"为本著搭建了理论与实践相结合的平台，让我们把实践经验上升到理论层面。感谢副院长桑仲刚对以上项目的申报、运行及本著的完成提供了建设性的指导。感谢院长贾俊民提供了大量的天水"五大文化"原始语料，使其成为我们翻译参考借鉴的模板。感谢《伏羲庙志》作者、历史学院教授刘雁翔在百忙中为专著作序，再一次给我们的研究指明了方向。感谢同事安登贤、许胜男无私的帮助使我们从感性认识上升到理性认识。

历时两年的写作经历了许多困难。在浩瀚的信息里选择语境相似的景点资料花费了大量时间，再用语言学理论进行重构、翻译、描写和解释倍感压力。为实现源语文本和译语文本语域匹配，我们几易译文，合作讨论最佳选择。尽管几乎走遍了天水"五大文化"涉及的所有景点，但受域外旅游经历所限，有些景点的信息可能不太全面。书中提供的门票和交通信息仅供参考。如有出入，请以实际情况为准。欢迎读者批评指正。

本著第一章总论以及第二章天水伏羲文化描写与解释、第三章天水大地湾文化描写与解释由马英莲完成，共计约8万字；第四章天水秦文化描写与解释、第五章天水三国文化描写与解释和第六章天水石窟文化描写与解释由龚金霞完成，共计约13万字；另外天水"五大文化"补充英语语料由二人合作完成。

作　者

二○一七年元月于西安